BIG MUSHY HAPPY LUMP

A "Sarah's Scribbles" collection

Sarah Andersen

Andrews McMeel
PUBLISHING®

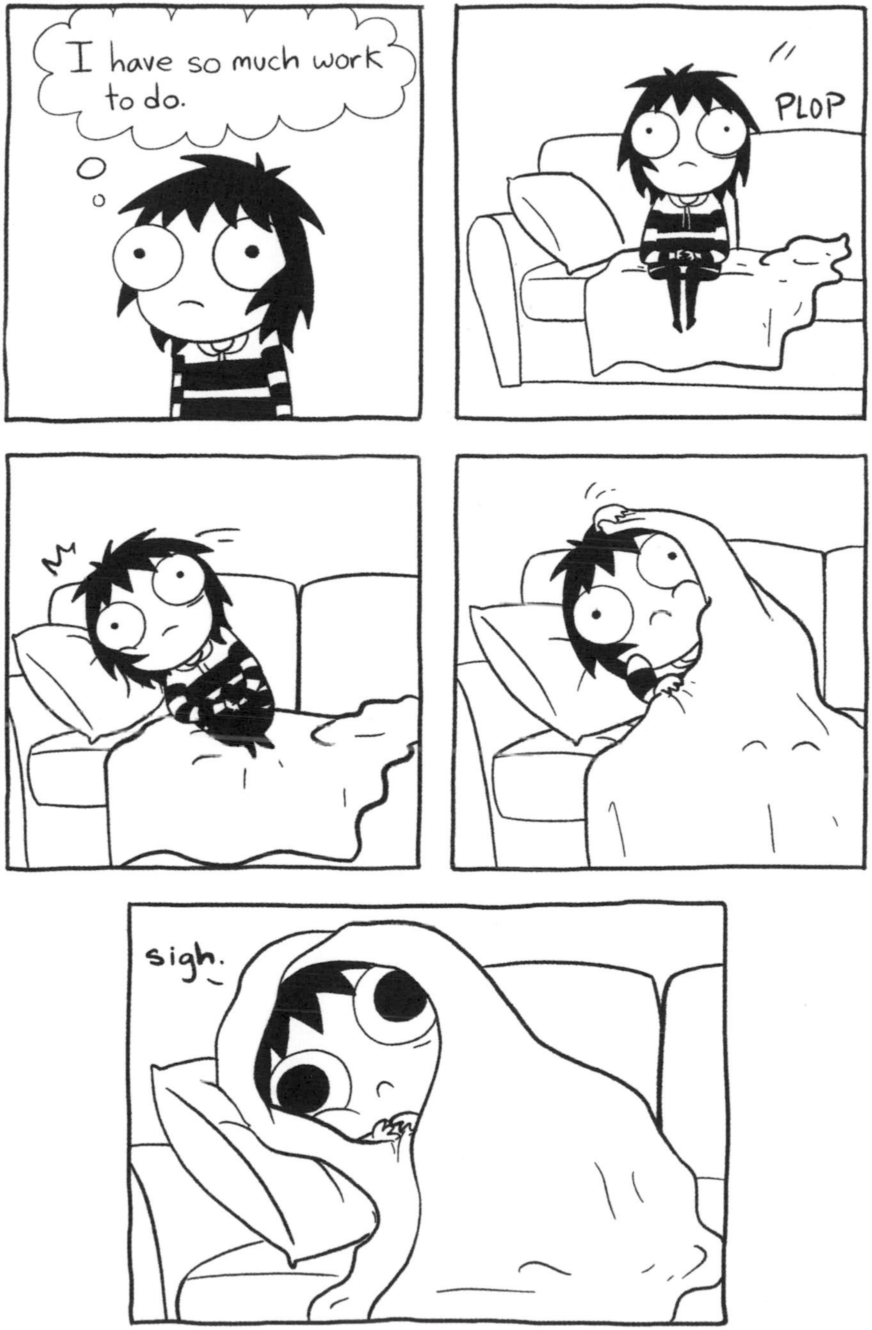
I have so much work to do.
PLOP
sigh.

COMPLIMENTS

MEN:

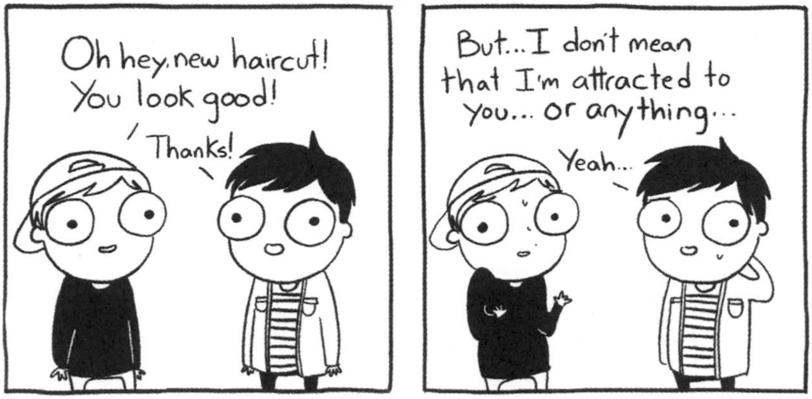

Oh hey, new haircut! You look good!
Thanks!
But... I don't mean that I'm attracted to you... or anything...
Yeah...

WOMEN:

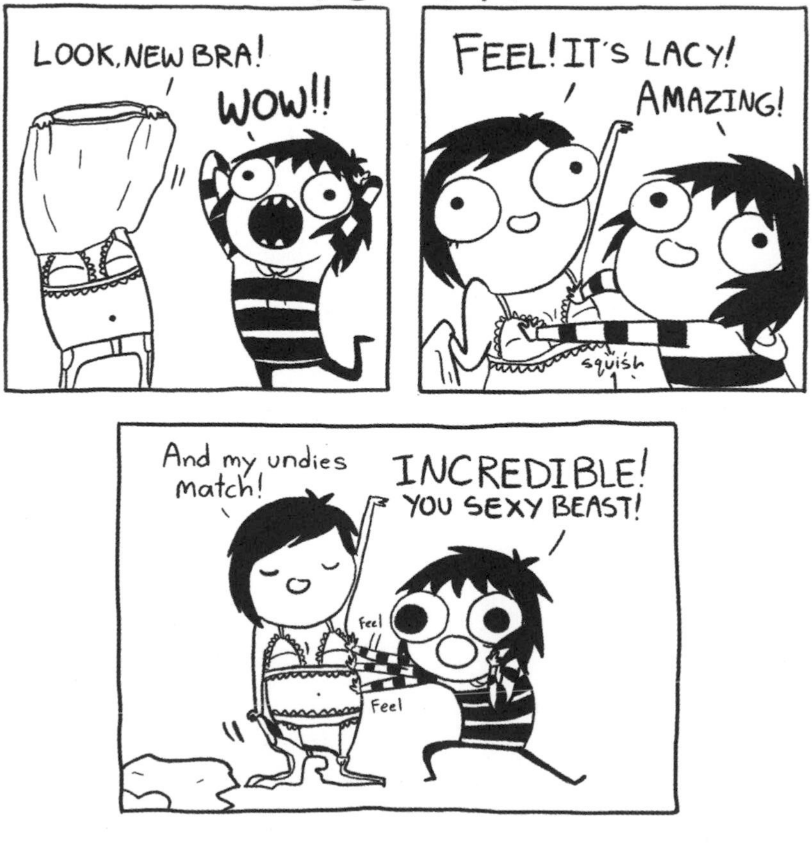

LOOK, NEW BRA!
WOW!!
FEEL! IT'S LACY!
AMAZING!
squish
And my undies match!
INCREDIBLE! YOU SEXY BEAST!
Feel
Feel

ME AT HOME

ME AT HOME ALONE

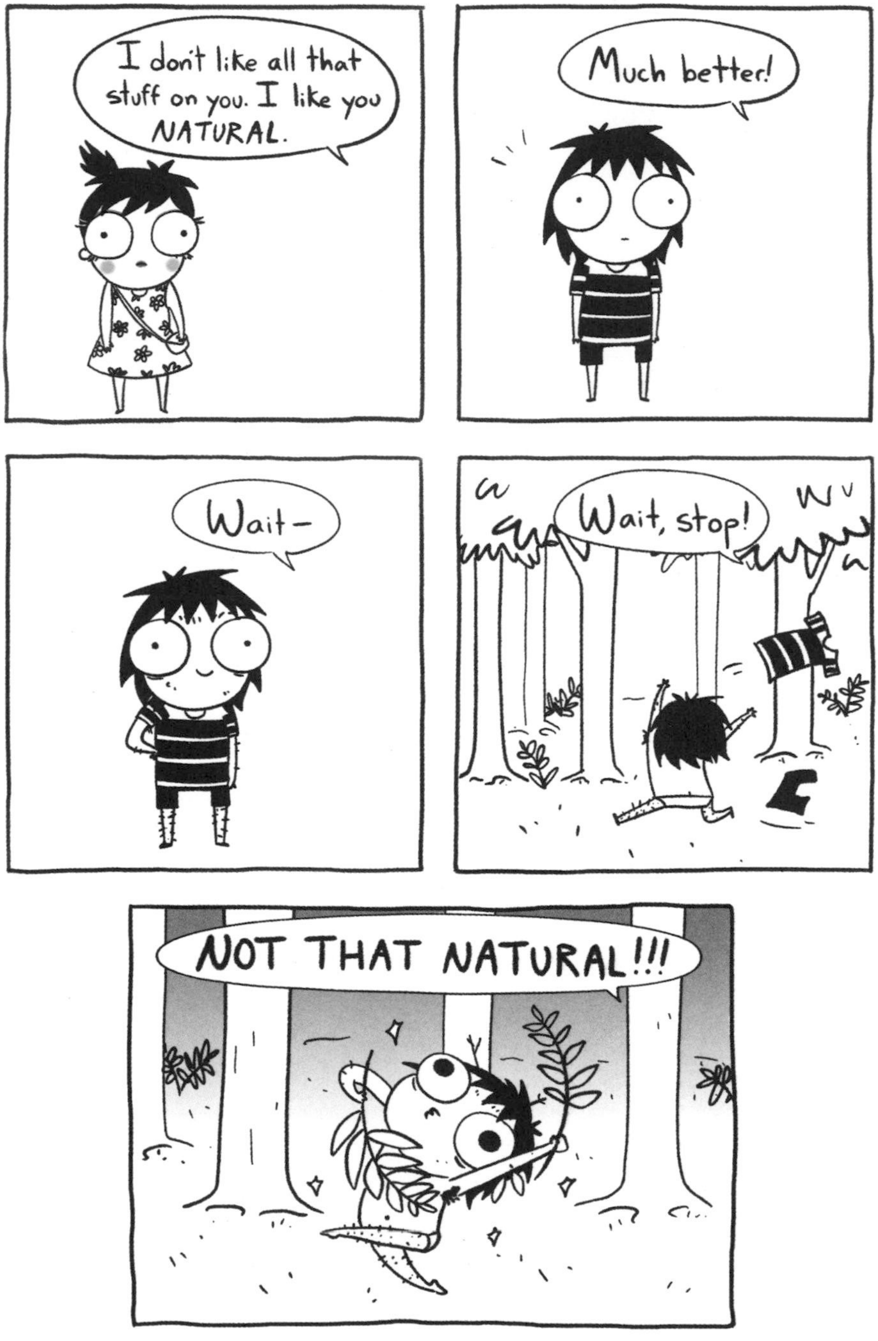
I don't like all that stuff on you. I like you NATURAL.
Much better!
Wait-
Wait, stop!
NOT THAT NATURAL!!!

WHY FEMALE FRIENDSHIPS ARE IMPORTANT

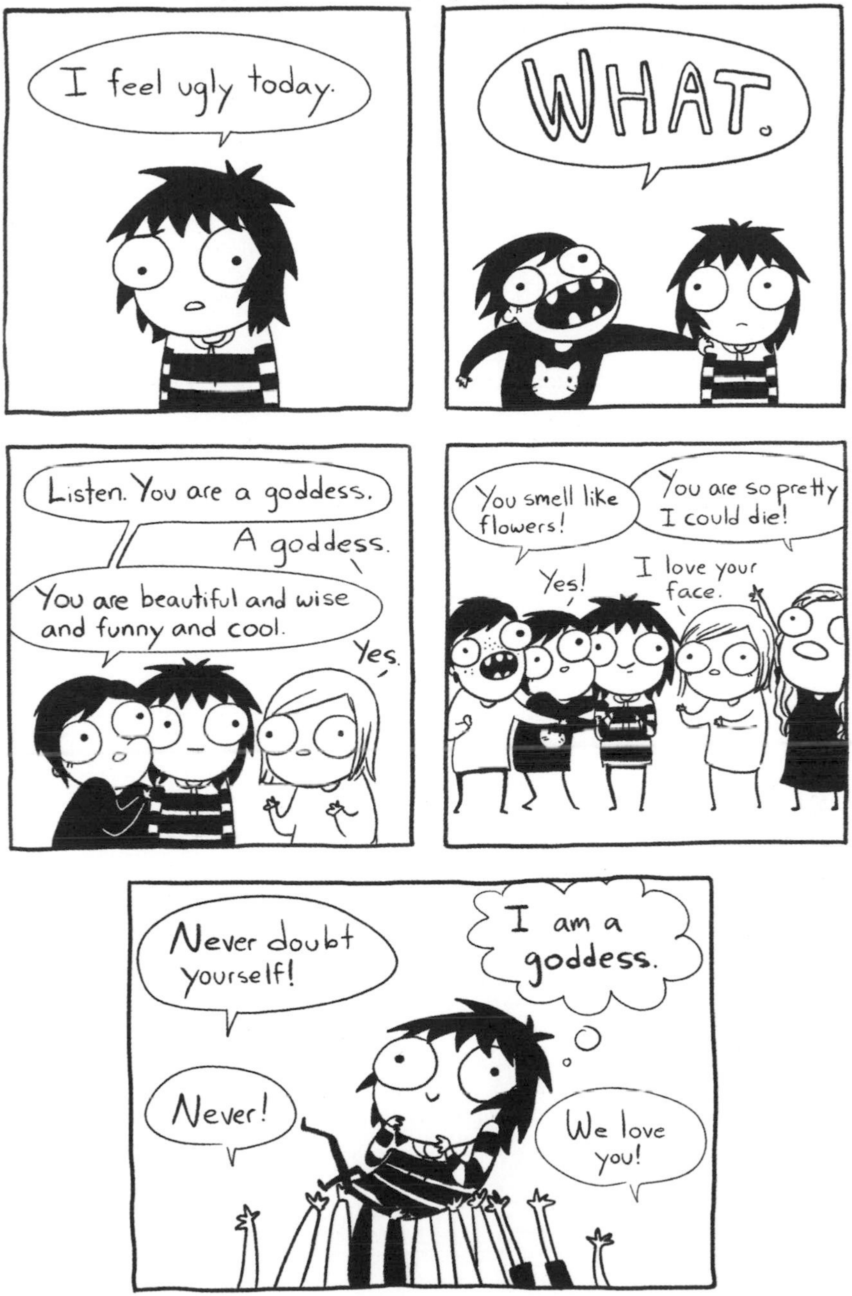

I feel ugly today.
WHAT.
Listen. You are a goddess.
A goddess.
You are beautiful and wise and funny and cool.
Yes.
You smell like flowers!
You are so pretty I could die!
Yes!
I love your face.
Never doubt yourself!
I am a goddess.
Never!
We love you!

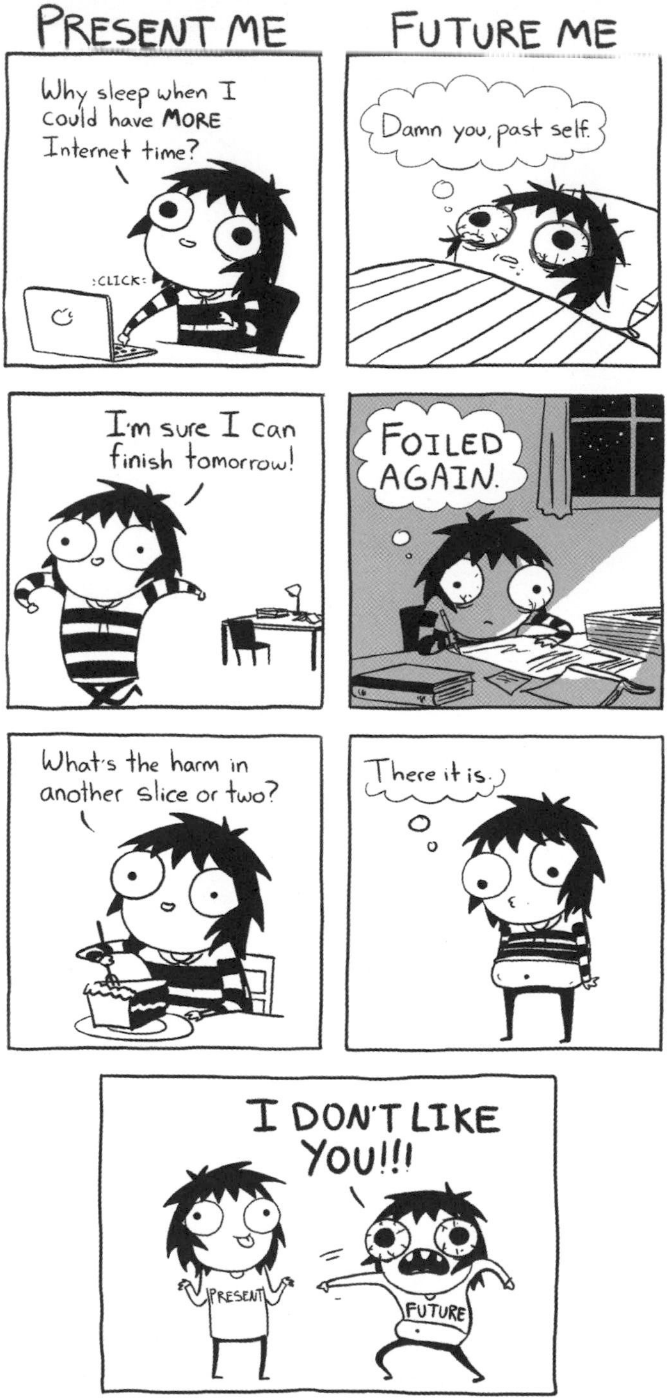
PRESENT ME
FUTURE ME
Why sleep when I could have MORE Internet time?
:CLICK:
Damn you, past self.
I'm sure I can finish tomorrow!
FOILED AGAIN.
What's the harm in another slice or two?
There it is.
I DON'T LIKE YOU!!!
PRESENT
FUTURE

MY SELF-ESTEEM

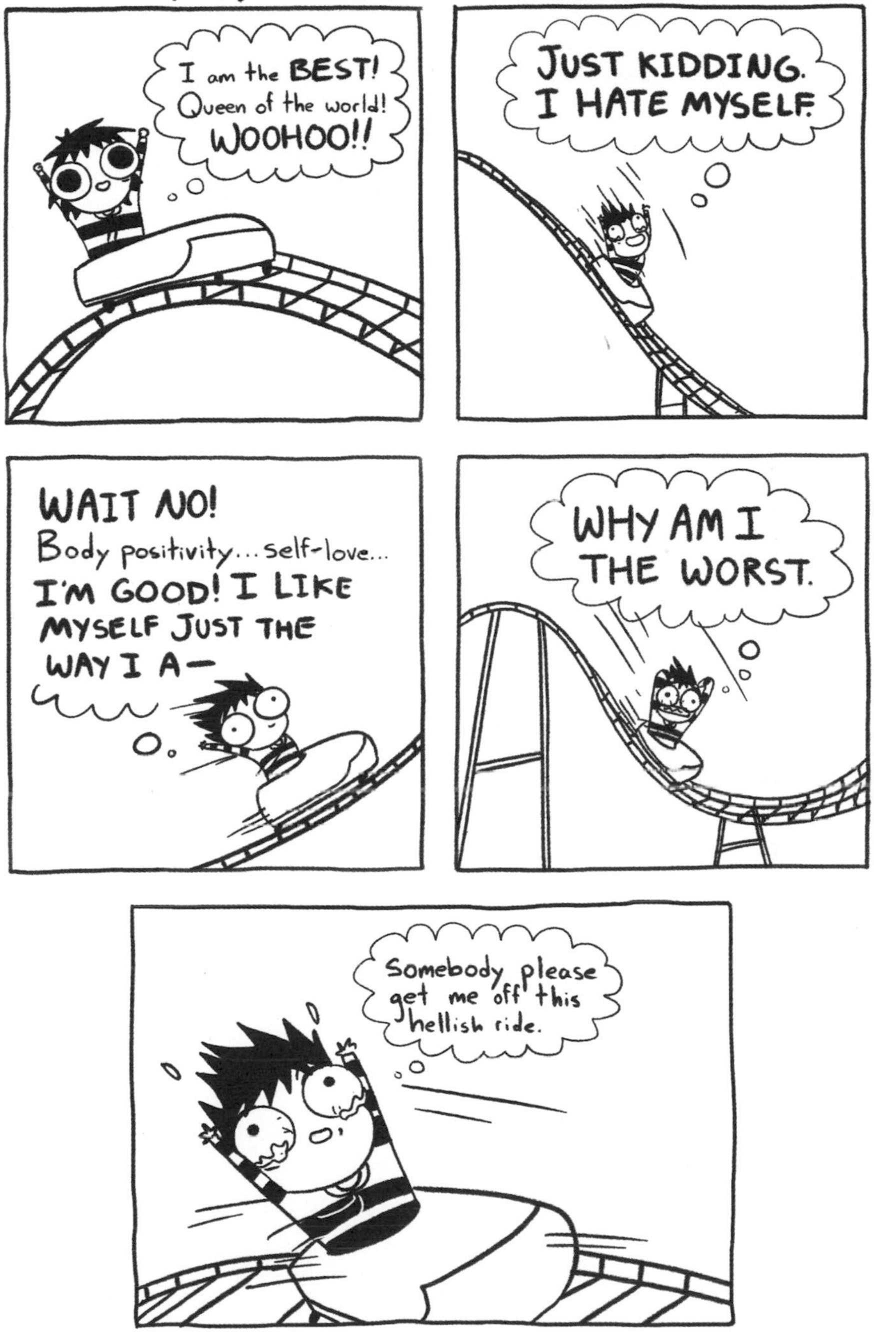
I am the BEST! Queen of the world! WOOHOO!!
JUST KIDDING. I HATE MYSELF.
WAIT NO! Body positivity... self-love... I'M GOOD! I LIKE MYSELF JUST THE WAY I A—
WHY AM I THE WORST.
Somebody please get me off this hellish ride.

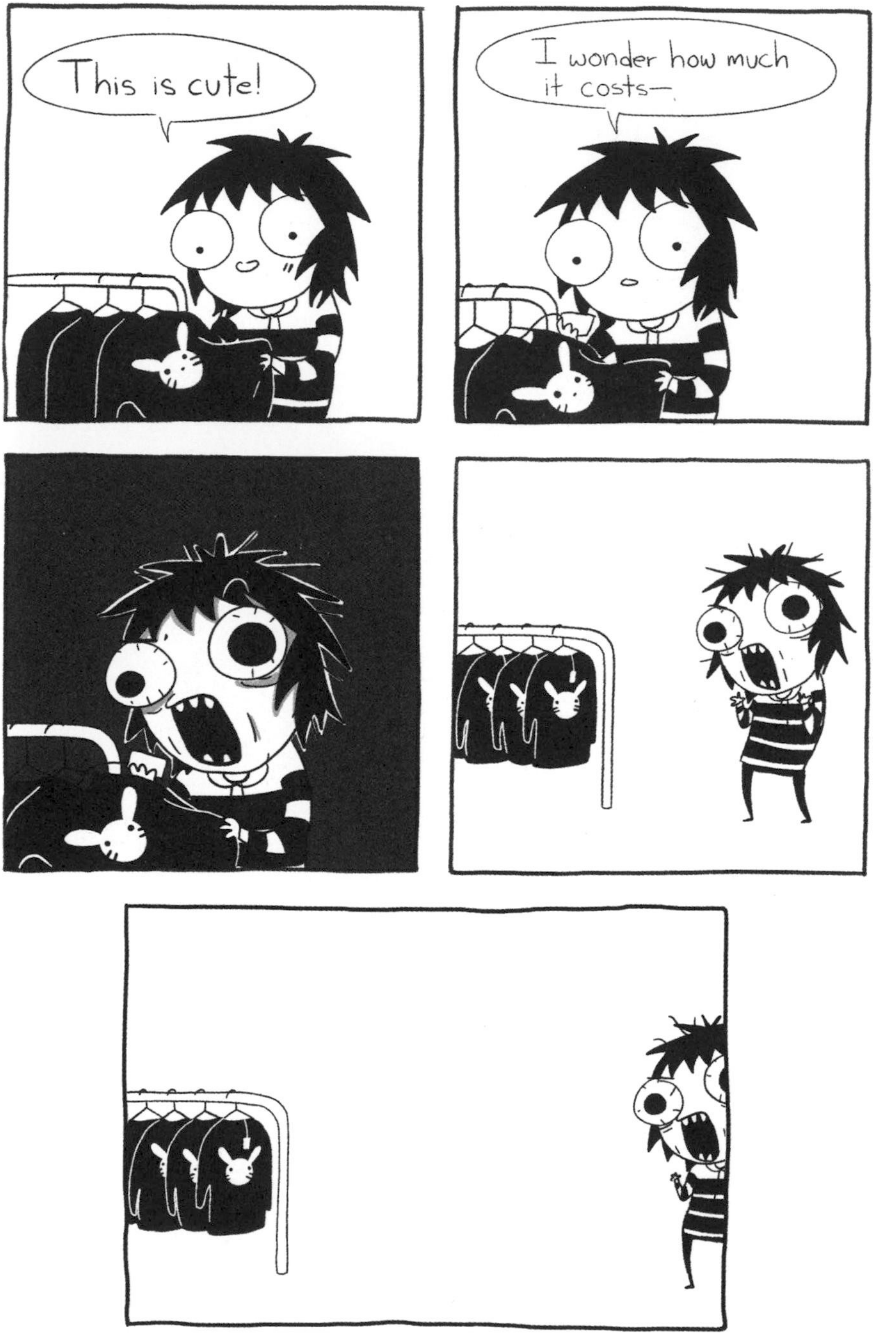
This is cute!
I wonder how much it costs—

ALTERNATIVE BOYFRIEND USES

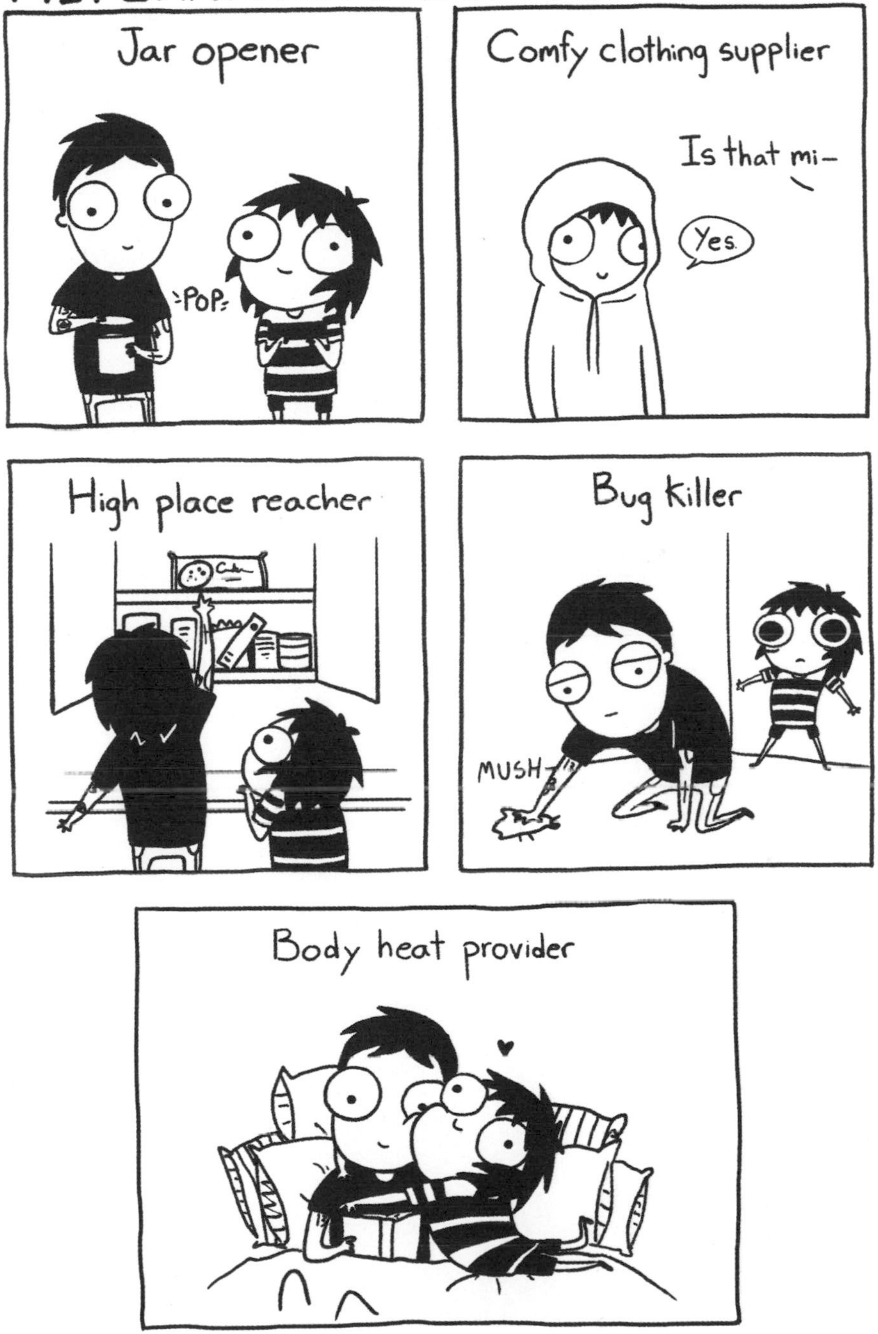
Jar opener
POP
Comfy clothing supplier
Is that mi–
Yes.
High place reacher
Bug killer
MUSH
Body heat provider

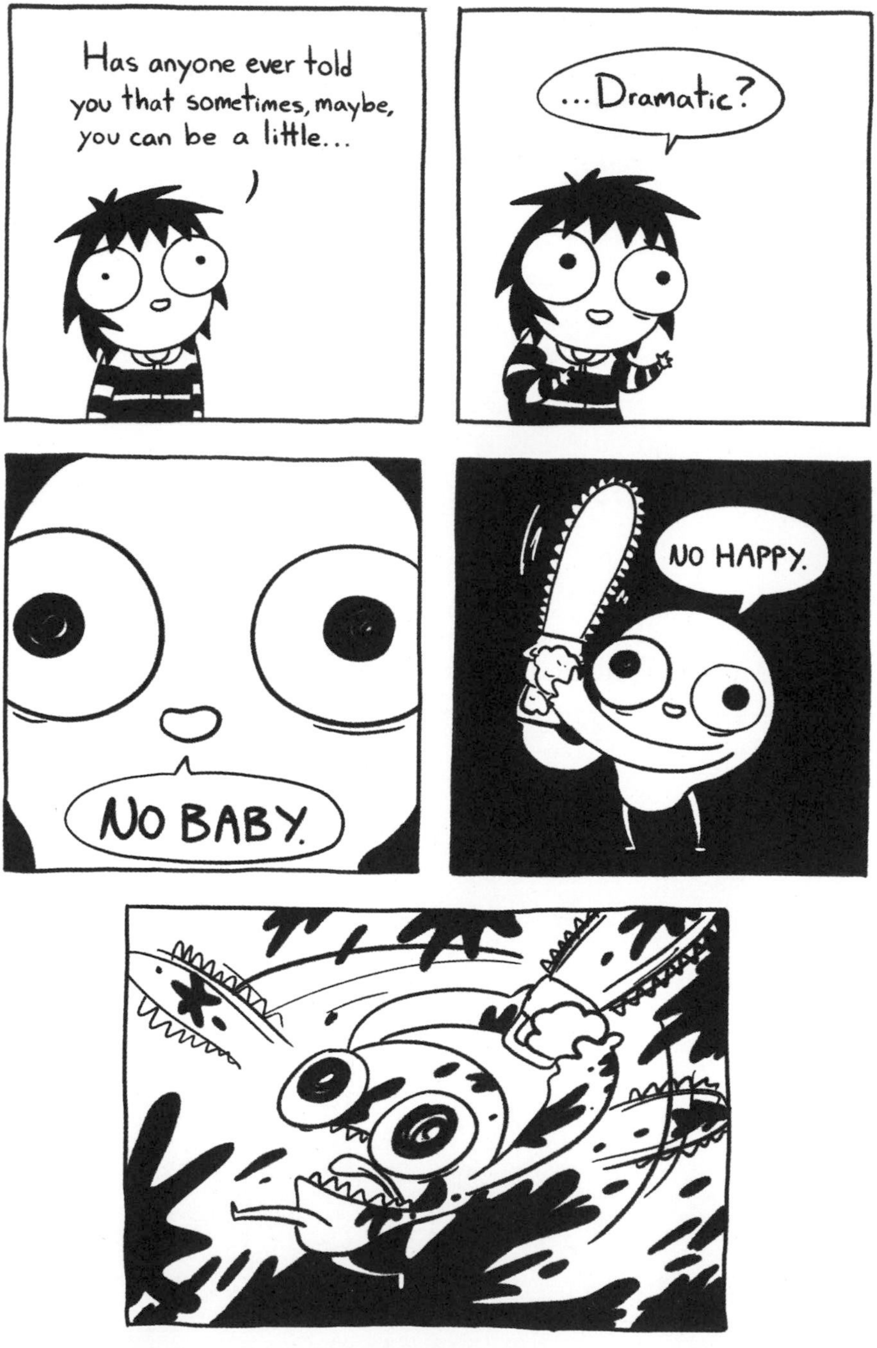
Has anyone ever told you that sometimes, maybe, you can be a little...
...Dramatic?
NO BABY.
NO HAPPY.

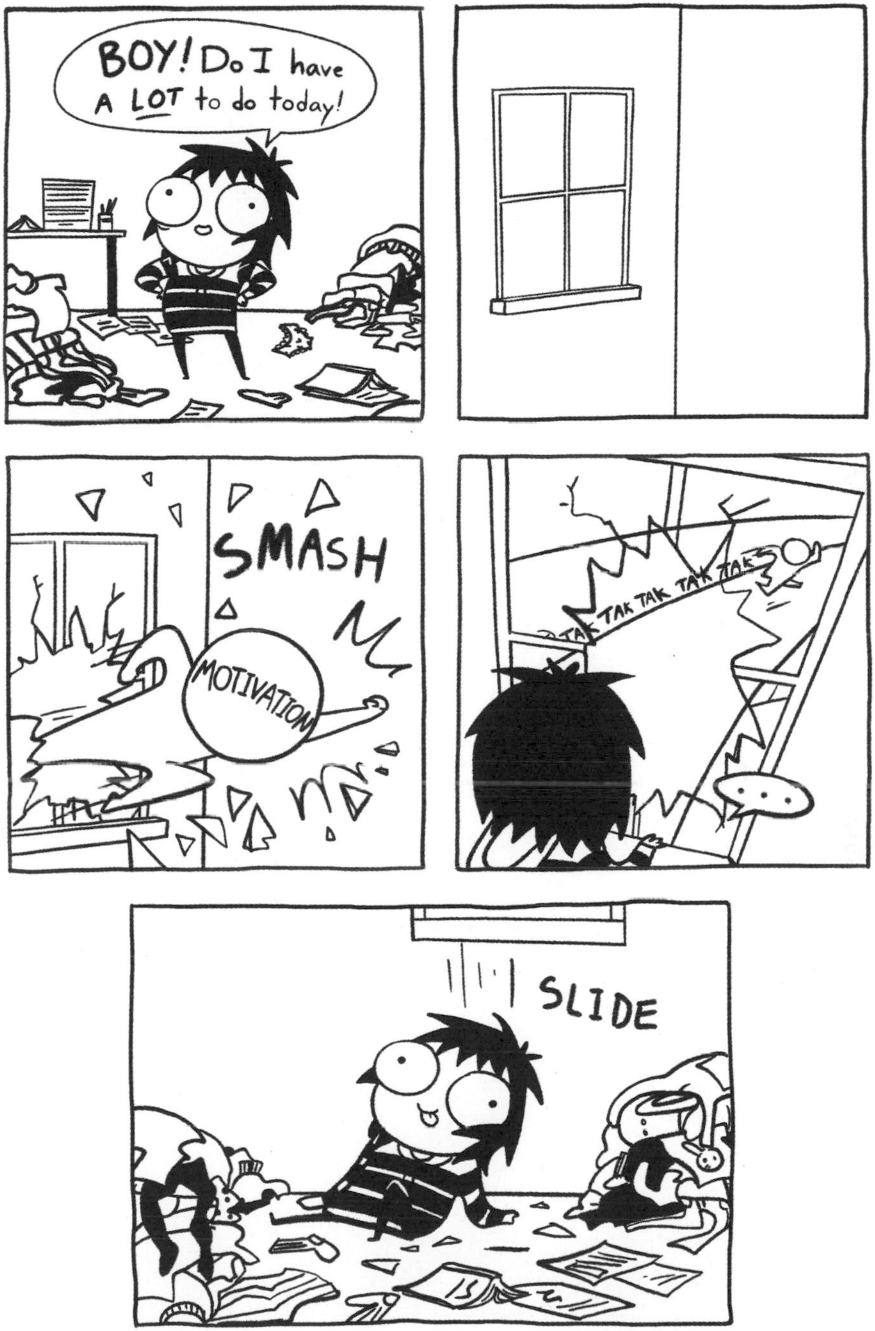
BOY! Do I have A LOT to do today!
SMASH
MOTIVATION
TAK TAK TAK TAK TAK
...
SLIDE

THERE ARE TWO TYPES OF PEOPLE

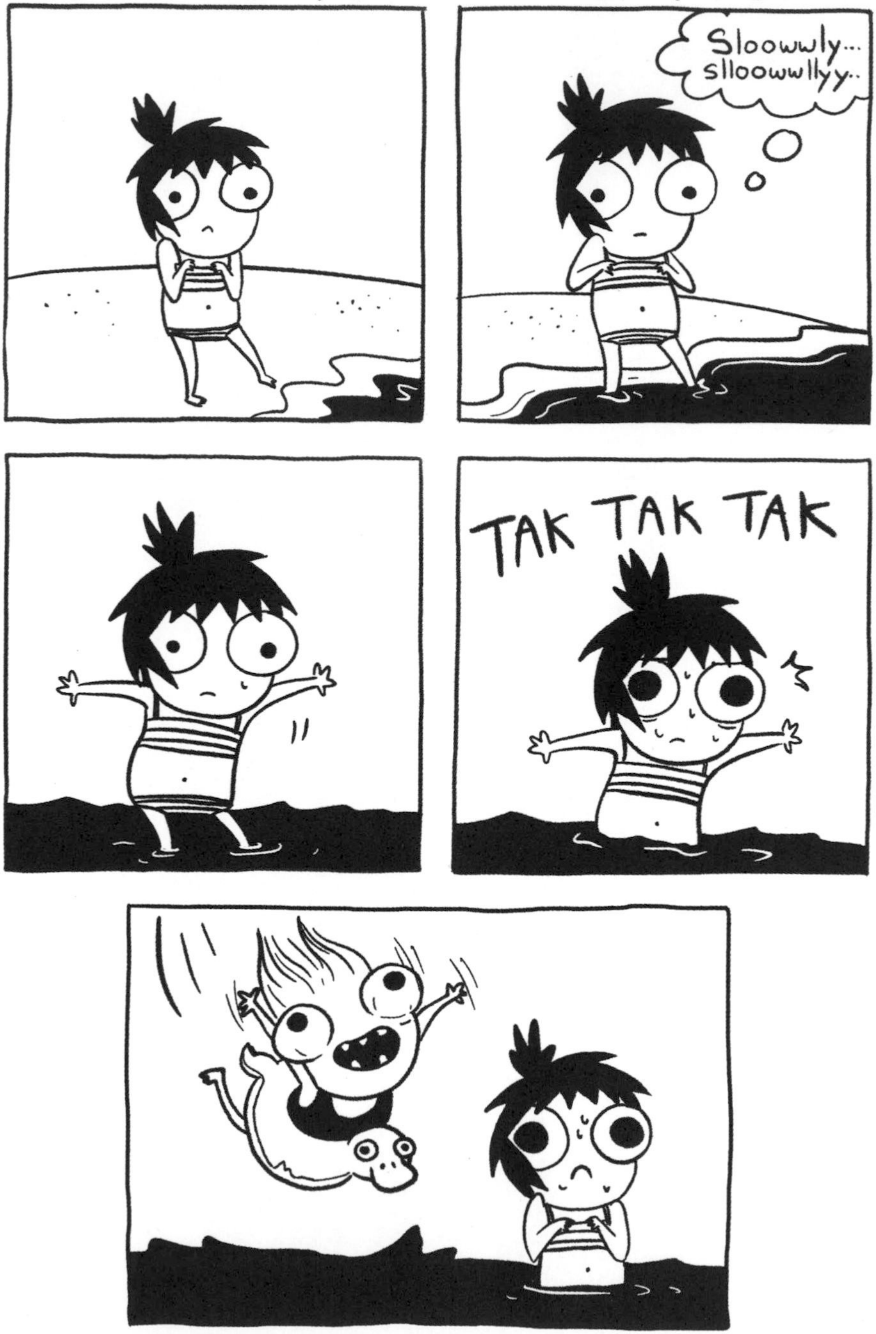
Sloowwly... slloowwllyy..
TAK TAK TAK

MALE PUBERTY

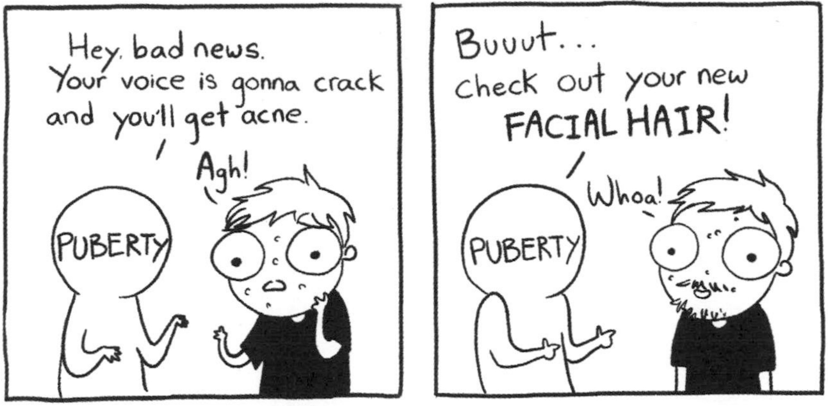
Hey, bad news. Your voice is gonna crack and you'll get acne.
Agh!
PUBERTY
Buuut... Check out your new FACIAL HAIR!
Whoa!
PUBERTY

FEMALE PUBERTY

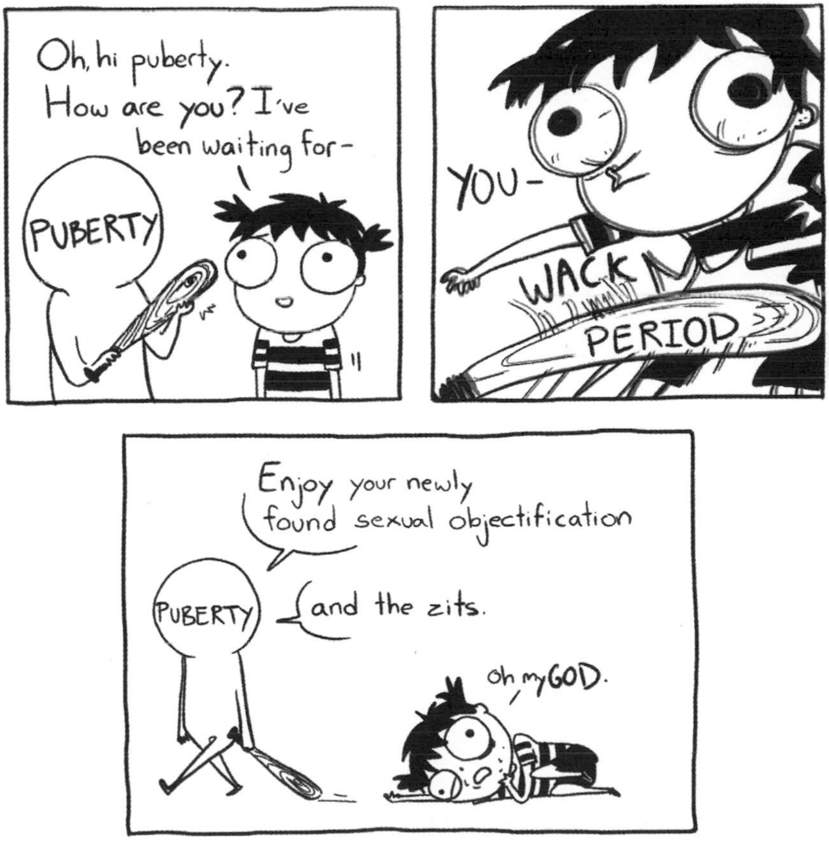
Oh, hi puberty. How are you? I've been waiting for-
PUBERTY
YOU-
WACK
PERIOD
Enjoy your newly found sexual objectification
and the zits.
PUBERTY
Oh my GOD.

How I Spend Money

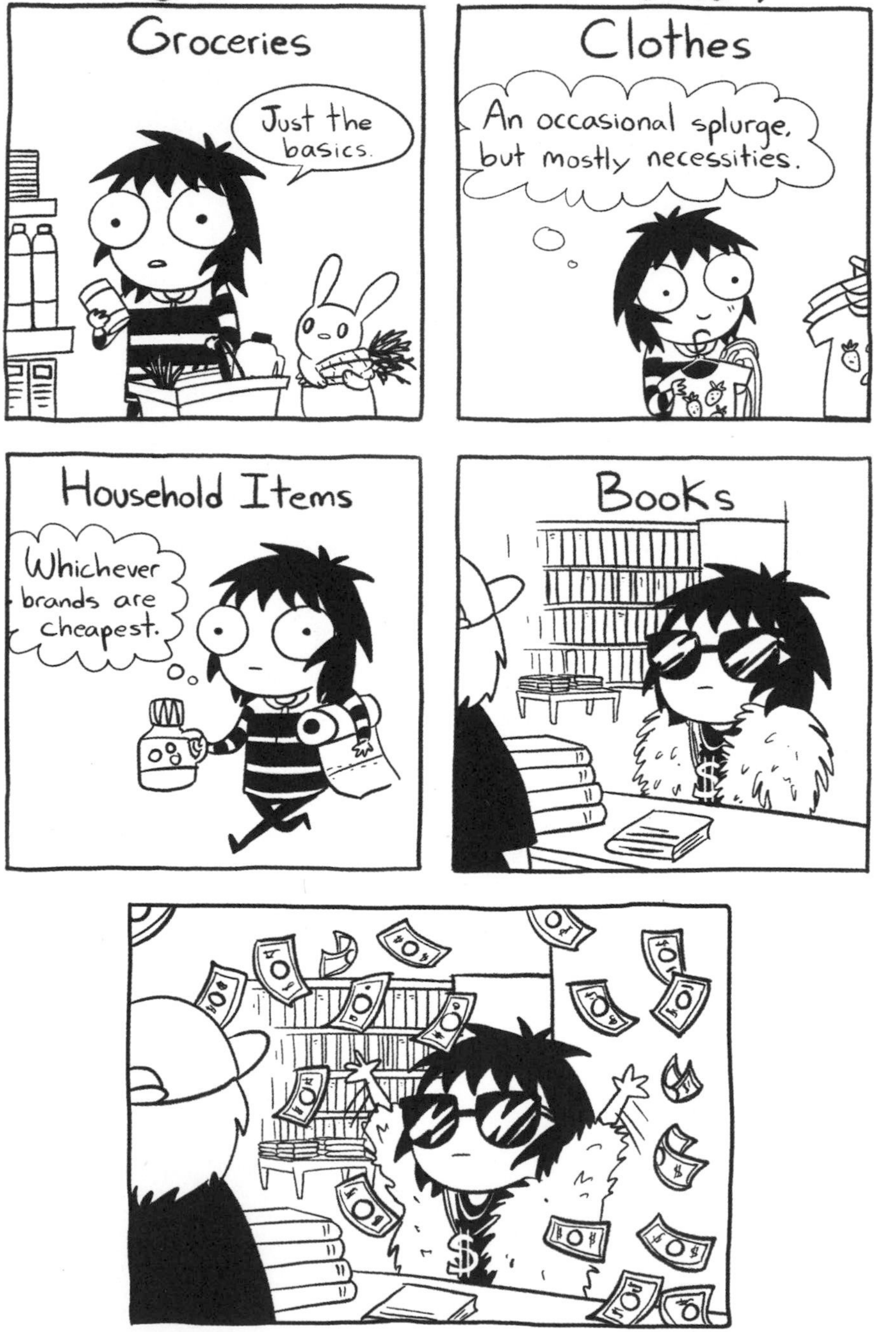
Groceries
Just the basics.
Clothes
An occasional splurge, but mostly necessities.
Household Items
Whichever brands are cheapest.
Books

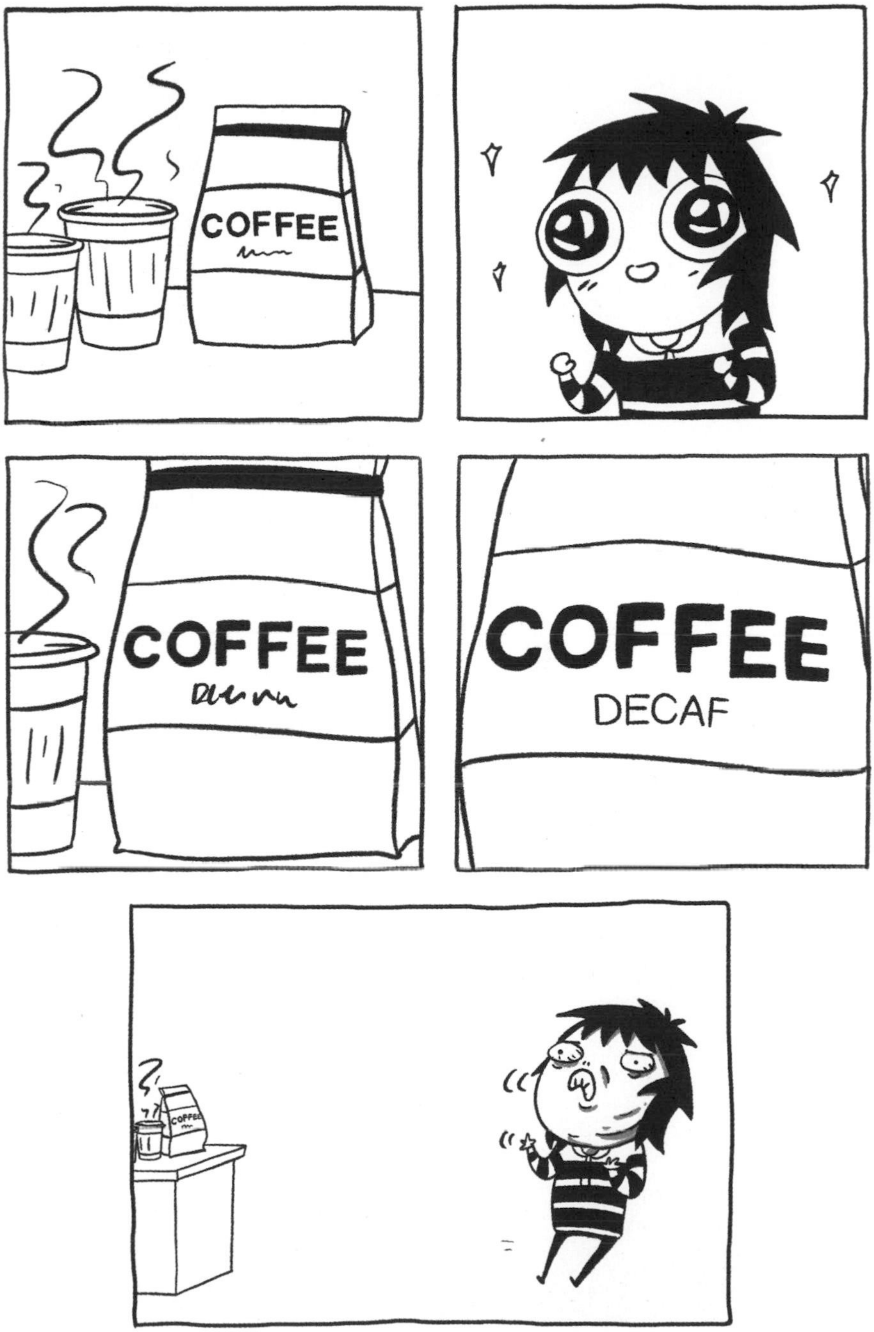
COFFEE
COFFEE
COFFEE
DECAF

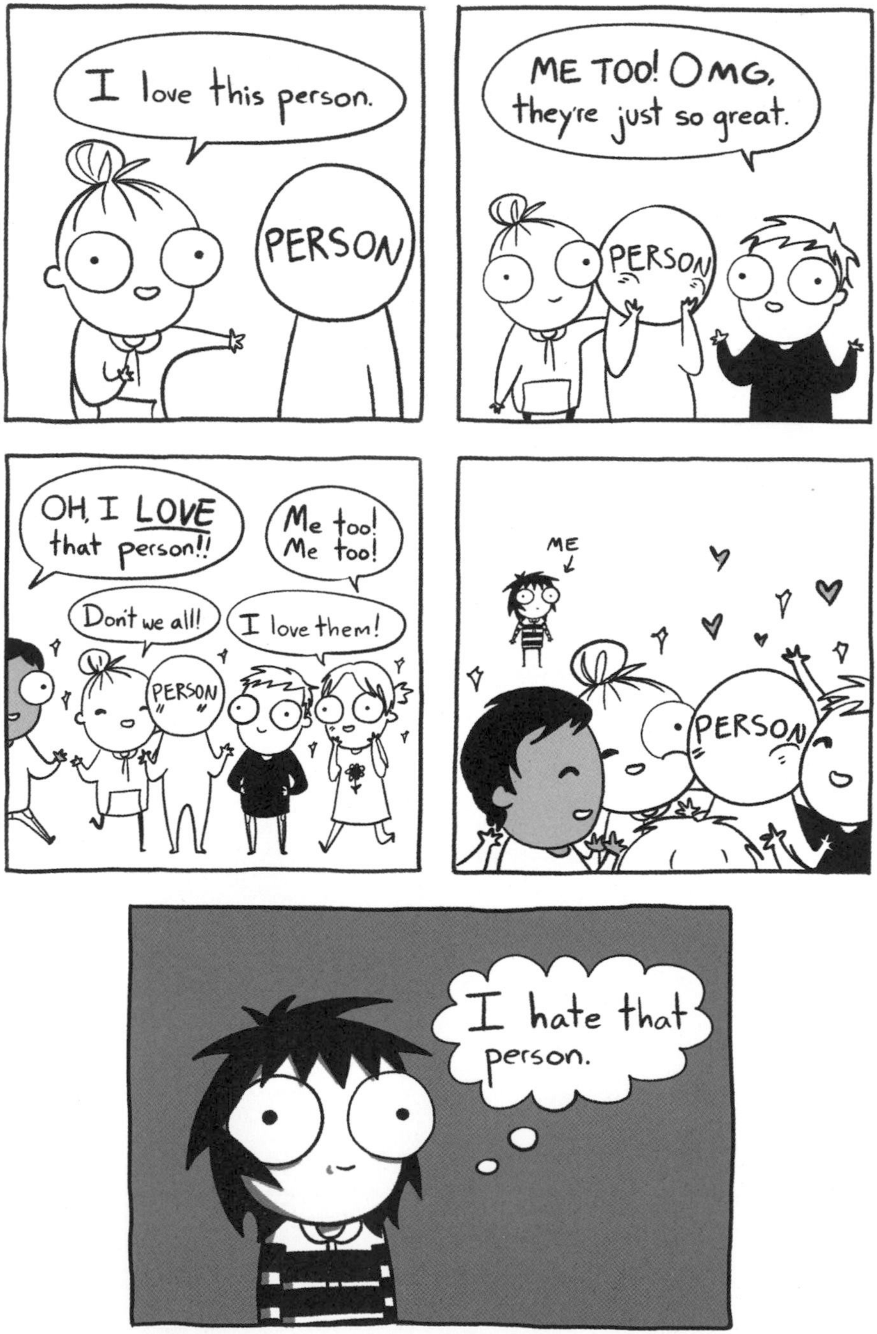
I love this person.
PERSON
ME TOO! OMG, they're just so great.
PERSON
OH, I LOVE that person!!
Me too! Me too!
Don't we all!
I love them!
PERSON
ME
PERSON
I hate that person.

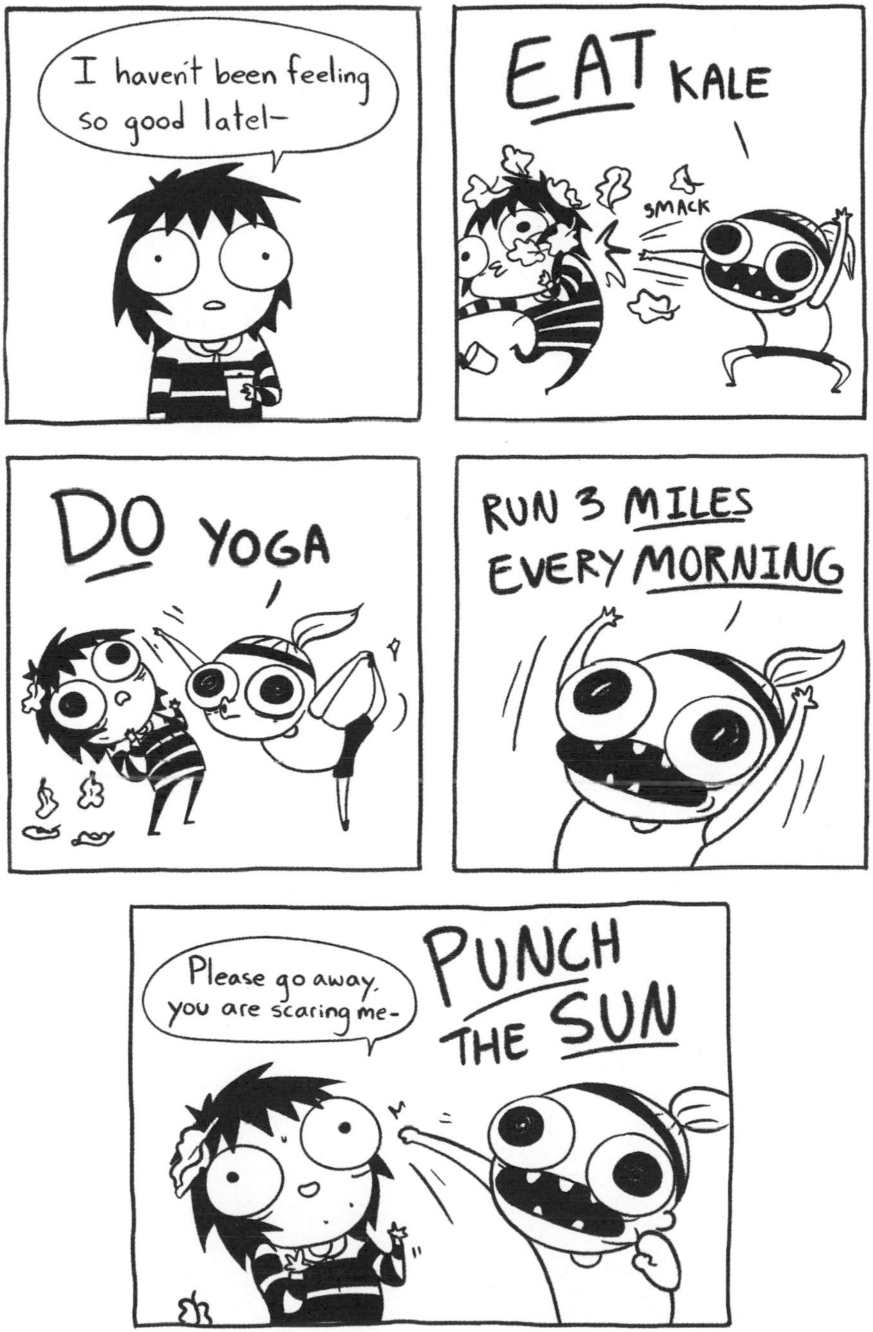
I haven't been feeling so good latel-
EAT KALE
SMACK
DO YOGA
RUN 3 MILES EVERY MORNING
Please go away, you are scaring me-
PUNCH THE SUN

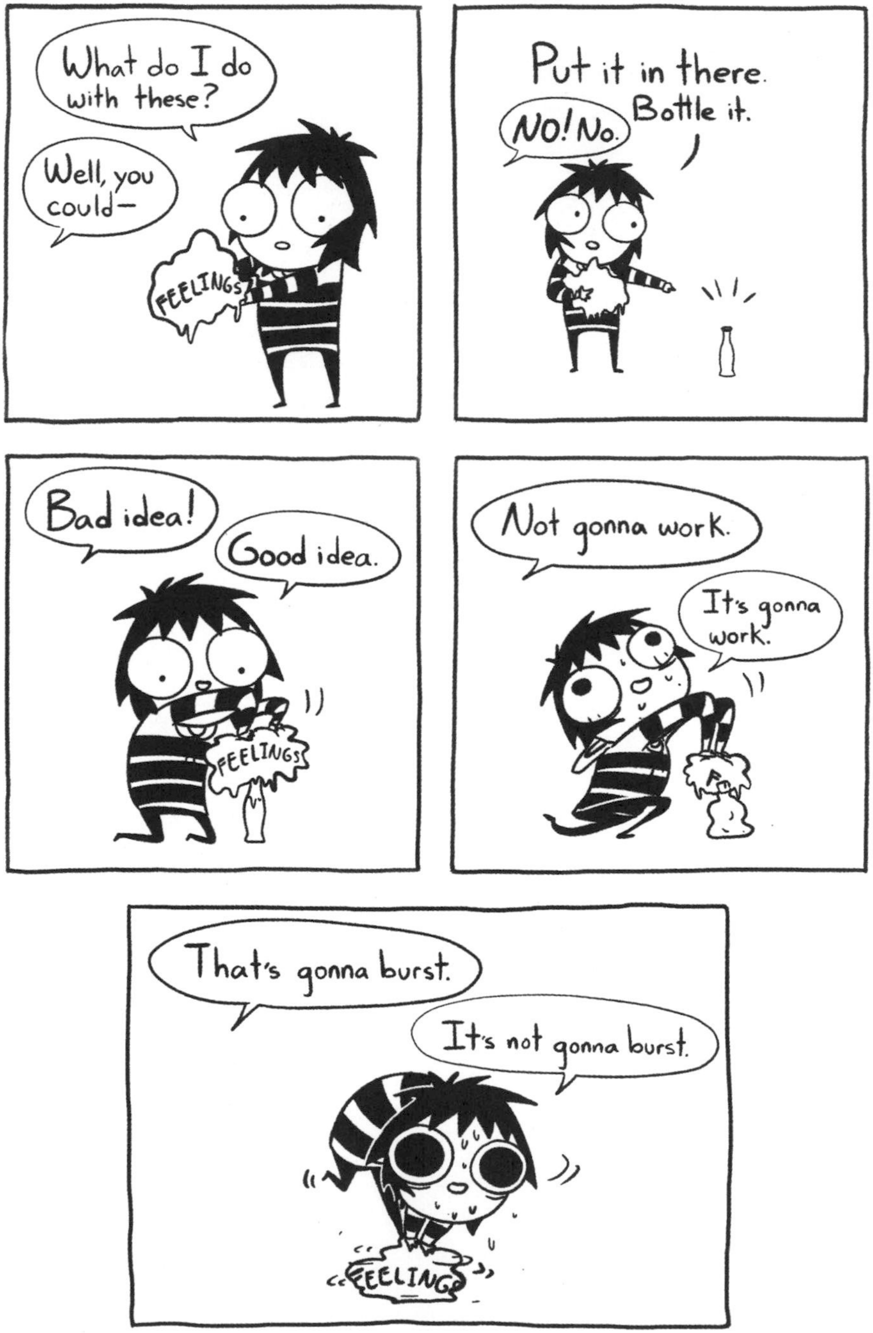
What do I do with these?
Well, you could—
FEELINGS
Put it in there.
NO! No.
Bottle it.
Bad idea!
Good idea.
FEELINGS
Not gonna work.
It's gonna work.
That's gonna burst.
It's not gonna burst.
FEELING

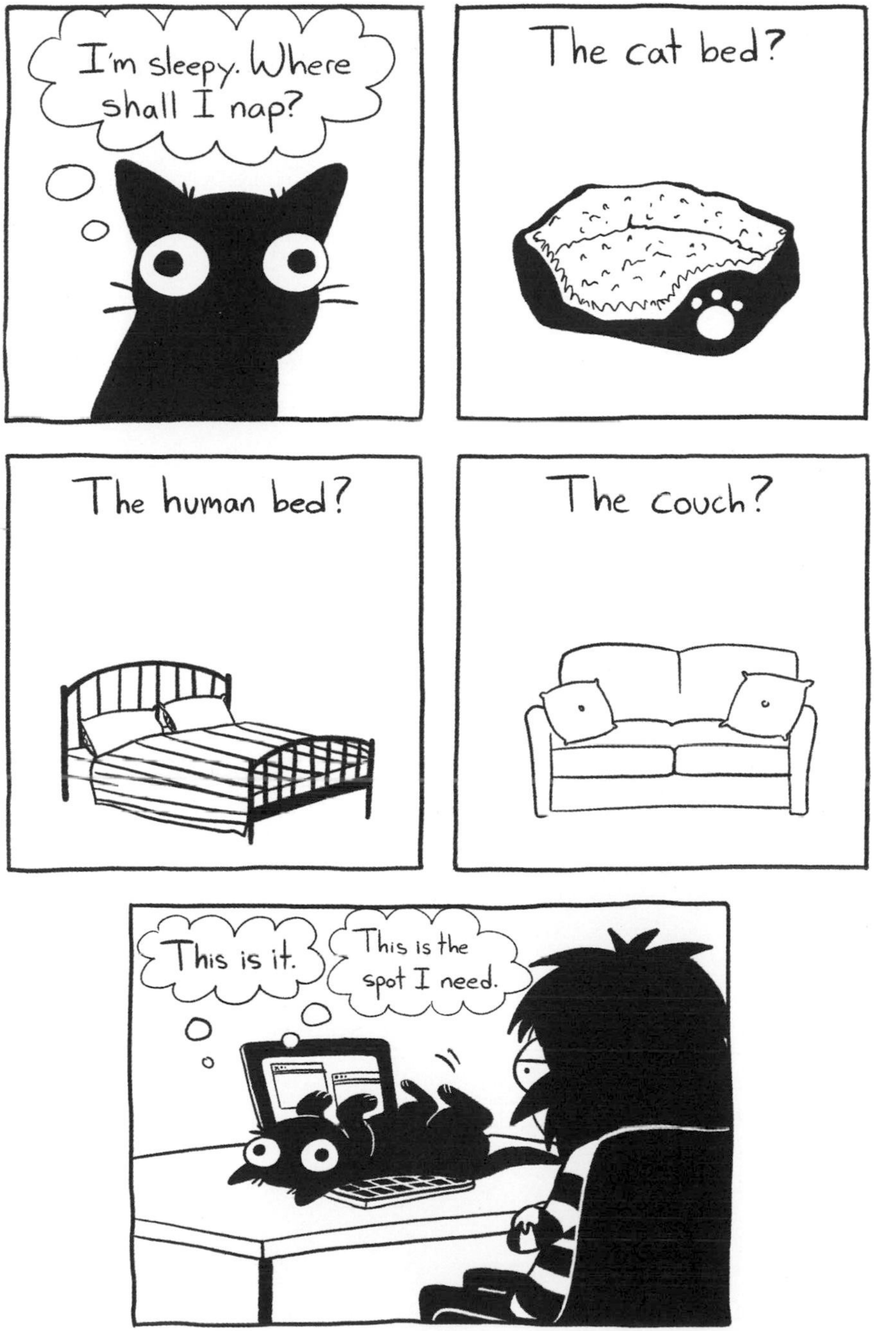
I'm sleepy. Where shall I nap?
The cat bed?
The human bed?
The couch?
This is it.
This is the spot I need.

FLIRTING

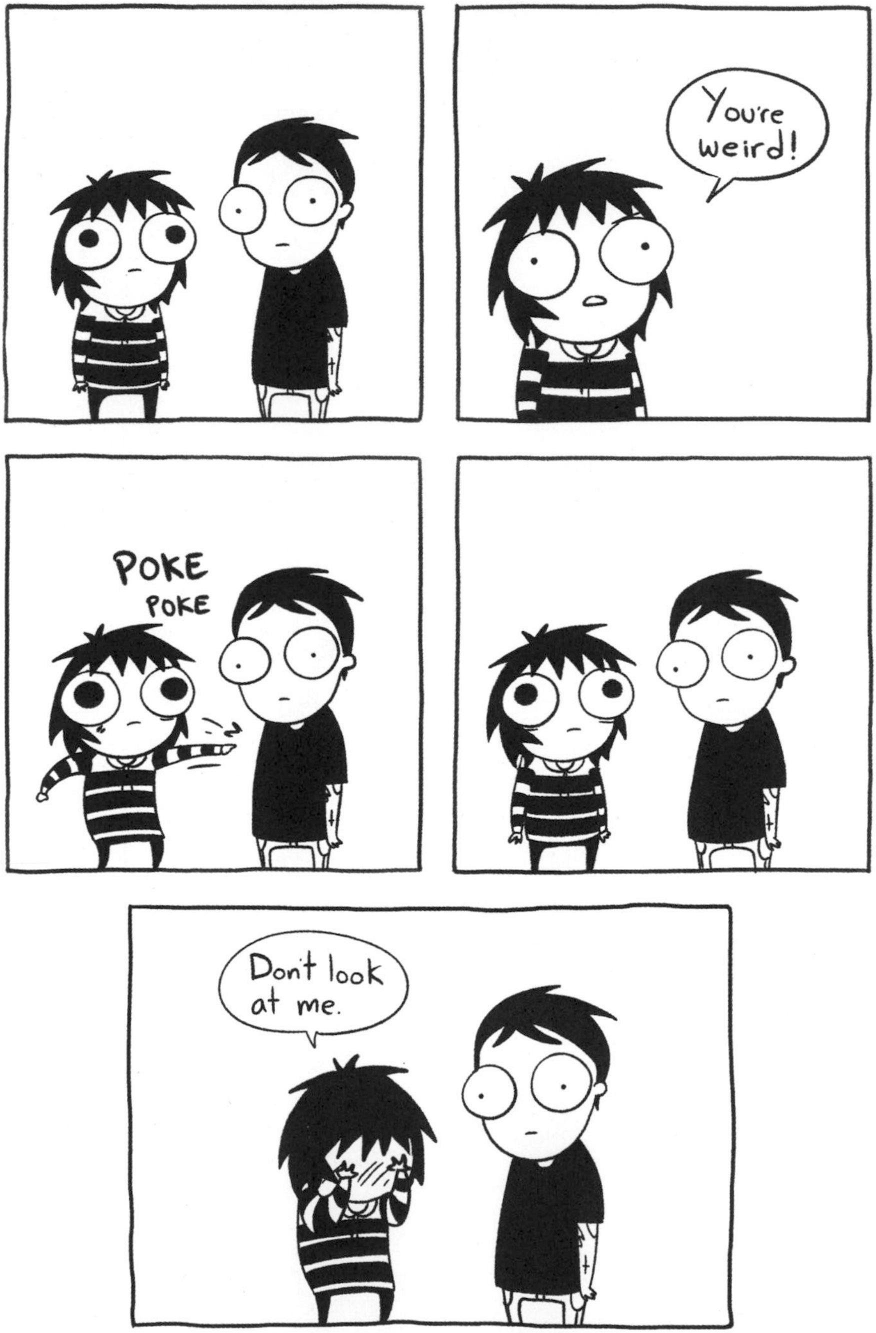
You're weird!
POKE
POKE
Don't look at me.

How Sundays Feel

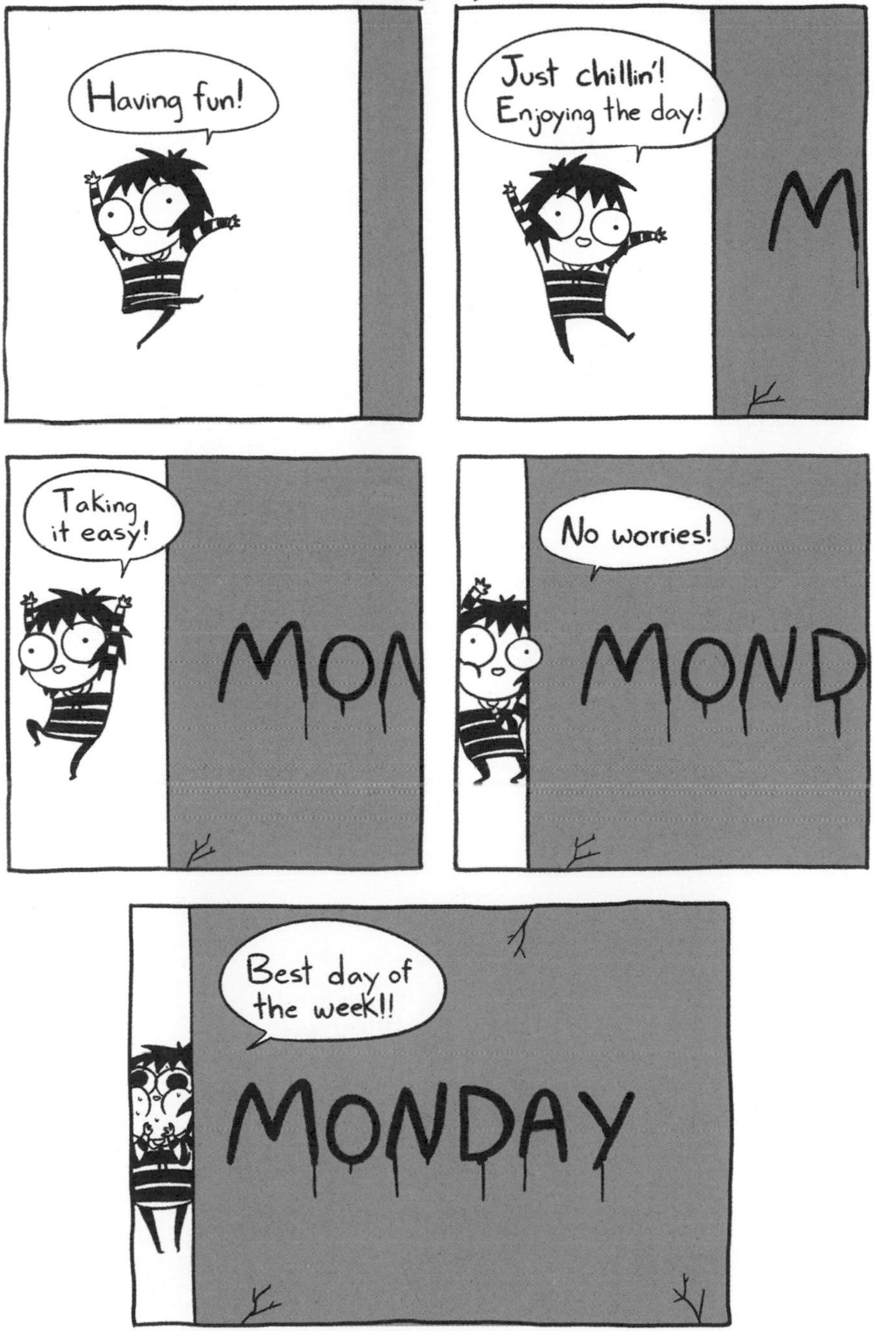
Having fun!
Just chillin'! Enjoying the day!
M
Taking it easy!
MON
No worries!
MOND
Best day of the week!!
MONDAY

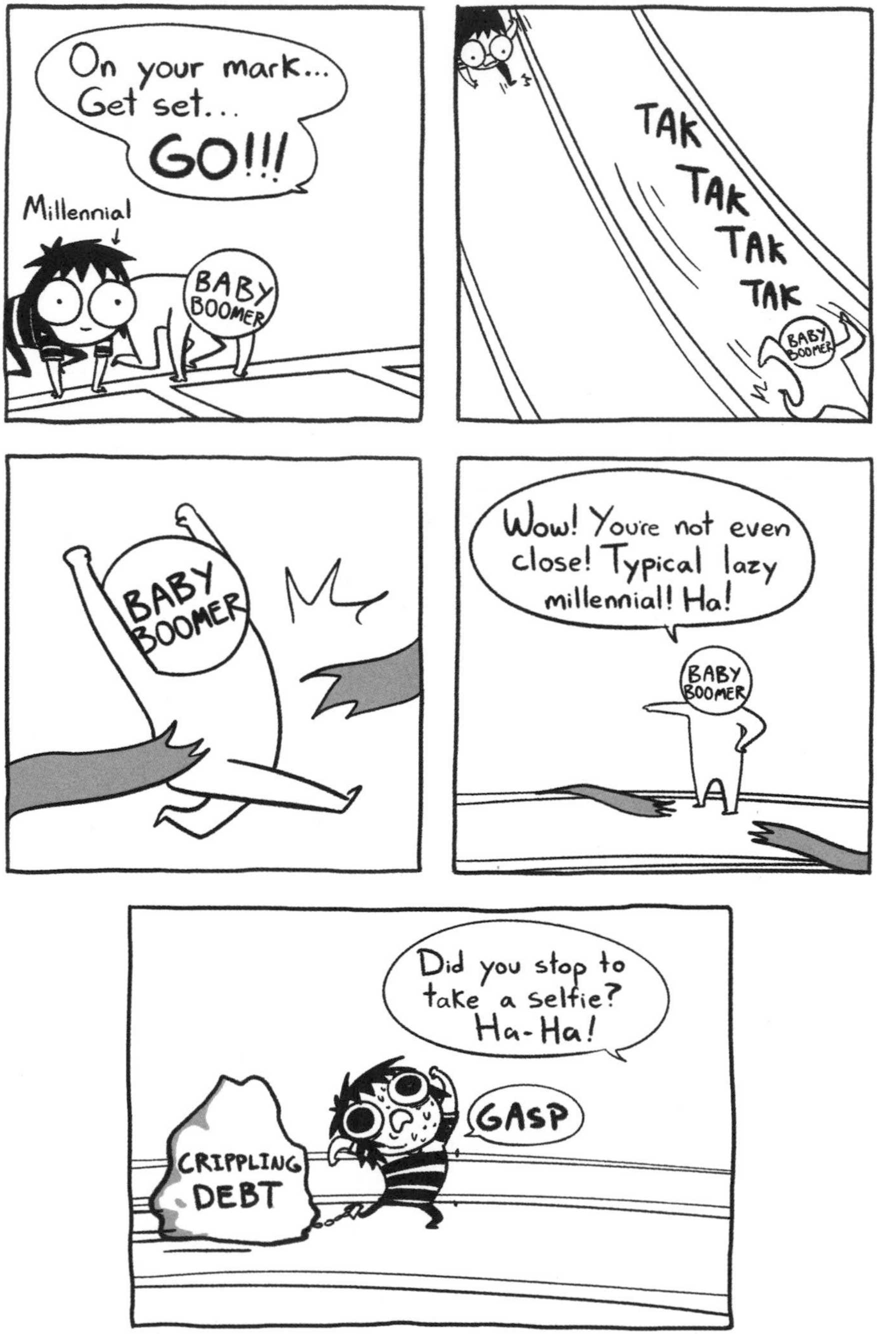
On your mark... Get set... GO!!!
Millennial
BABY BOOMER
TAK TAK TAK TAK
BABY BOOMER
BABY BOOMER
Wow! You're not even close! Typical lazy millennial! Ha!
BABY BOOMER
Did you stop to take a selfie? Ha-Ha!
GASP
CRIPPLING DEBT

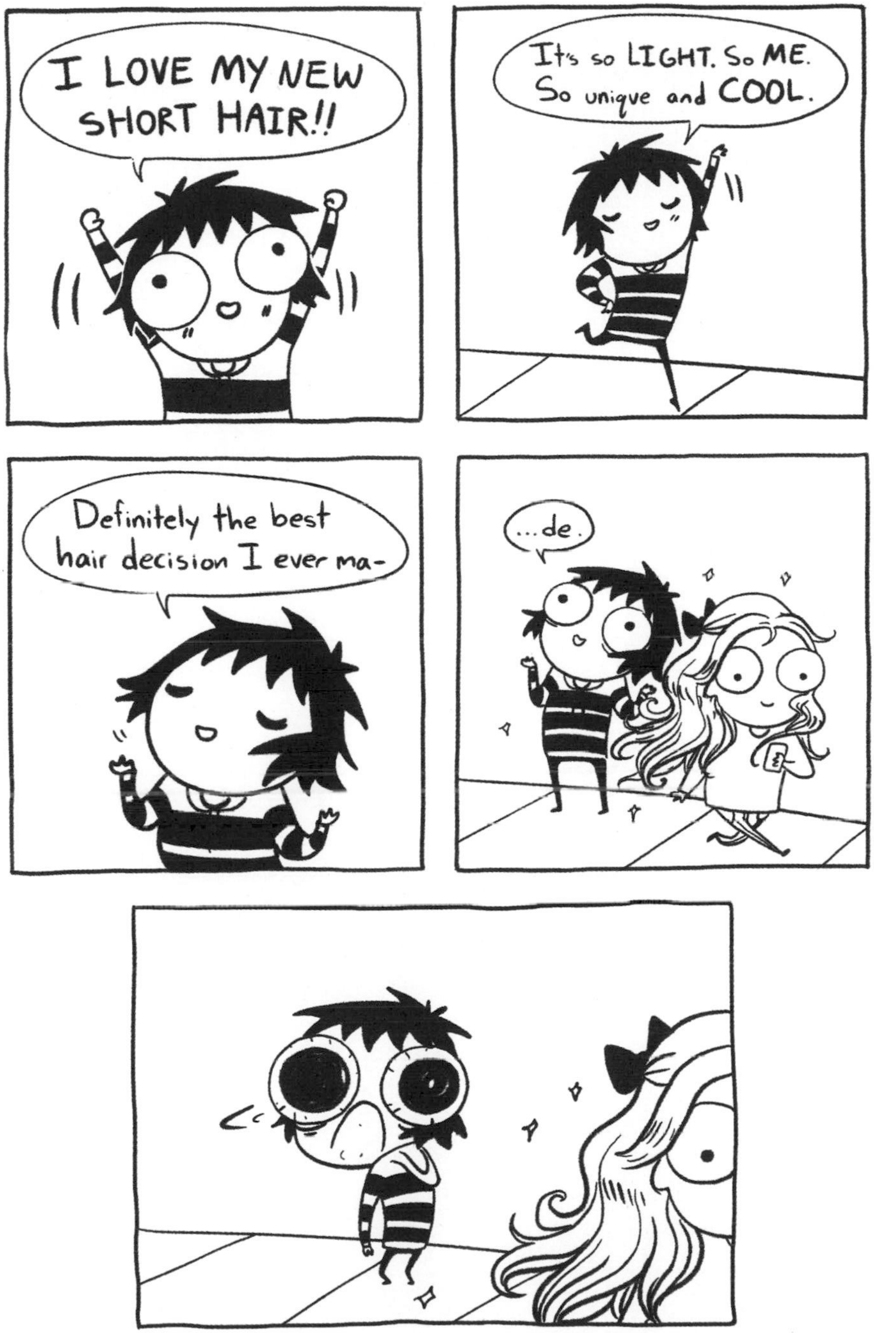
I LOVE MY NEW SHORT HAIR!!
It's so LIGHT. So ME. So unique and COOL.
Definitely the best hair decision I ever ma-
...de.

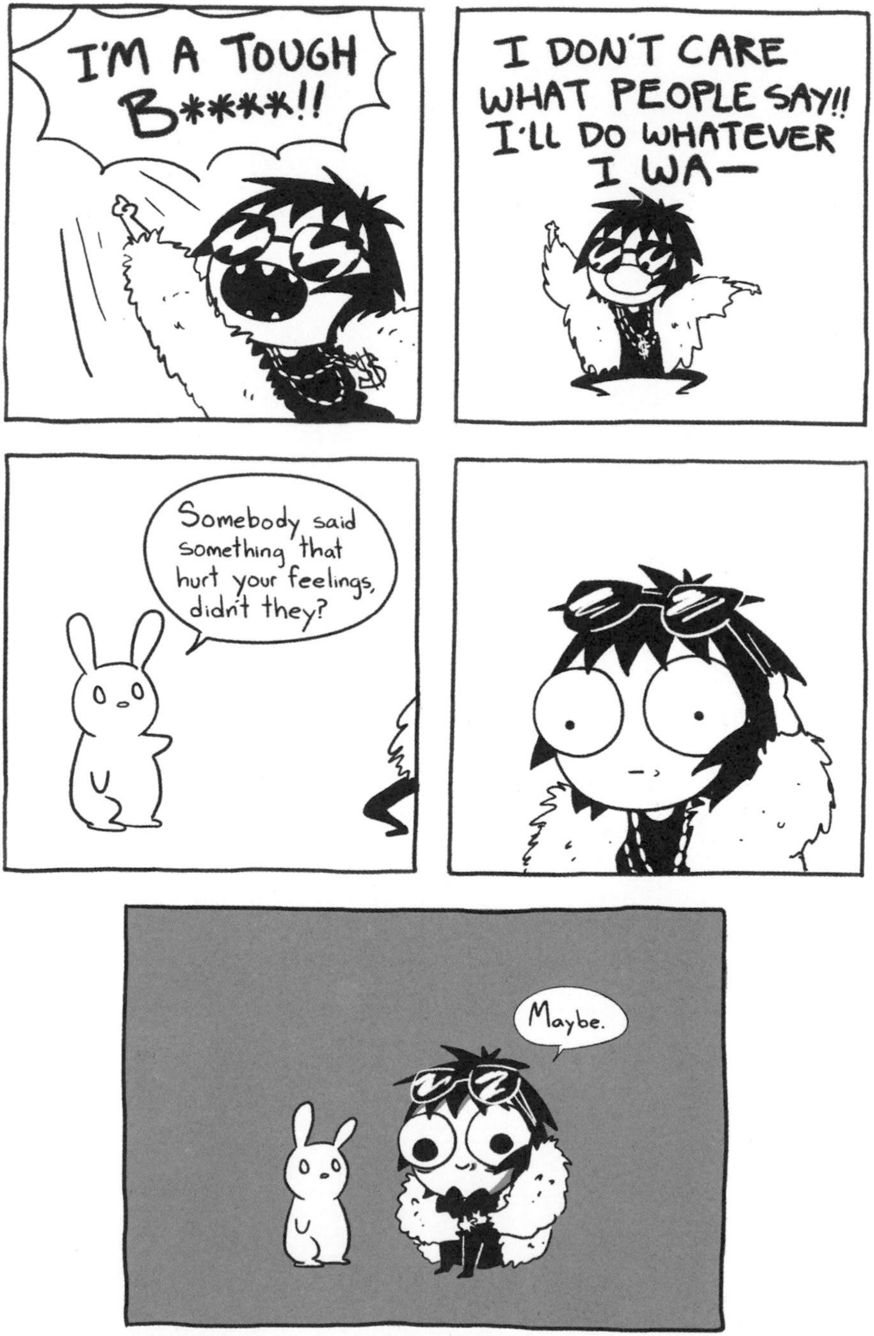
I'M A TOUGH B****!!
I DON'T CARE WHAT PEOPLE SAY!! I'LL DO WHATEVER I WA—
Somebody said something that hurt your feelings, didn't they?
Maybe.

MEN AT BARS

This chick is SO into me. She's giving me all the right signs!
BLAH BLAH BLAH
I should definitely keep talking to her.
AH AH AH
NO
BLAH BLAH BLAH
NO NO NO NO NO NO
NO
NO
NO

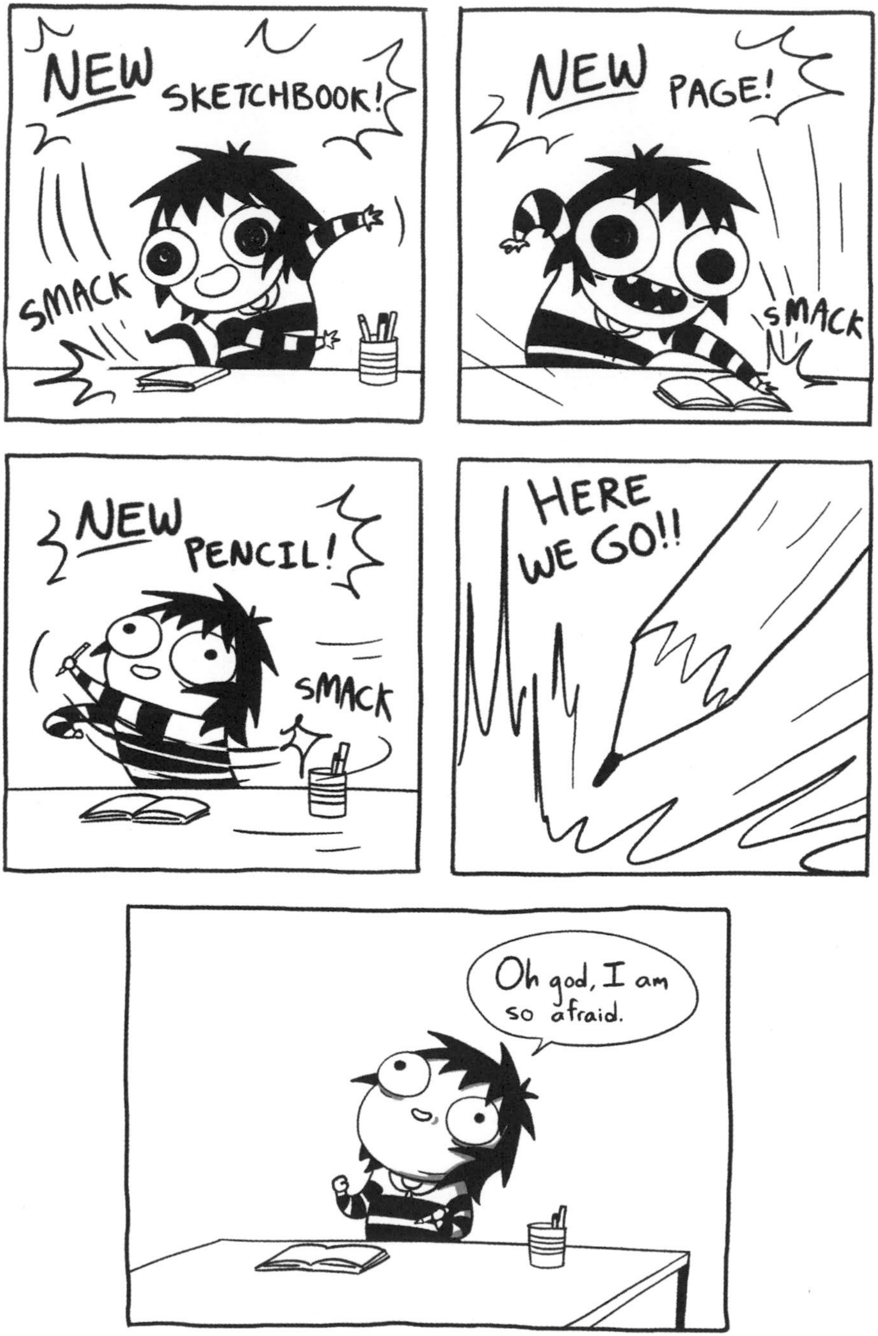
NEW SKETCHBOOK!
SMACK
NEW PAGE!
SMACK
NEW PENCIL!
SMACK
HERE WE GO!!
Oh god, I am so afraid.

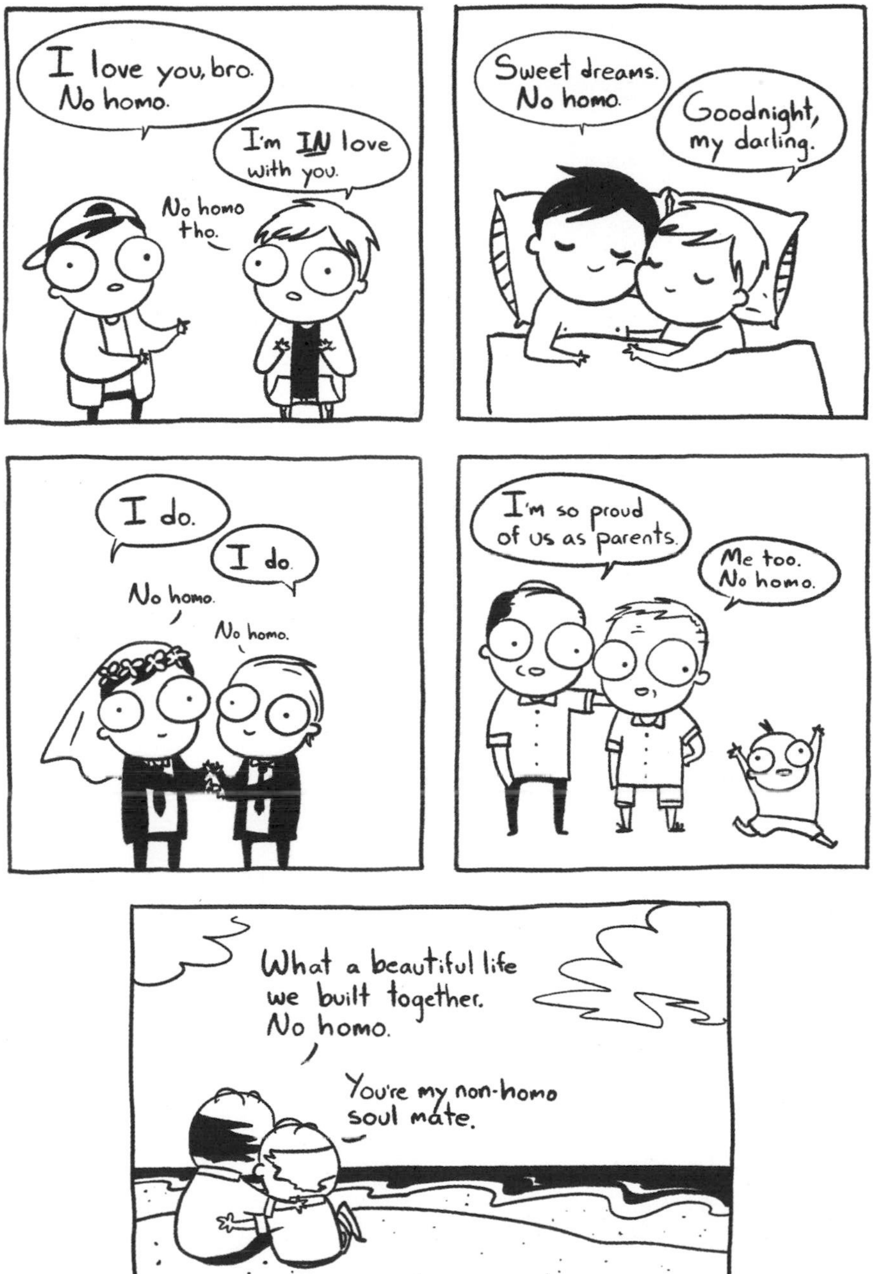
I love you, bro. No homo.
I'm IN love with you.
No homo tho.
Sweet dreams. No homo.
Goodnight, my darling.
I do.
I do.
No homo.
No homo.
I'm so proud of us as parents.
Me too. No homo.
What a beautiful life we built together. No homo.
You're my non-homo soul mate.

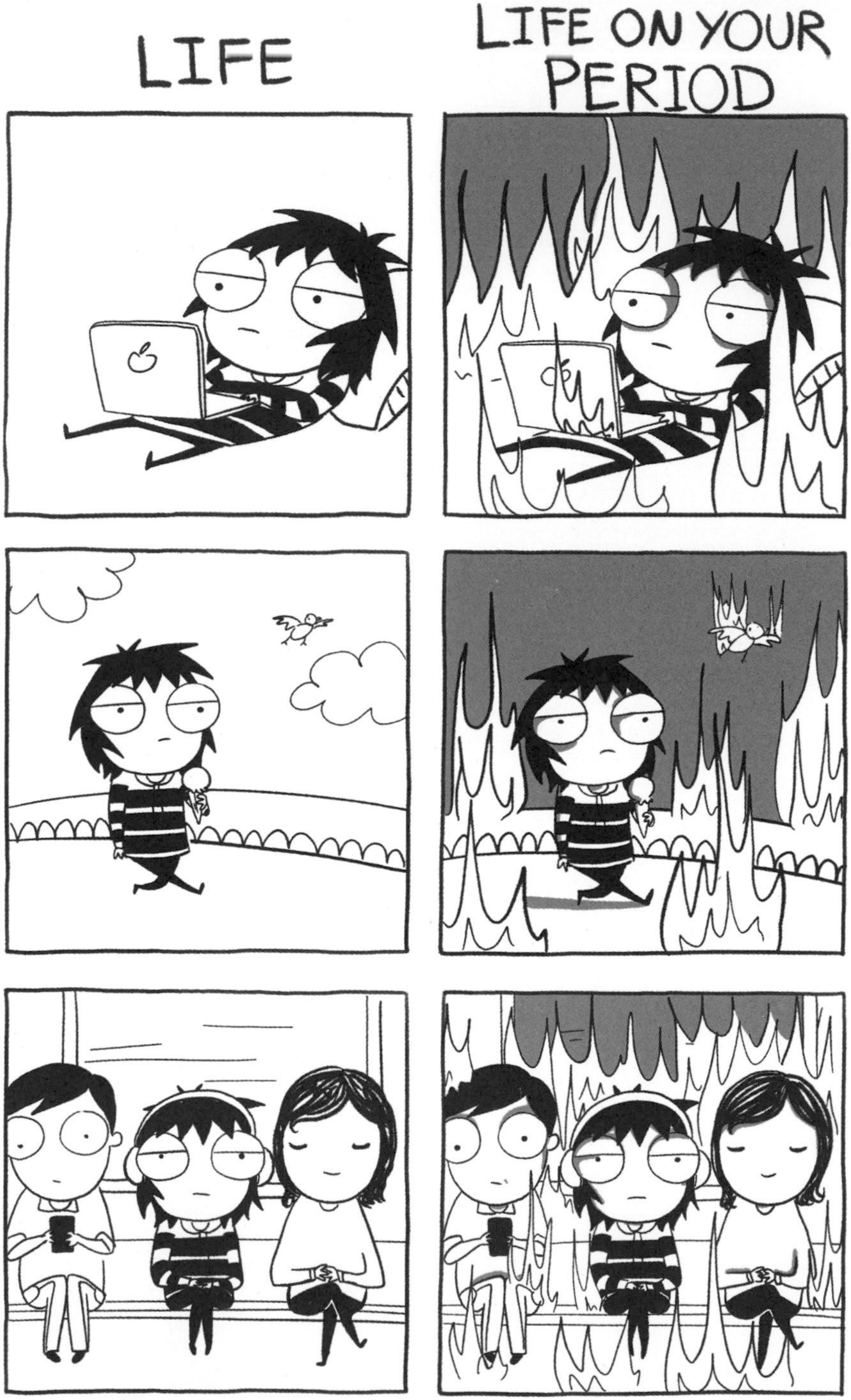
LIFE
LIFE ON YOUR PERIOD

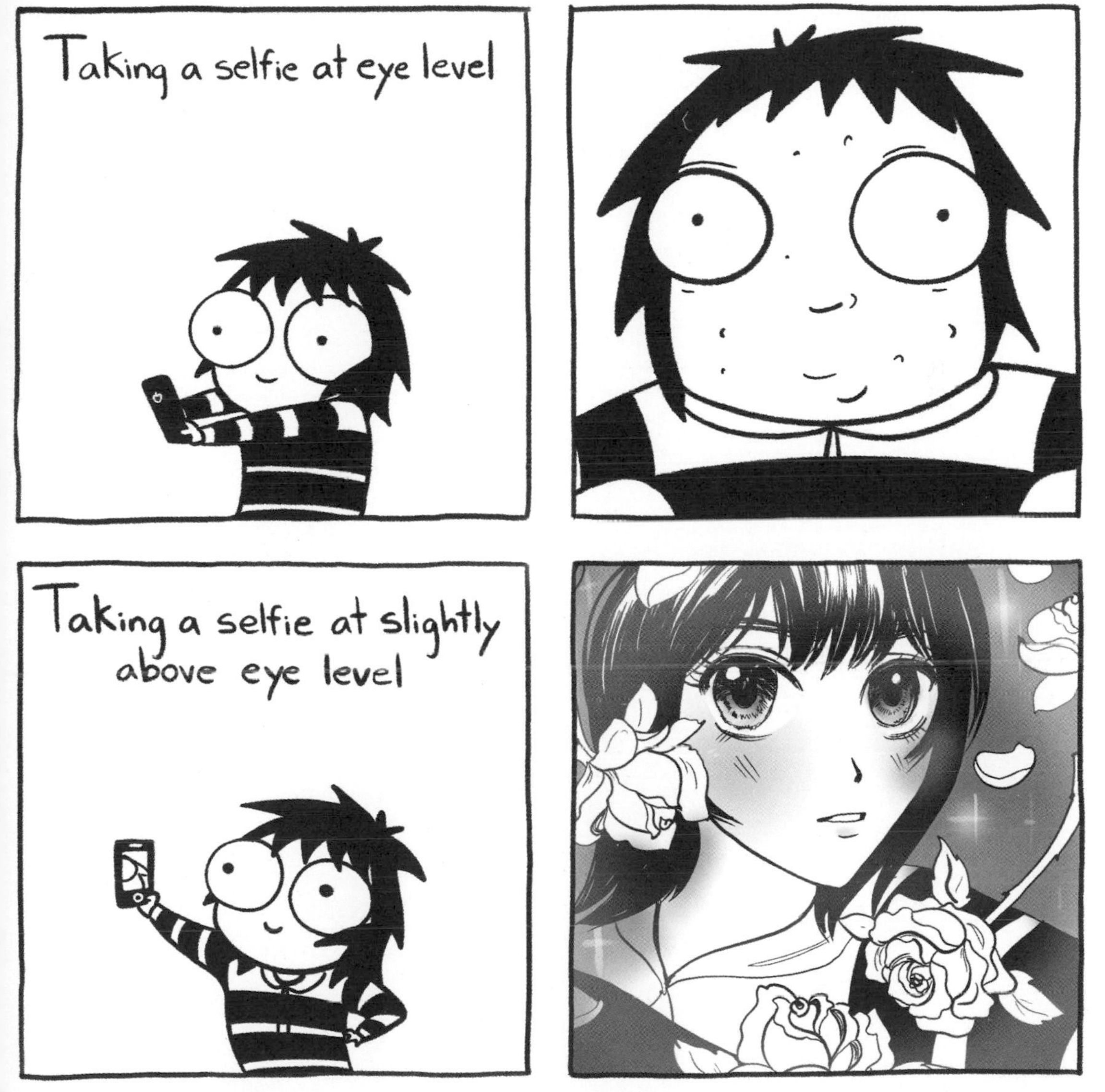
Taking a selfie at eye level
Taking a selfie at slightly above eye level

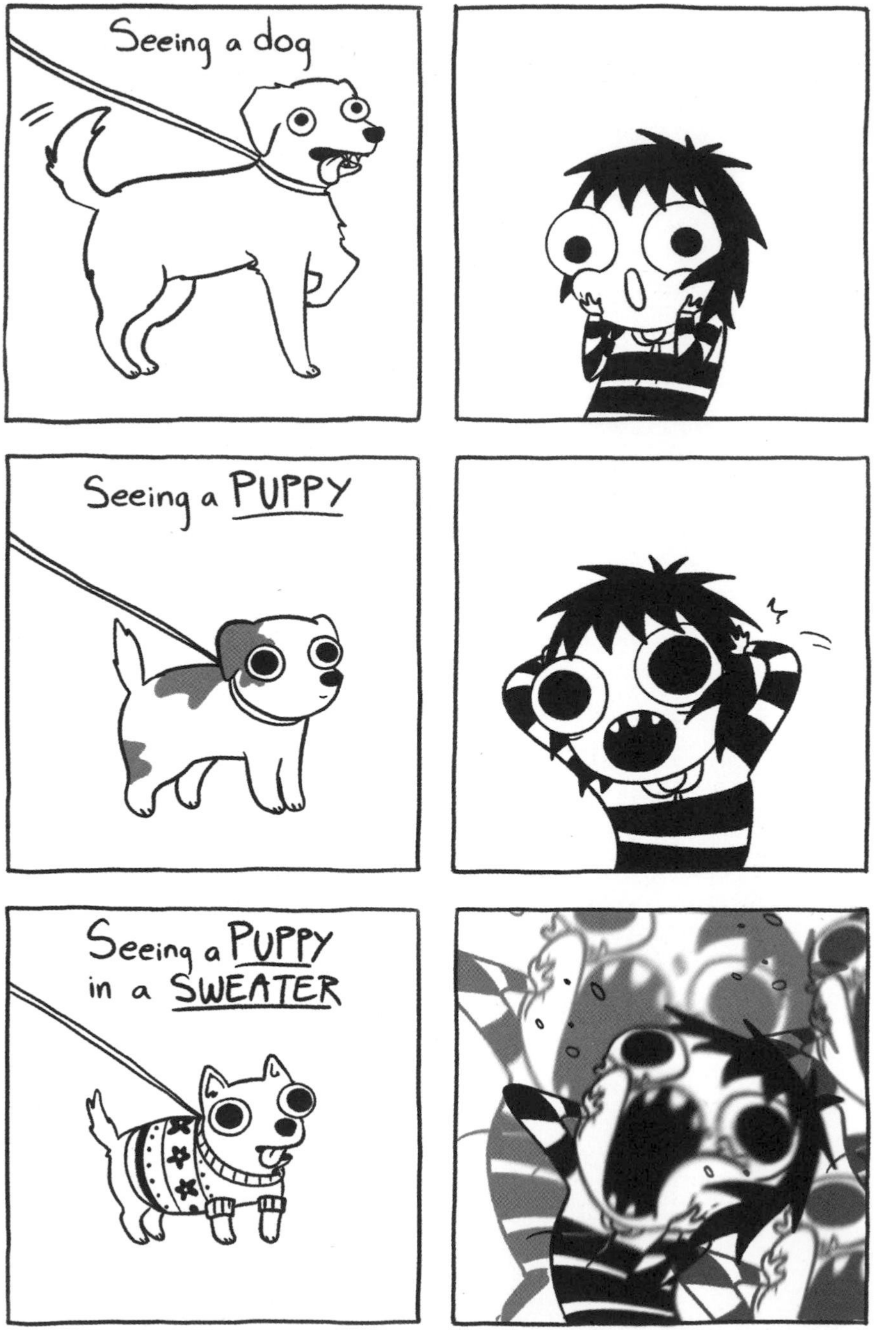
Seeing a dog
Seeing a PUPPY
Seeing a PUPPY in a SWEATER

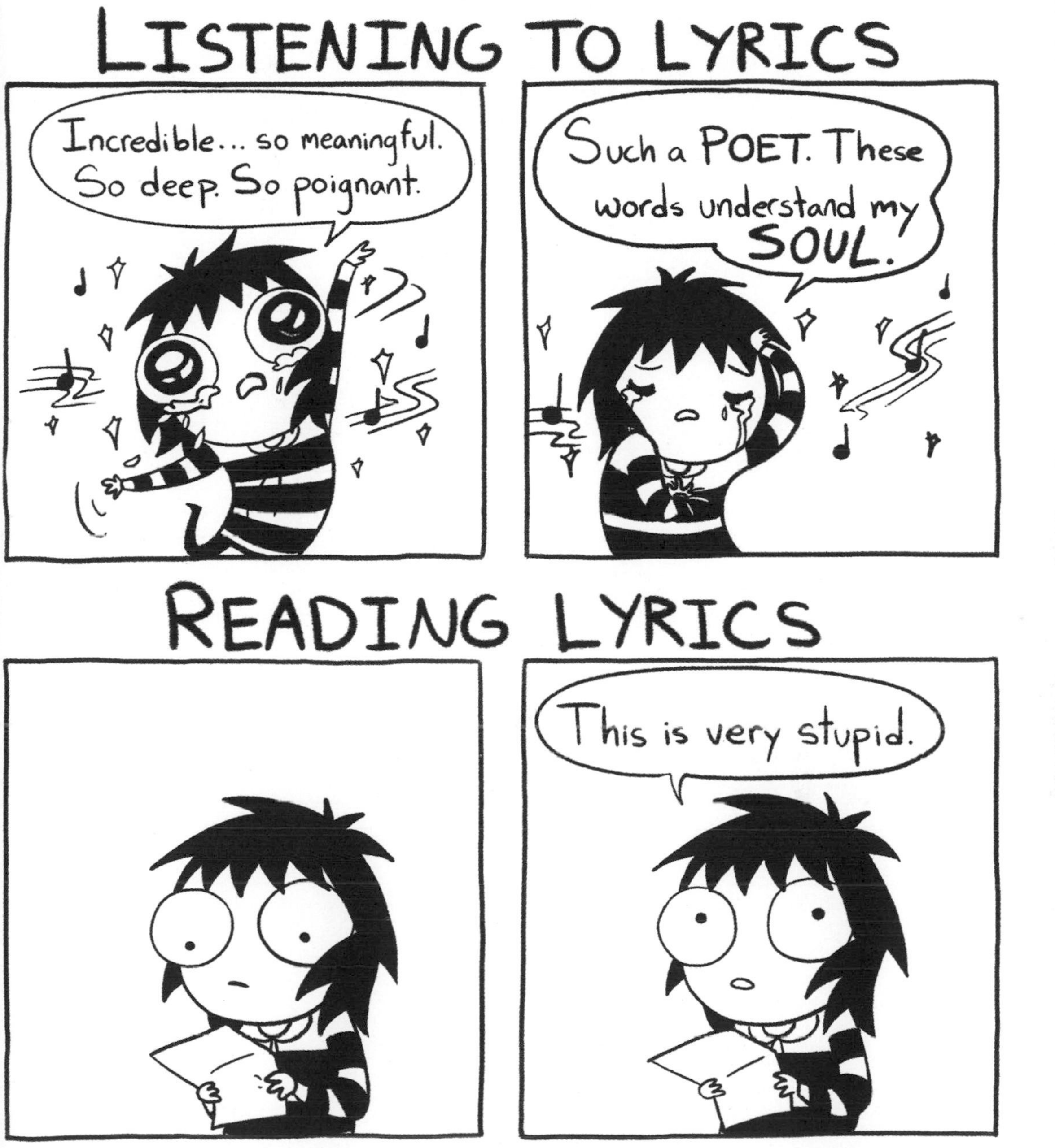
LISTENING TO LYRICS
Incredible... so meaningful. So deep. So poignant.
Such a POET. These words understand my SOUL.
READING LYRICS
This is very stupid.

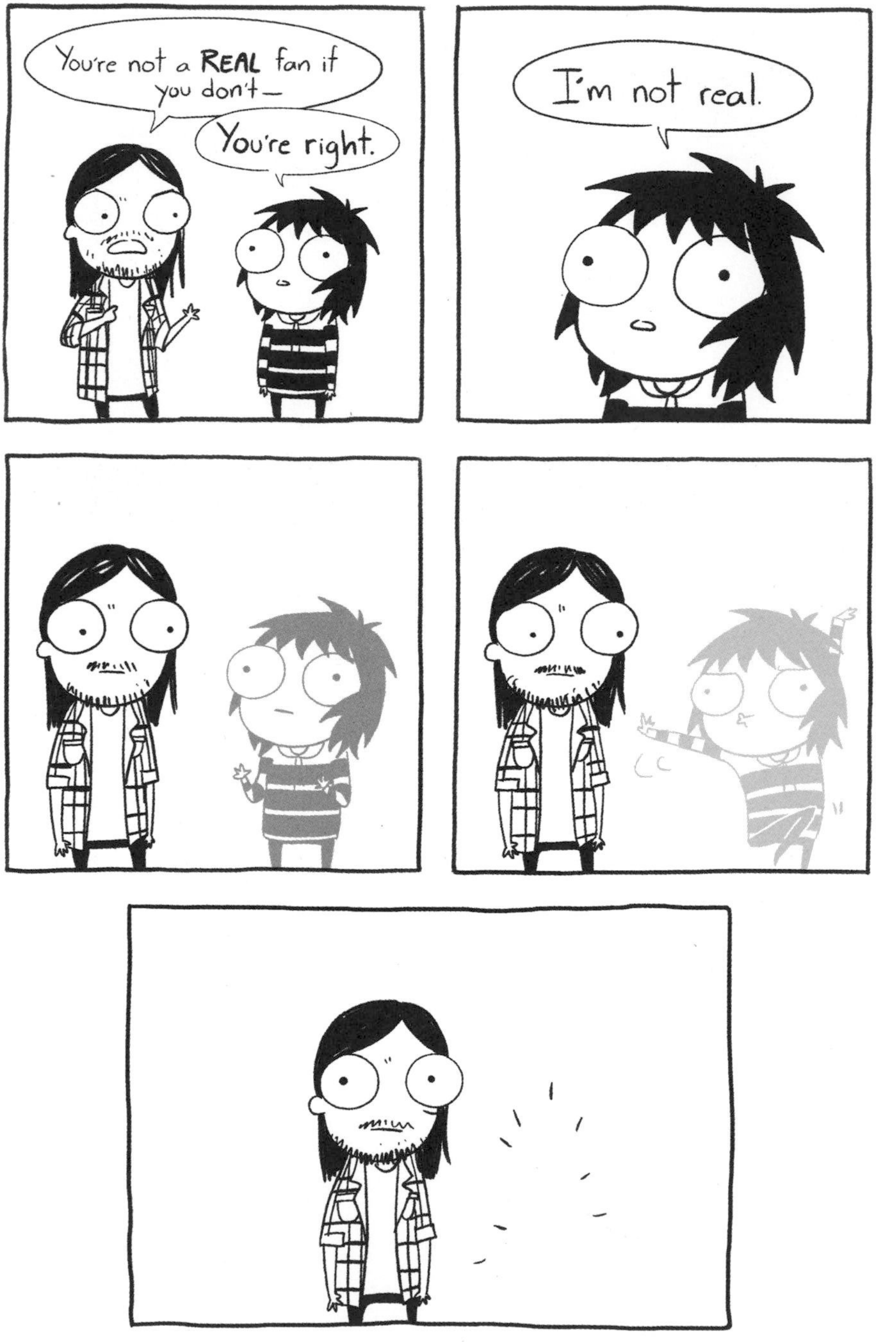
You're not a REAL fan if you don't—
You're right.
I'm not real.

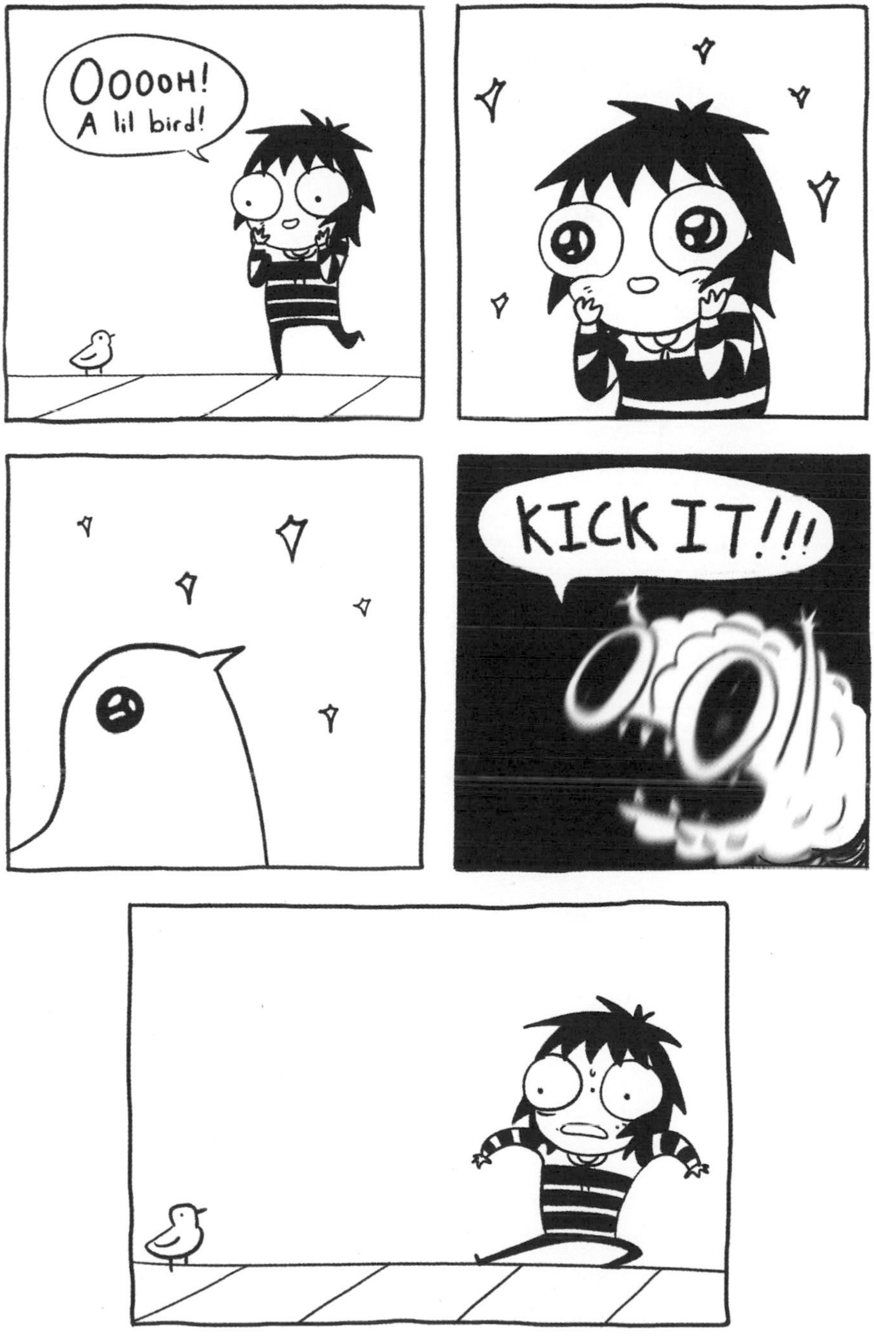
OOOOH!
A lil bird!
KICK IT!!!

TALKING ABOUT CELEBRITIES

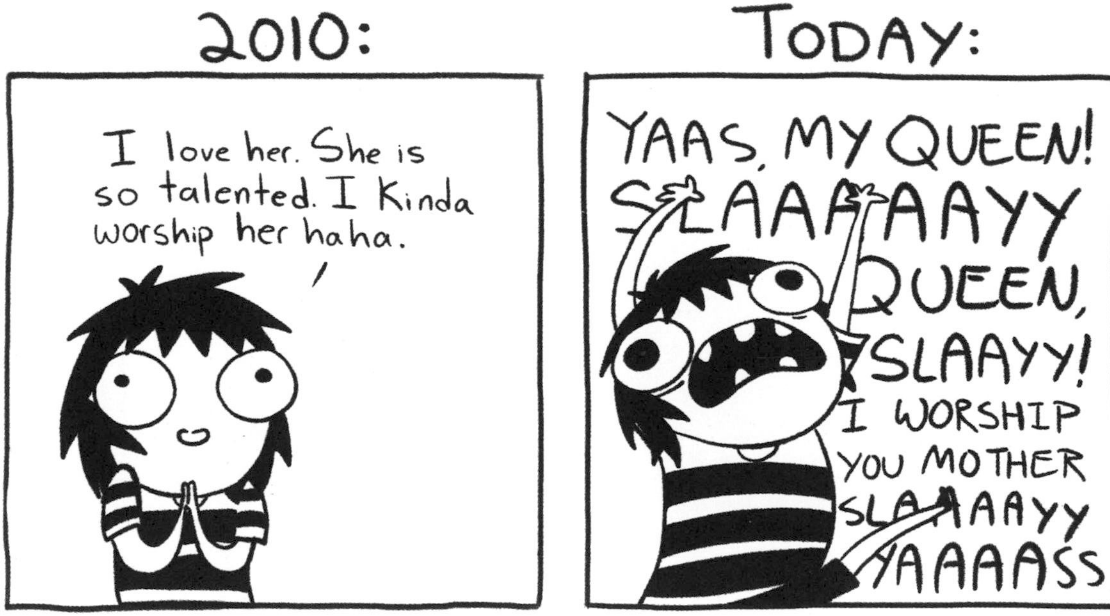

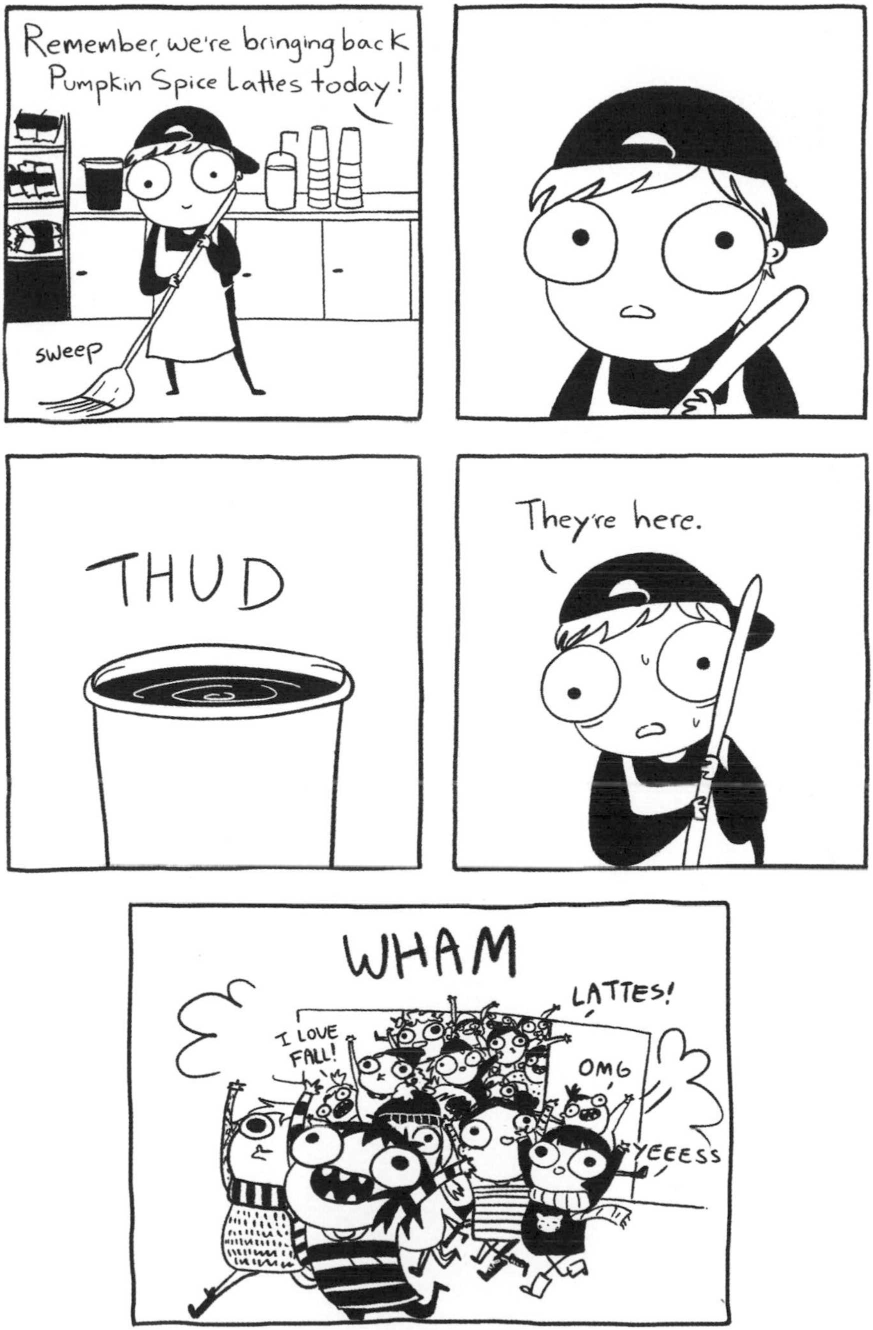
Remember, we're bringing back Pumpkin Spice Lattes today!
sweep
THUD
They're here.
WHAM
I LOVE FALL!
LATTES!
OMG
YEEESS

COSTUMES TO SCARE MILLENNIALS

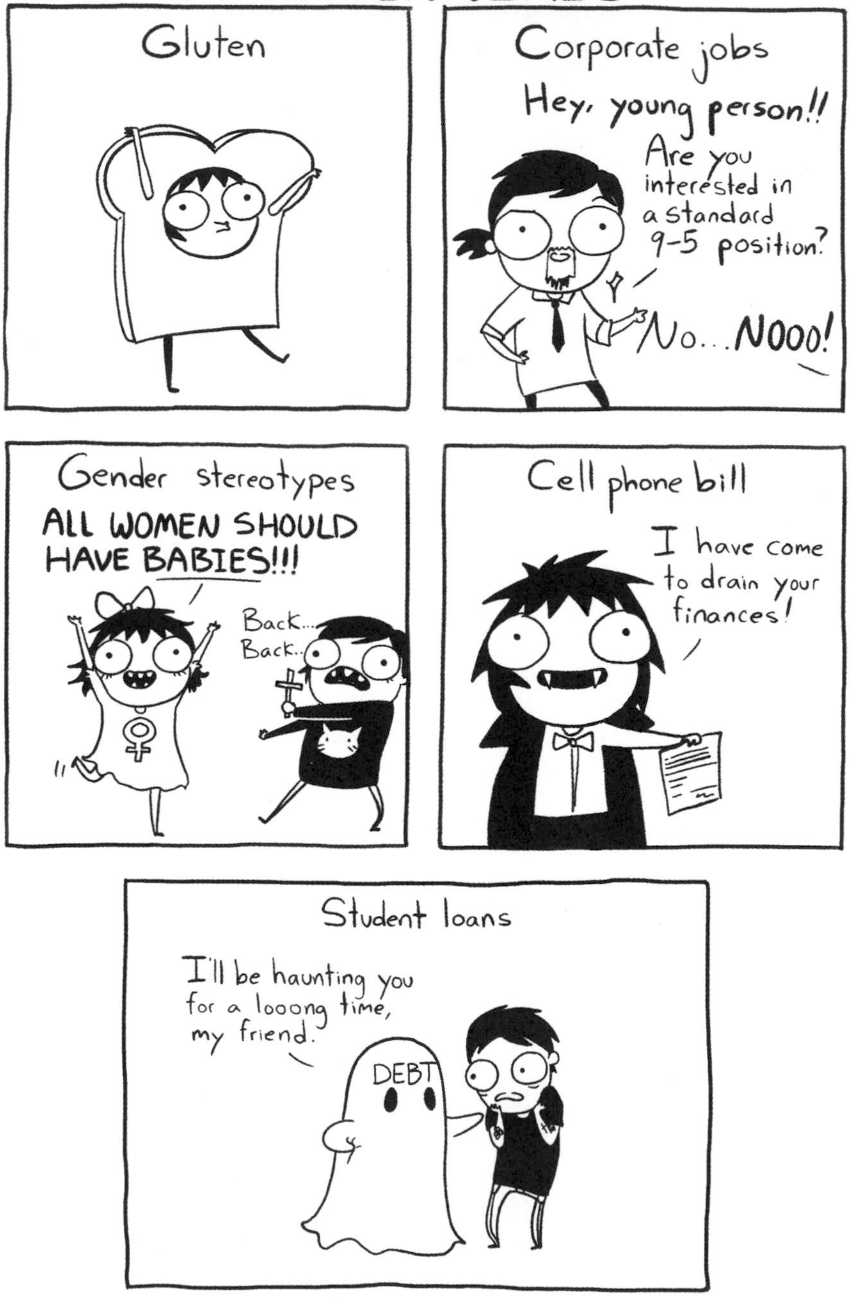
Gluten
Corporate jobs
Hey, young person!!
Are you interested in a standard 9-5 position?
No... NOOO!
Gender stereotypes
ALL WOMEN SHOULD HAVE BABIES!!!
Back... Back...
Cell phone bill
I have come to drain your finances!
Student loans
I'll be haunting you for a looong time, my friend.
DEBT

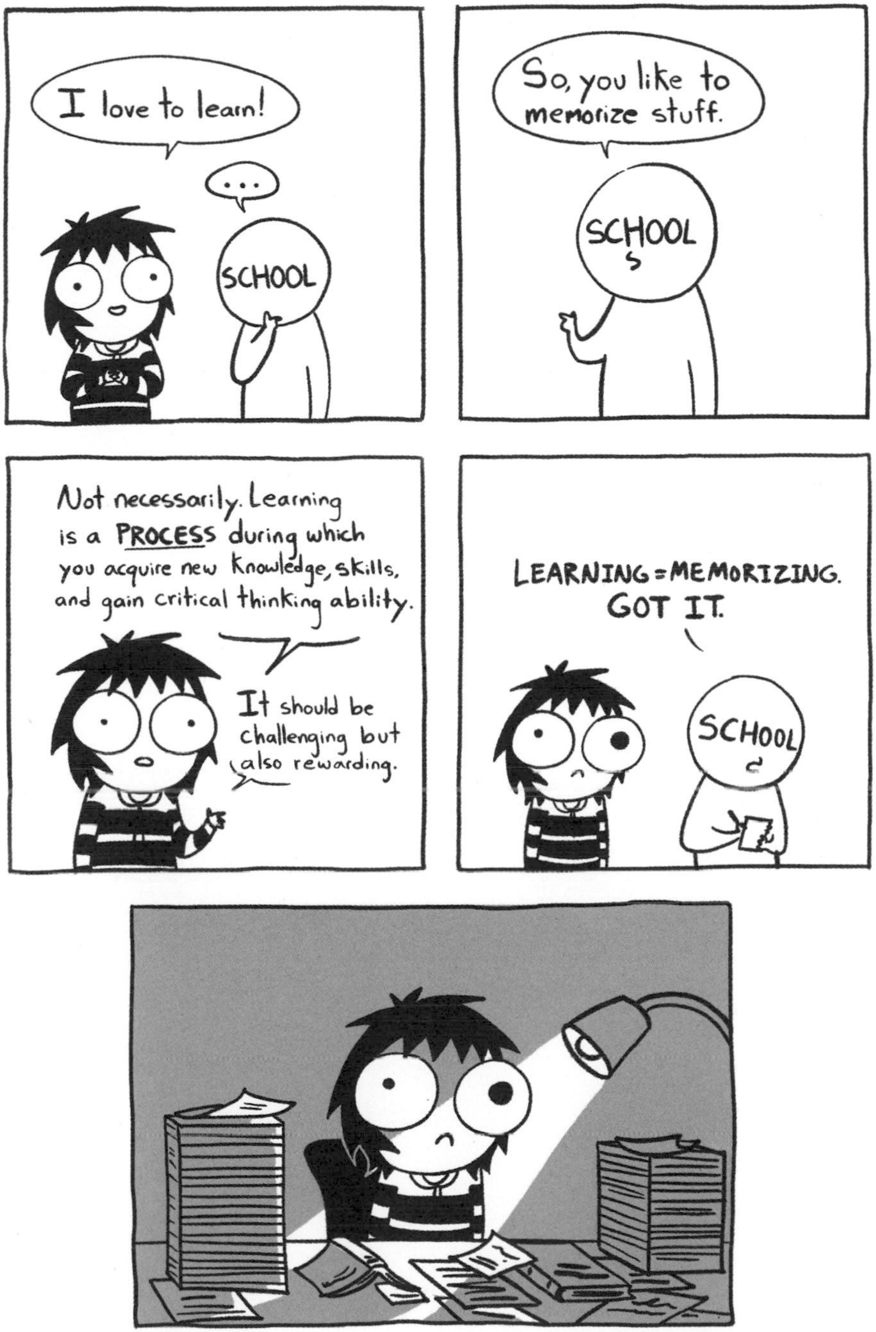
I love to learn!
...
SCHOOL
So, you like to memorize stuff.
SCHOOL
Not necessarily. Learning is a PROCESS during which you acquire new knowledge, skills, and gain critical thinking ability.
It should be challenging but also rewarding.
LEARNING = MEMORIZING. GOT IT.
SCHOOL

HOW THE ANIMAL KINGDOM SAYS "DON'T TALK TO ME"

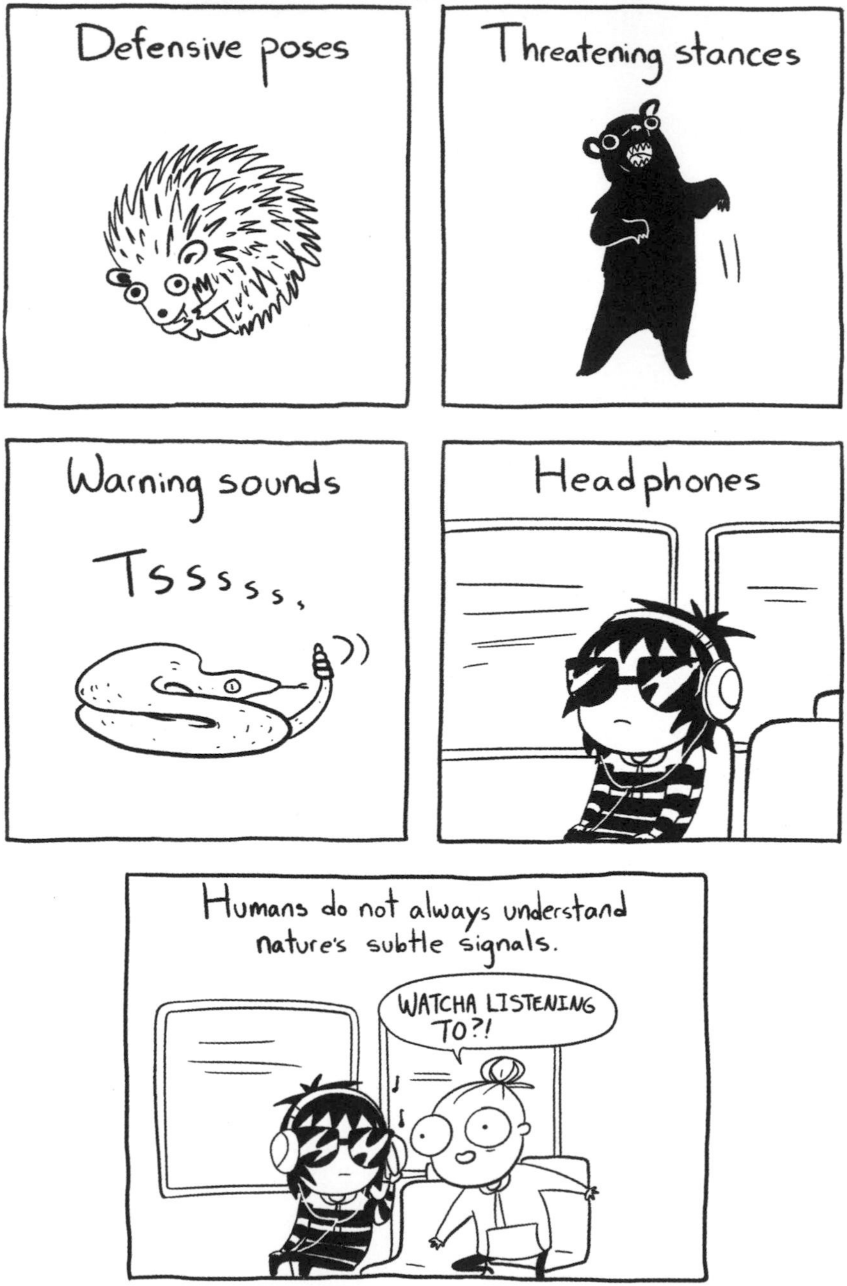
Defensive poses
Threatening stances
Warning sounds
Tsssss,
Headphones
Humans do not always understand nature's subtle signals.
WATCHA LISTENING TO?!

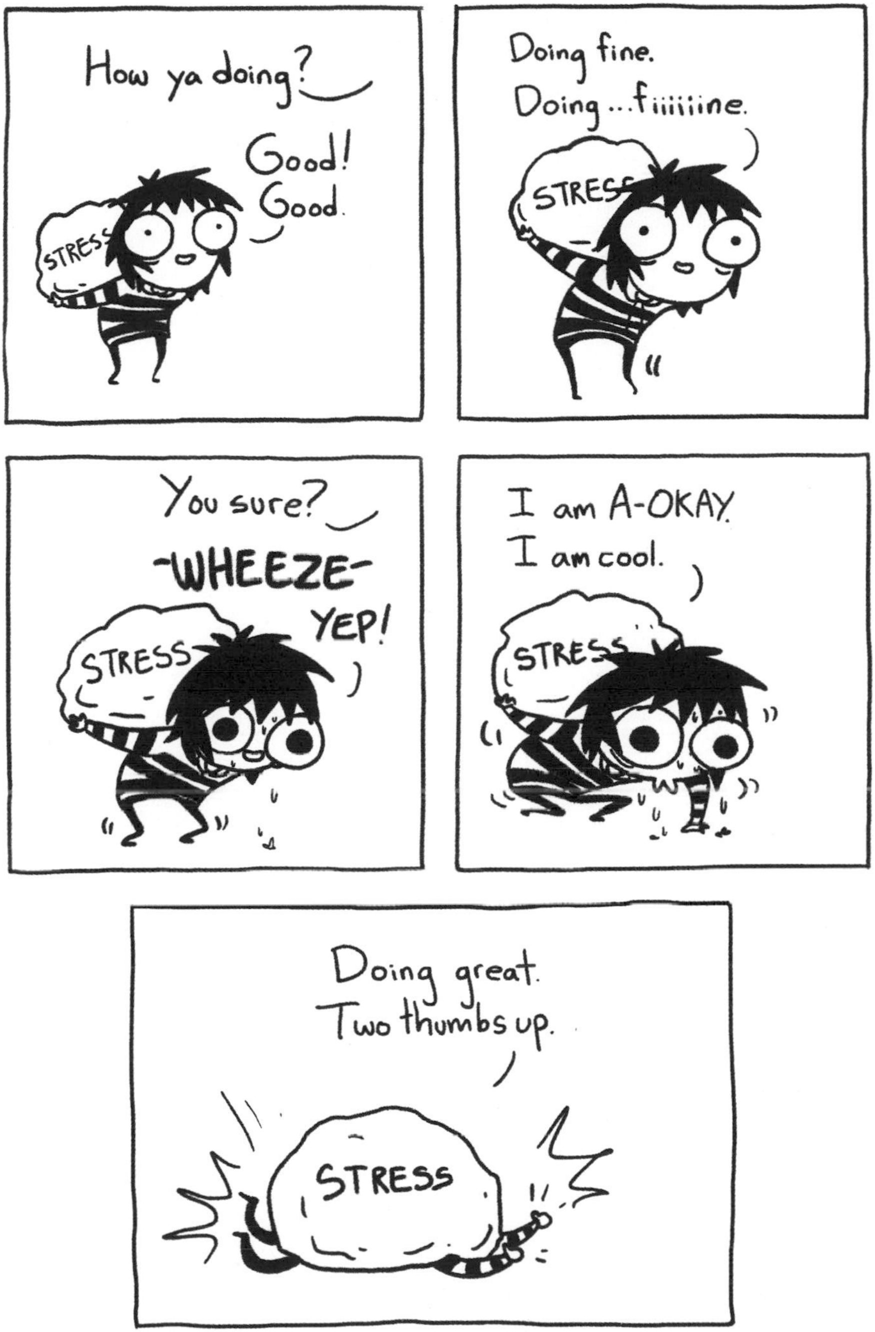
How ya doing?
Good! Good.
STRESS
Doing fine. Doing ...fiiiiiine.
STRESS
You sure?
-WHEEZE-
YEP!
STRESS
I am A-OKAY. I am cool.
STRESS
Doing great. Two thumbs up.
STRESS

HOW IT LOOKS HOW IT FEELS

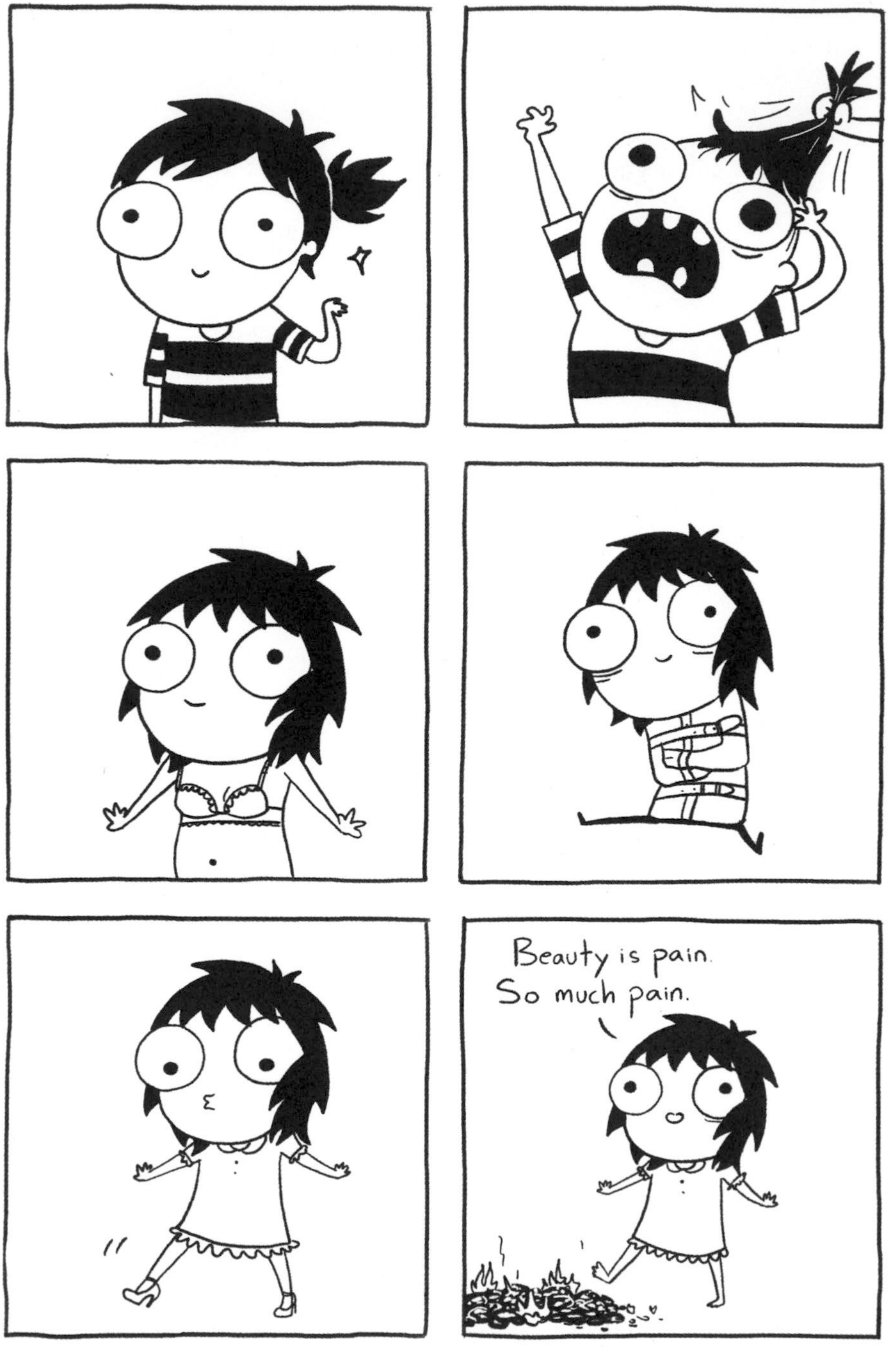
Beauty is pain.
So much pain.

STREET HARASSMENT

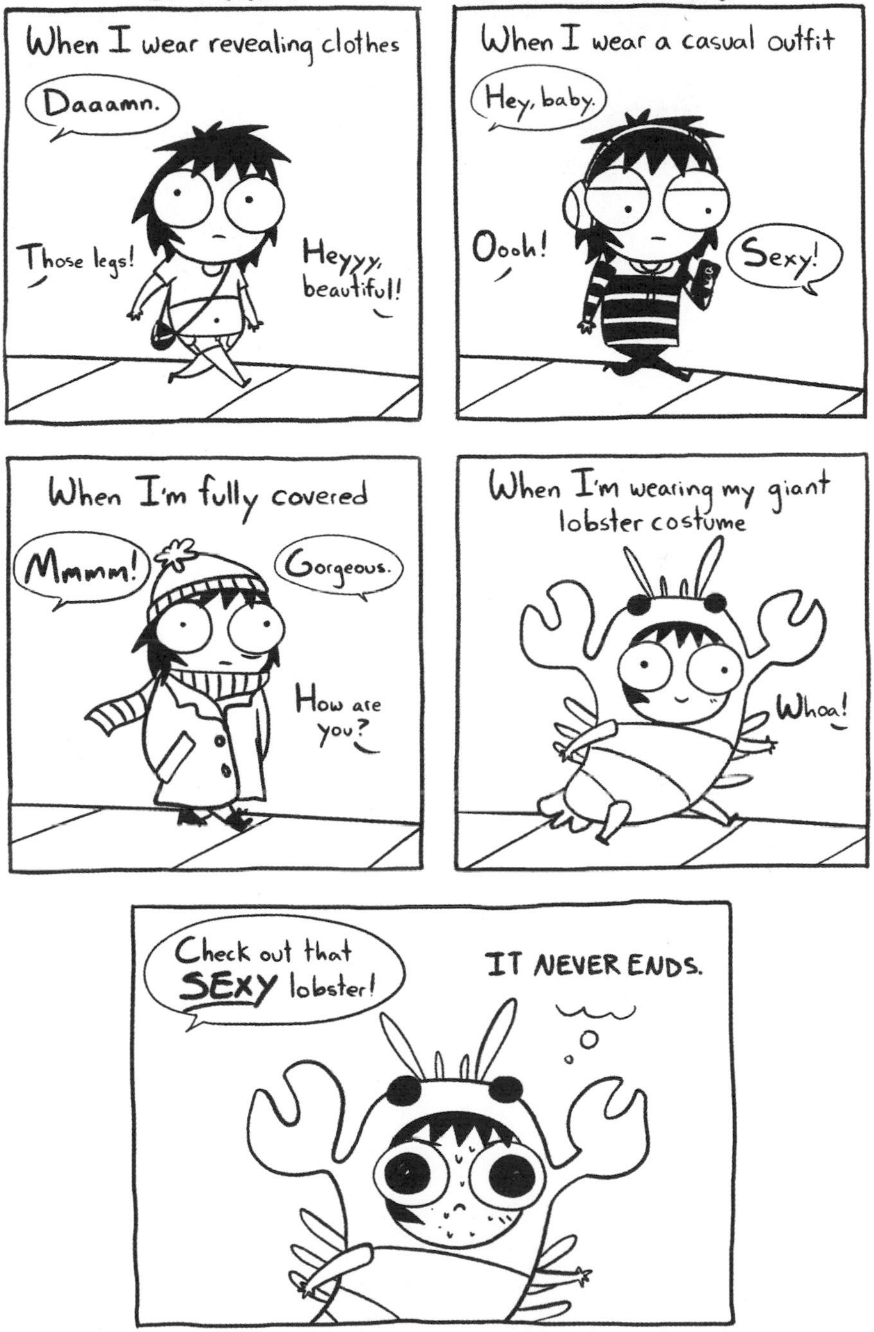
When I wear revealing clothes
Daaamn.
Those legs!
Heyyy, beautiful!
When I wear a casual outfit
Hey, baby.
Oooh!
Sexy!
When I'm fully covered
Mmmm!
Gorgeous.
How are you?
When I'm wearing my giant lobster costume
Whoa!
Check out that SEXY lobster!
IT NEVER ENDS.

MAN BUN

MAN BUN

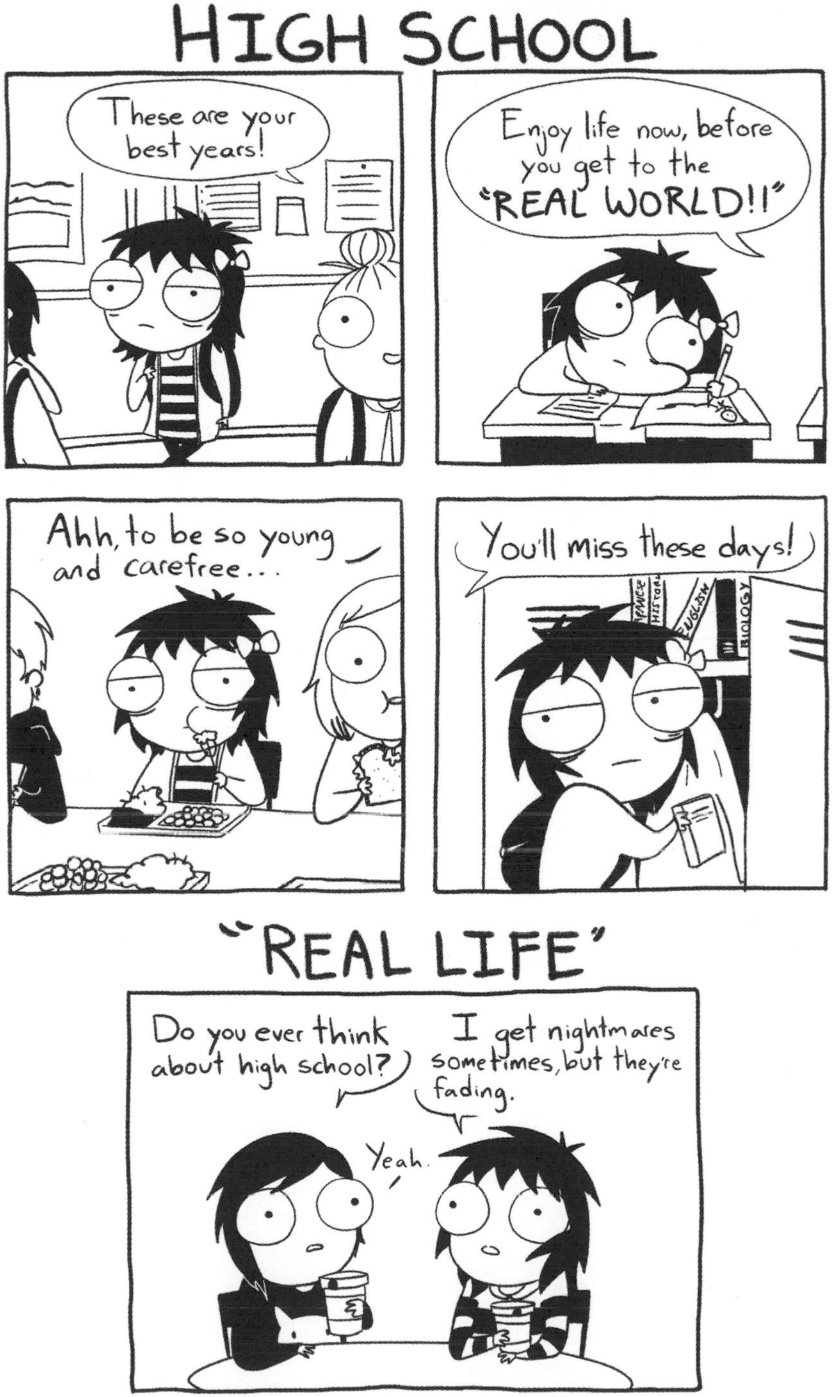
HIGH SCHOOL
These are your best years!
Enjoy life now, before you get to the "REAL WORLD!!"
Ahh, to be so young and carefree...
You'll miss these days!
ENGLISH
BIOLOGY
"REAL LIFE"
Do you ever think about high school?
I get nightmares sometimes, but they're fading.
Yeah.

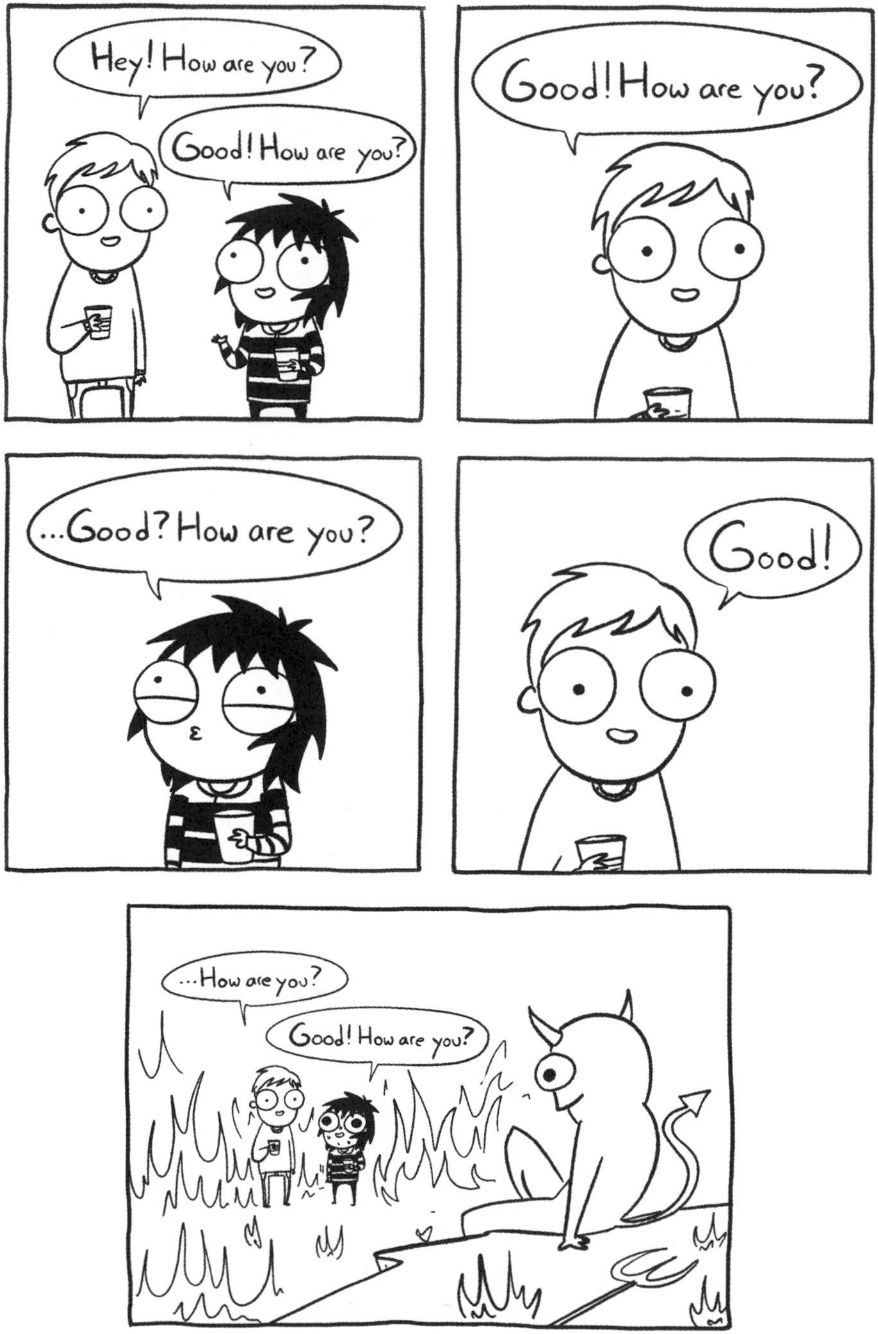
Hey! How are you?
Good! How are you?
Good! How are you?
...Good? How are you?
Good!
...How are you?
Good! How are you?

"DESCRIBE YOUR STYLE"

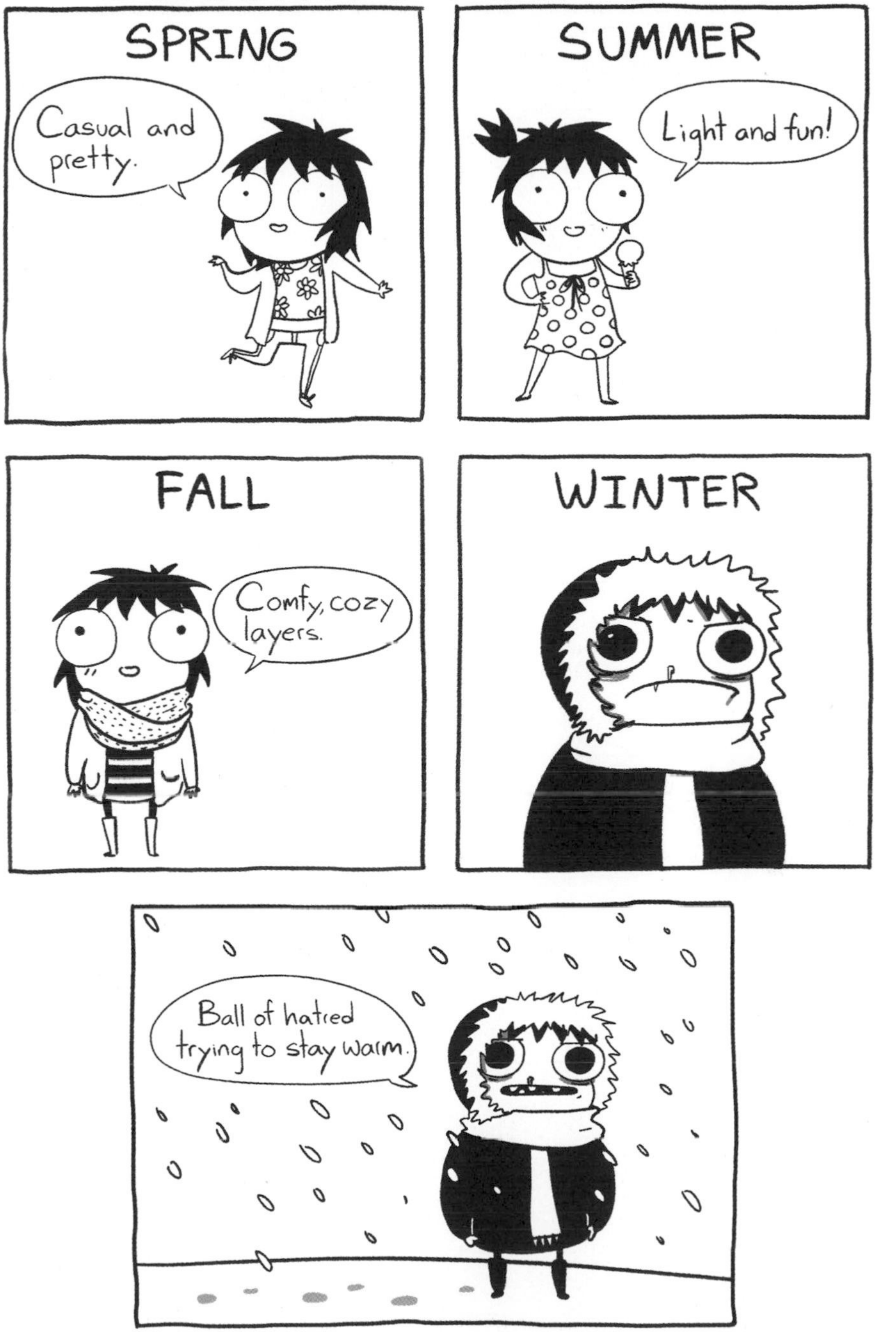
SPRING
Casual and pretty.
SUMMER
Light and fun!
FALL
Comfy, cozy layers.
WINTER
Ball of hatred trying to stay warm.

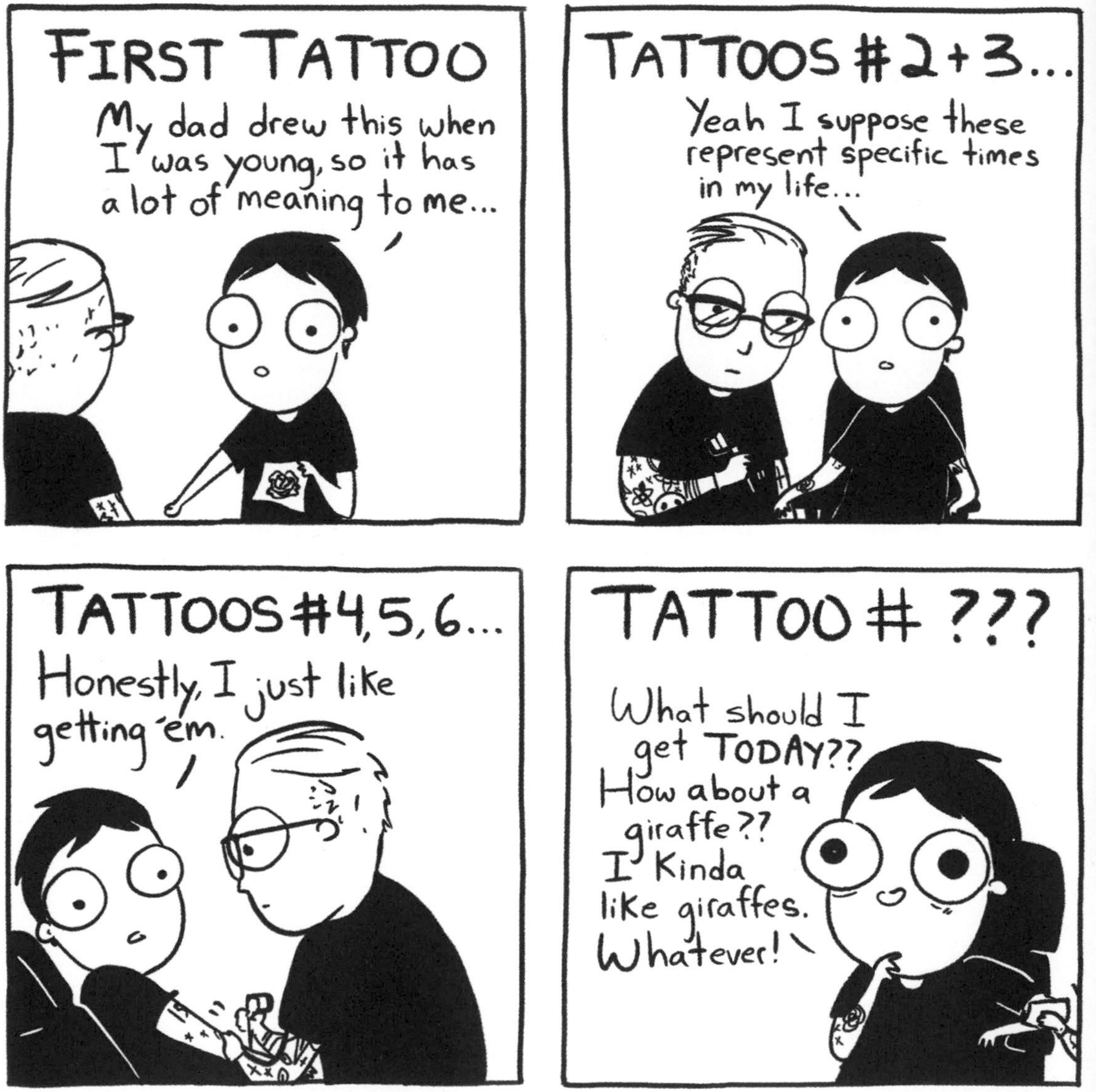
FIRST TATTOO
My dad drew this when I was young, so it has a lot of meaning to me...
TATTOOS #2+3...
Yeah I suppose these represent specific times in my life...
TATTOOS #4,5,6...
Honestly, I just like getting 'em.
TATTOO # ???
What should I get TODAY?? How about a giraffe?? I Kinda like giraffes. Whatever!

NICE

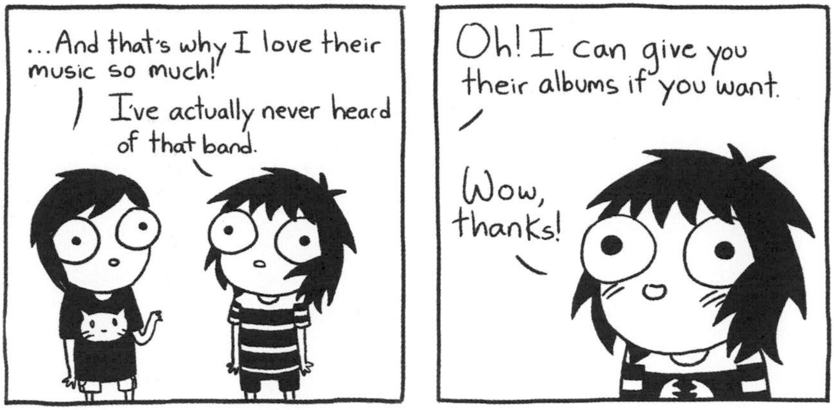

...And that's why I love their music so much!
I've actually never heard of that band.
Oh! I can give you their albums if you want.
Wow, thanks!

NOT NICE

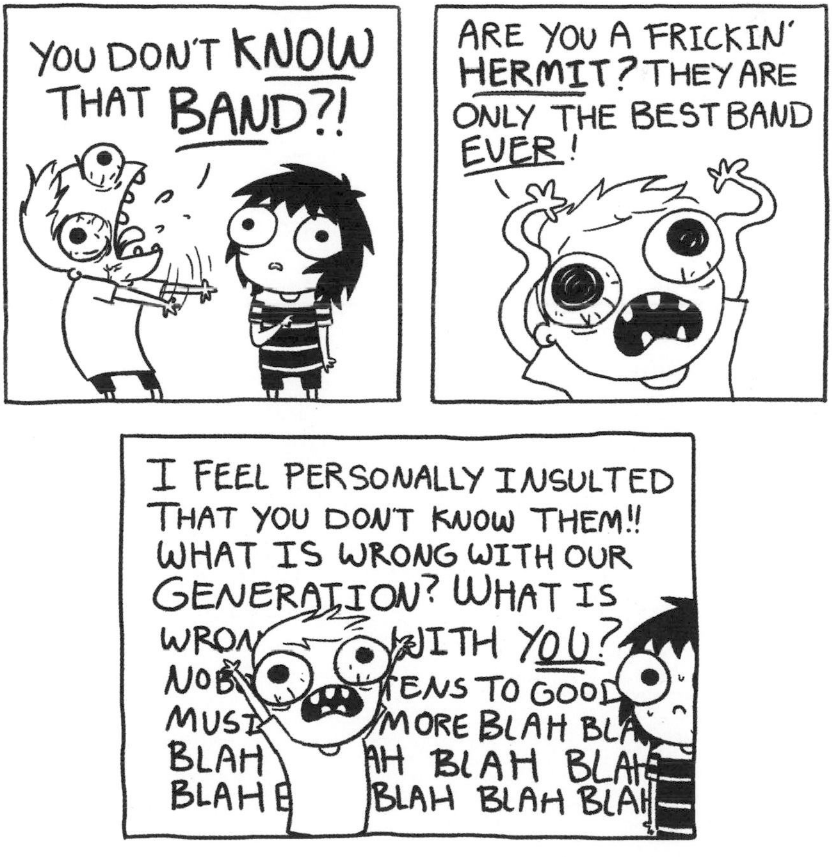

YOU DON'T KNOW THAT BAND?!
ARE YOU A FRICKIN' HERMIT? THEY ARE ONLY THE BEST BAND EVER!
I FEEL PERSONALLY INSULTED THAT YOU DON'T KNOW THEM!! WHAT IS WRONG WITH OUR GENERATION? WHAT IS
WRON WITH YOU?
NOB TENS TO GOOD
MUS MORE BLAH BLA
BLAH AH BLAH BLAH
BLAH BLAH BLAH BLA

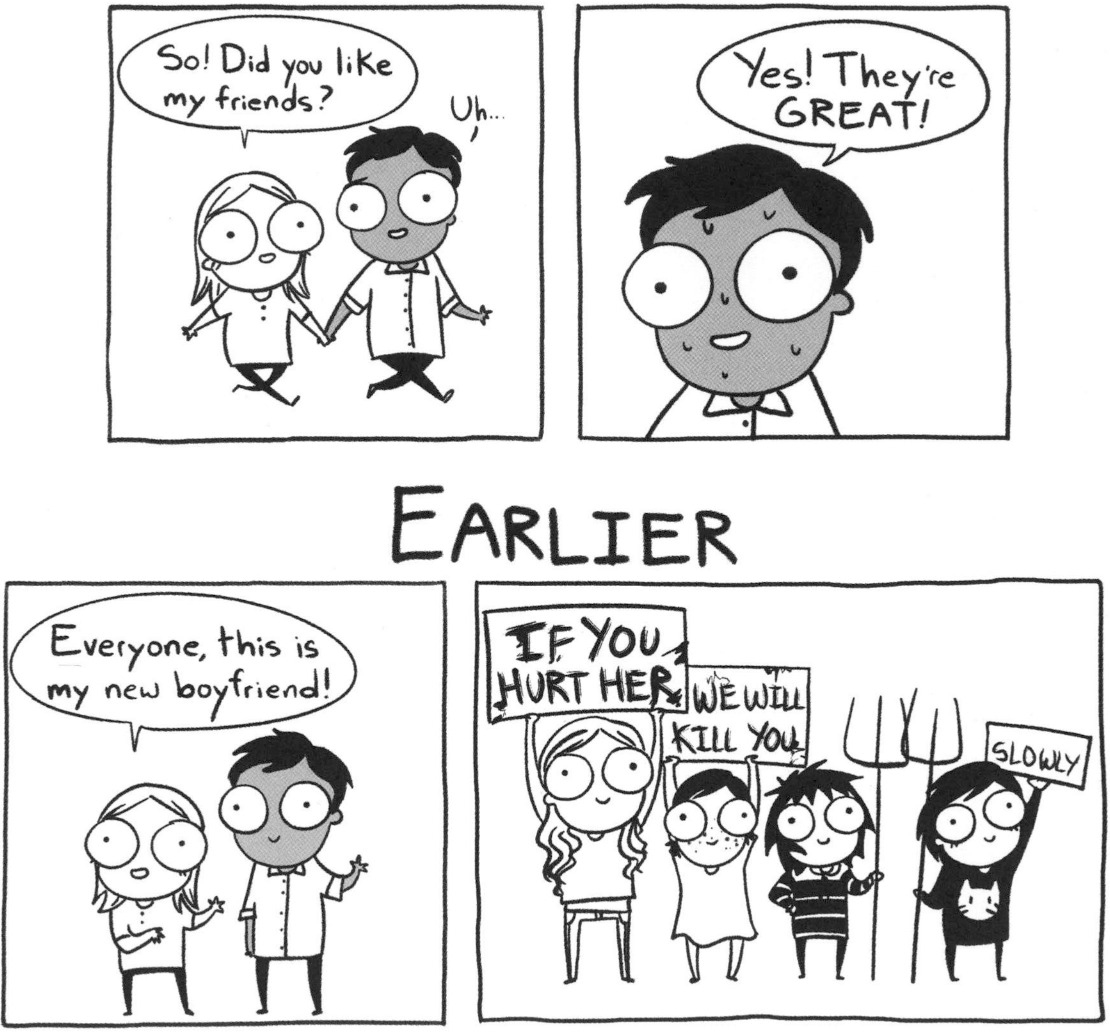
So! Did you like my friends?
Uh...
Yes! They're GREAT!
EARLIER
Everyone, this is my new boyfriend!
IF YOU HURT HER
WE WILL KILL YOU
SLOWLY

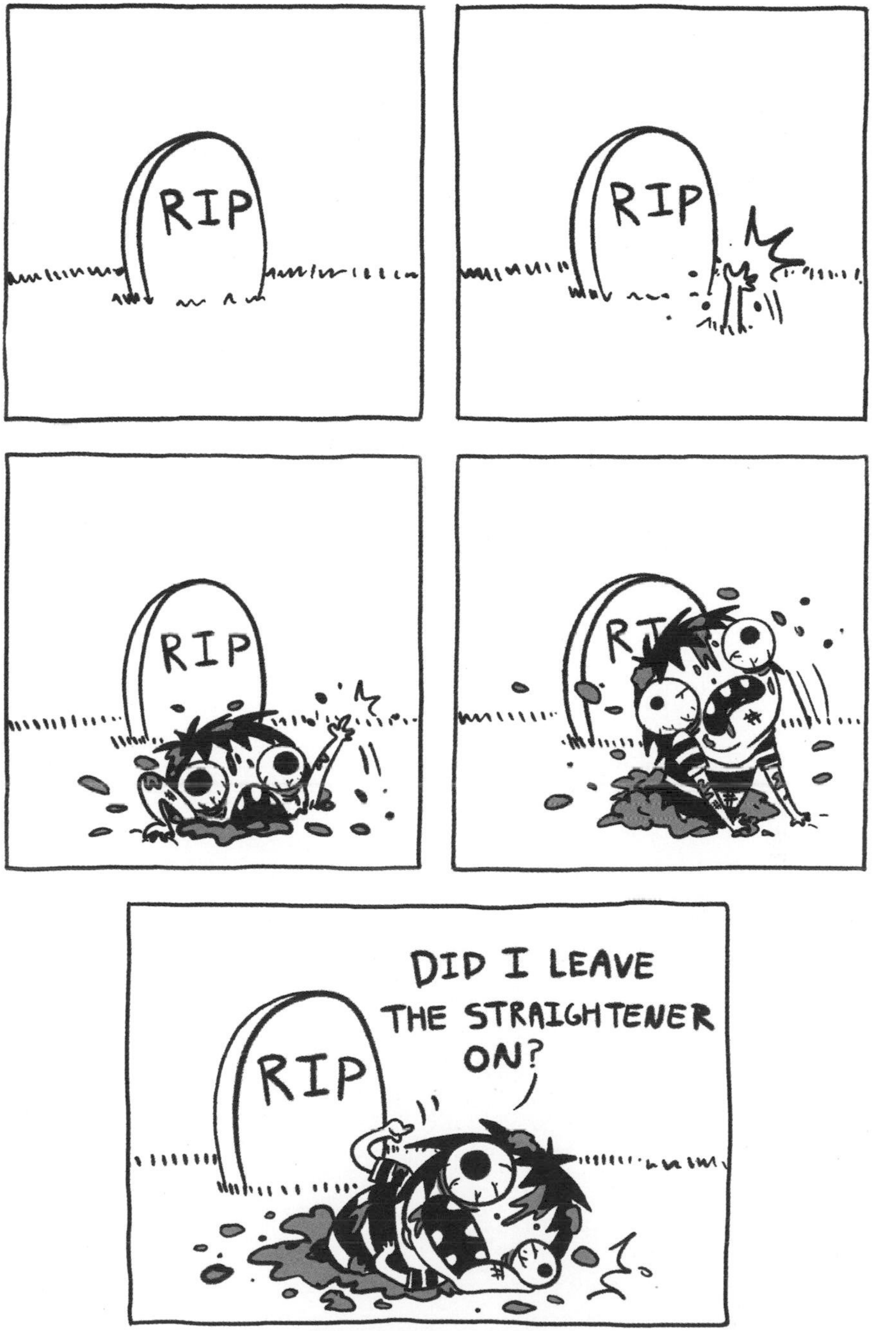
RIP
RIP
RIP
RIP
DID I LEAVE THE STRAIGHTENER ON?

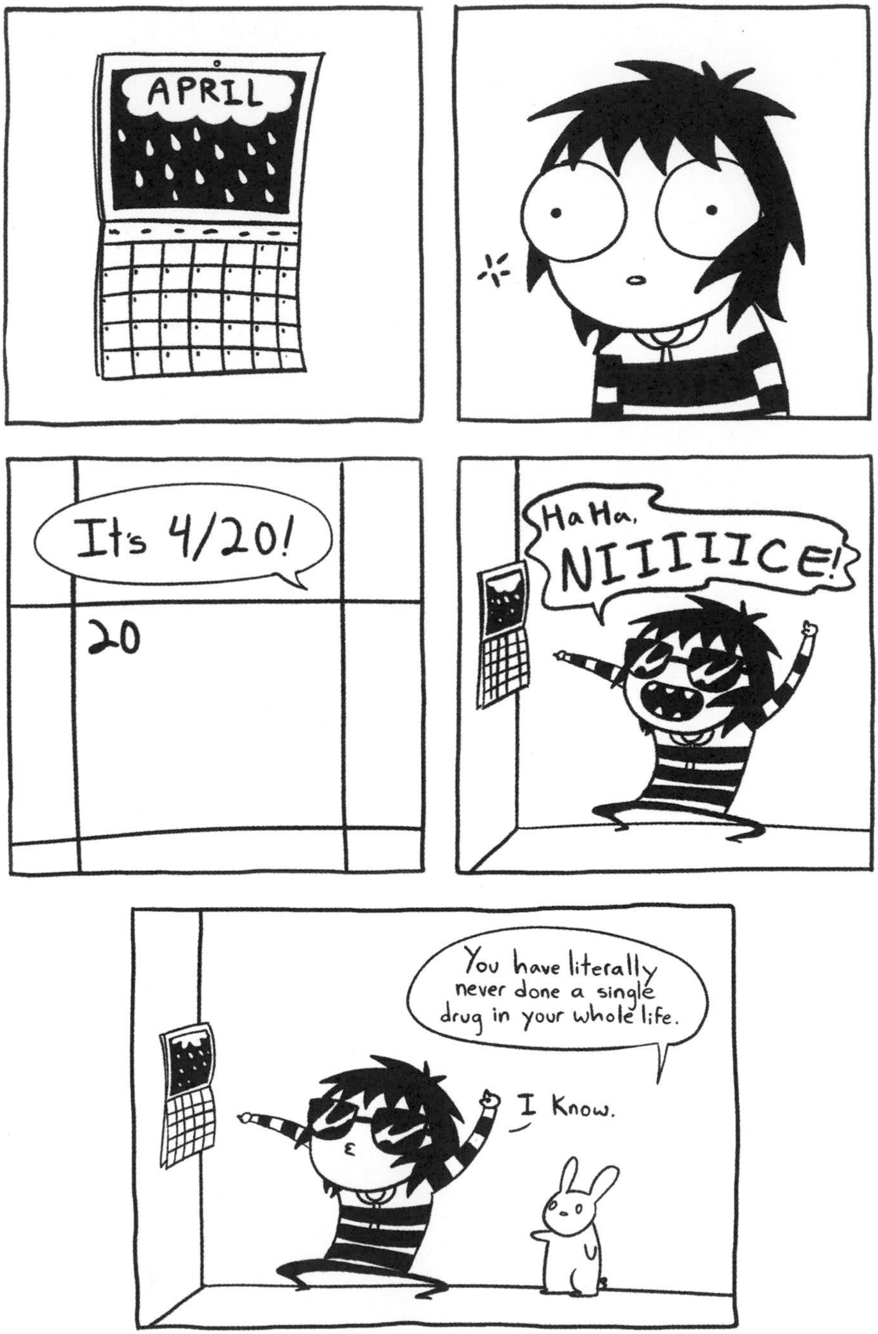
APRIL
It's 4/20!
20
Ha Ha,
NIIIIICE!
You have literally never done a single drug in your whole life.
I Know.

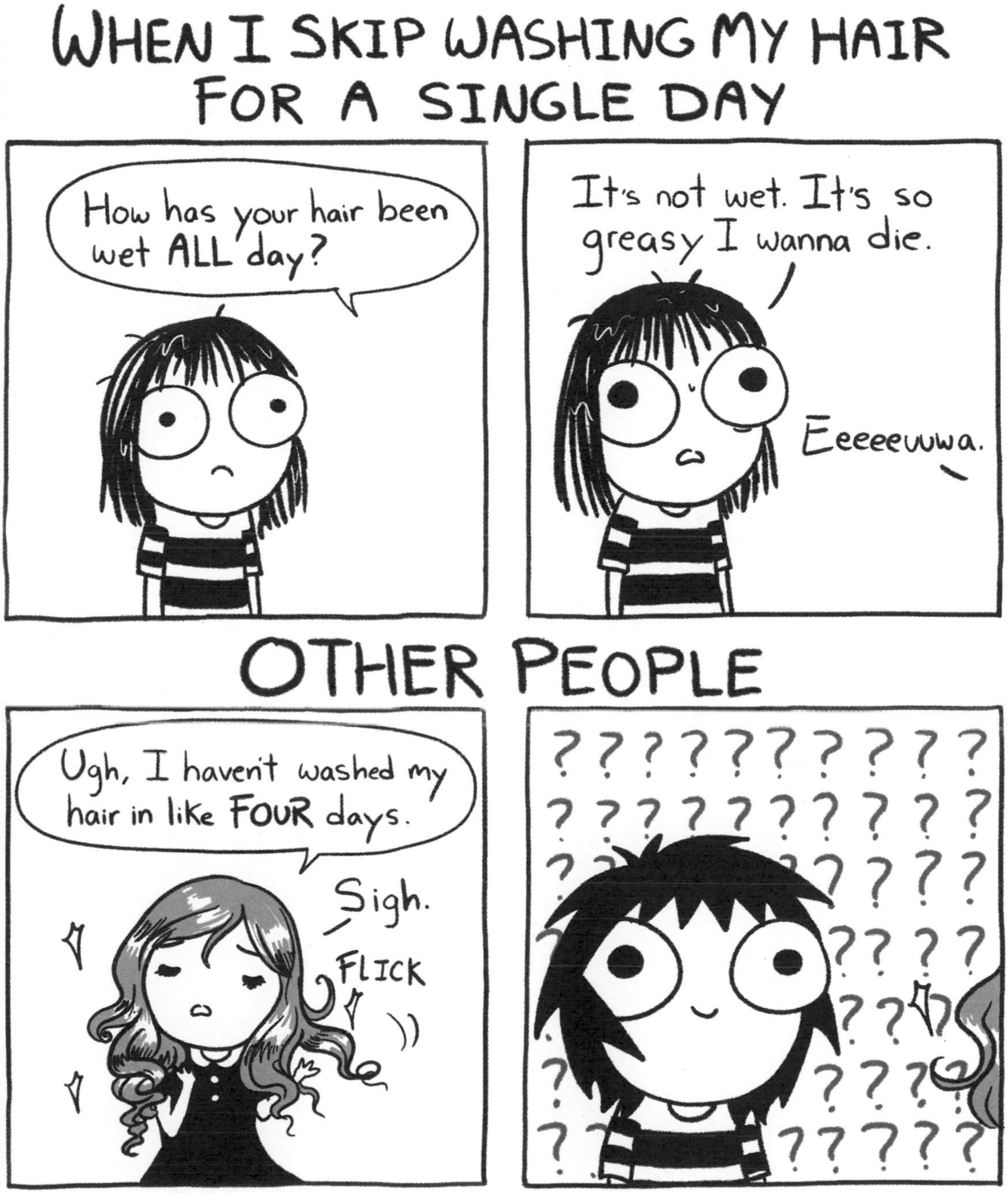
WHEN I SKIP WASHING MY HAIR FOR A SINGLE DAY
How has your hair been wet ALL day?
It's not wet. It's so greasy I wanna die.
Eeeeeuuwa.
OTHER PEOPLE
Ugh, I haven't washed my hair in like FOUR days.
Sigh.
FLICK
? ? ? ? ? ? ? ? ? ?

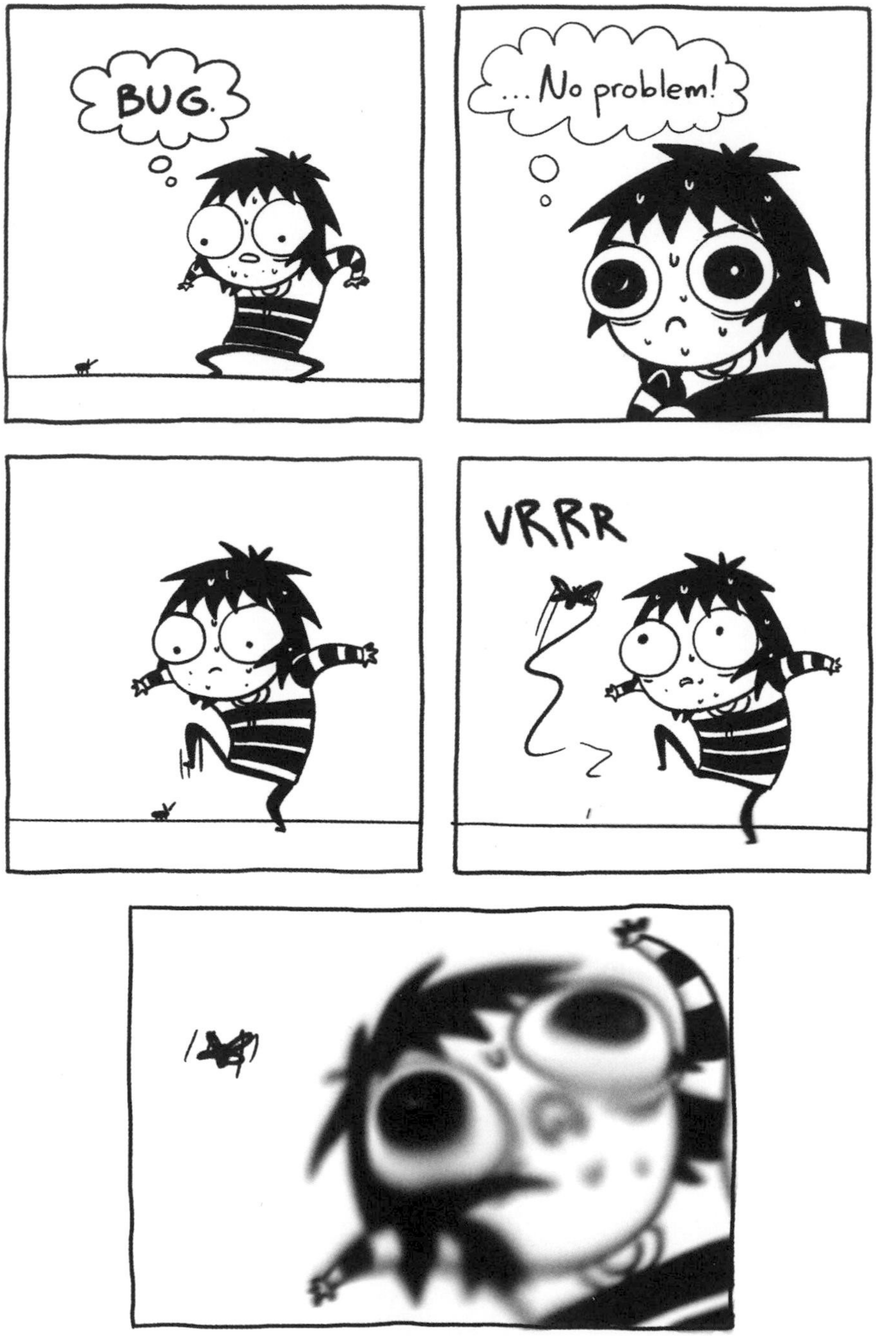
BUG.
...No problem!
VRRR

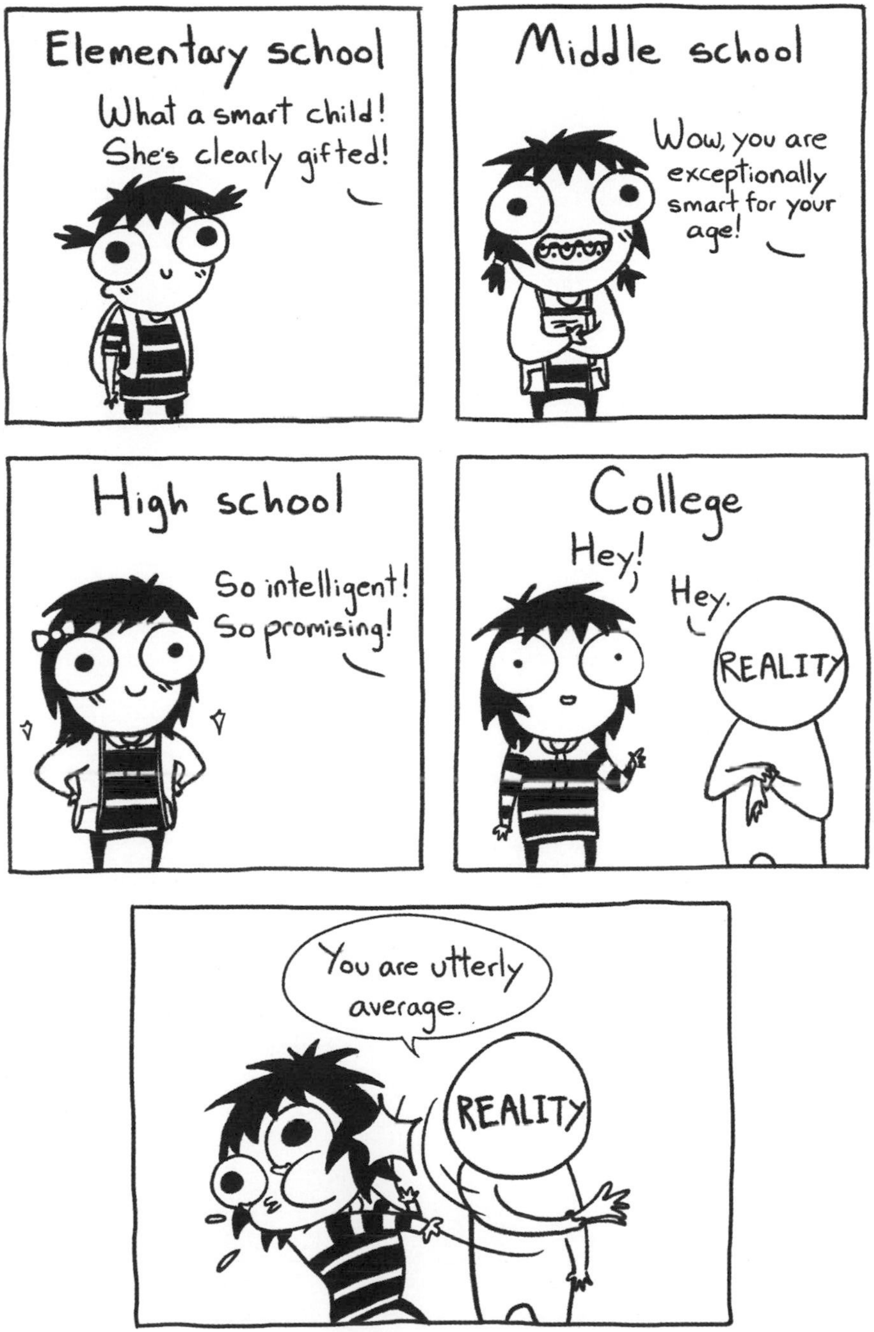
Elementary school
What a smart child! She's clearly gifted!
Middle school
Wow, you are exceptionally smart for your age!
High school
So intelligent! So promising!
College
Hey!
Hey.
REALITY
You are utterly average.
REALITY

HOW TO BECOME GOOD AT DRAWING

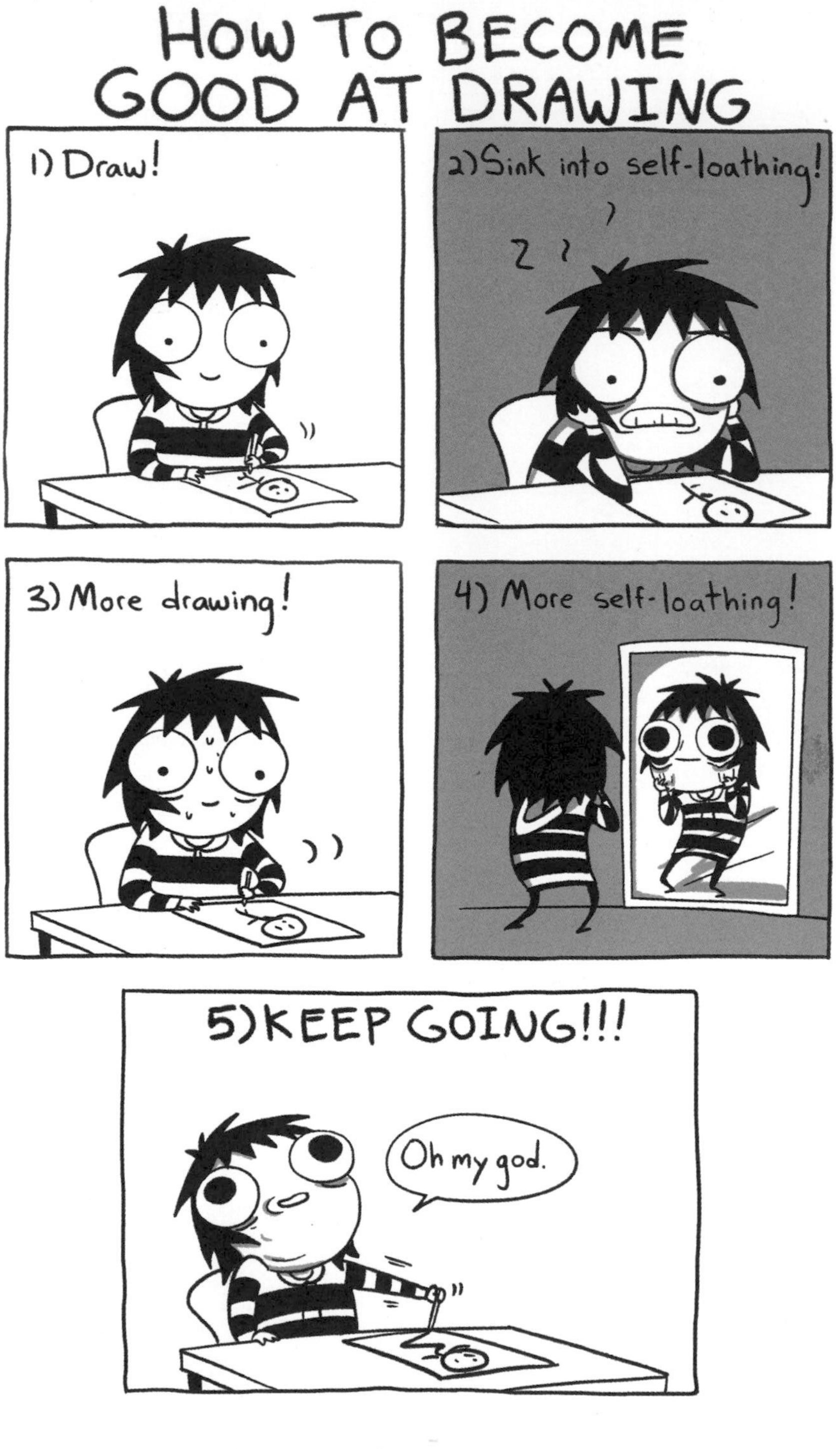
1) Draw!
2) Sink into self-loathing!
3) More drawing!
4) More self-loathing!
5) KEEP GOING!!!
Oh my god.

WHEN SOMEONE HURTS MY FEELINGS

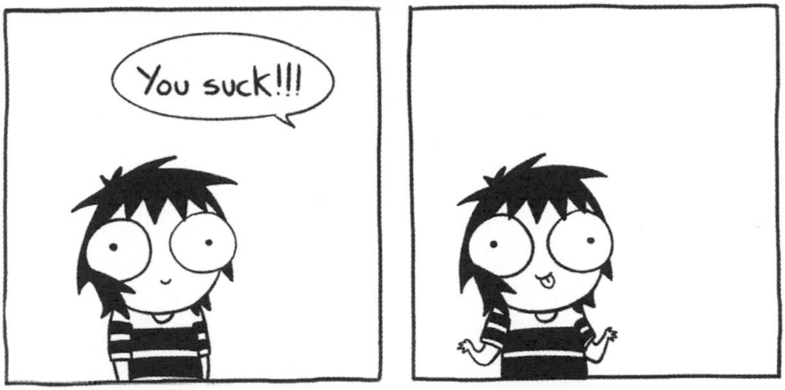
You suck!!!

WHEN SOMEONE HURTS MY FRIEND'S FEELINGS

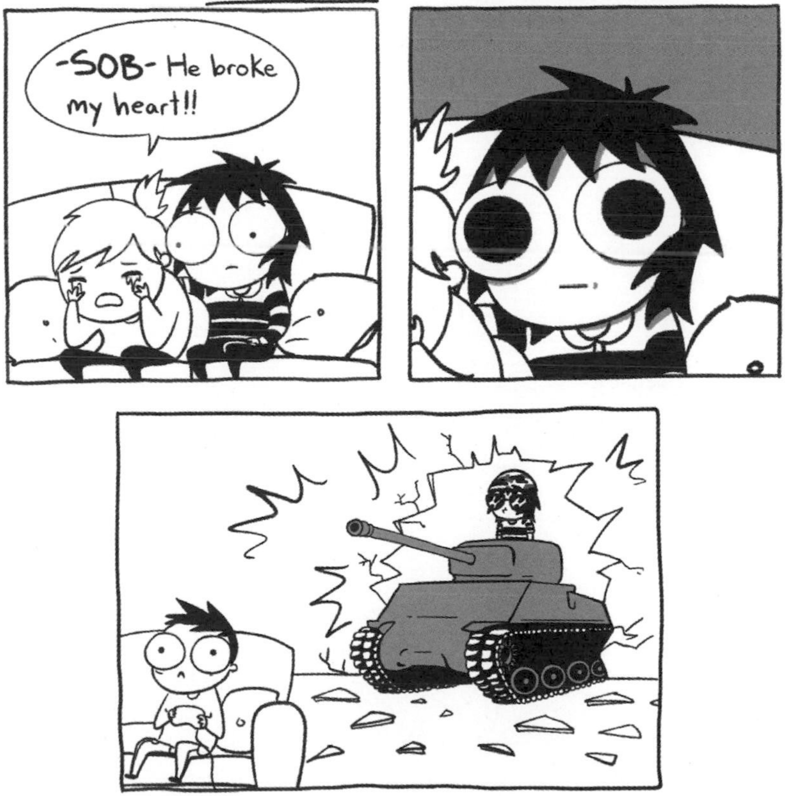
-SOB- He broke my heart!!

CUDDLING

WINTER: SUMMER:

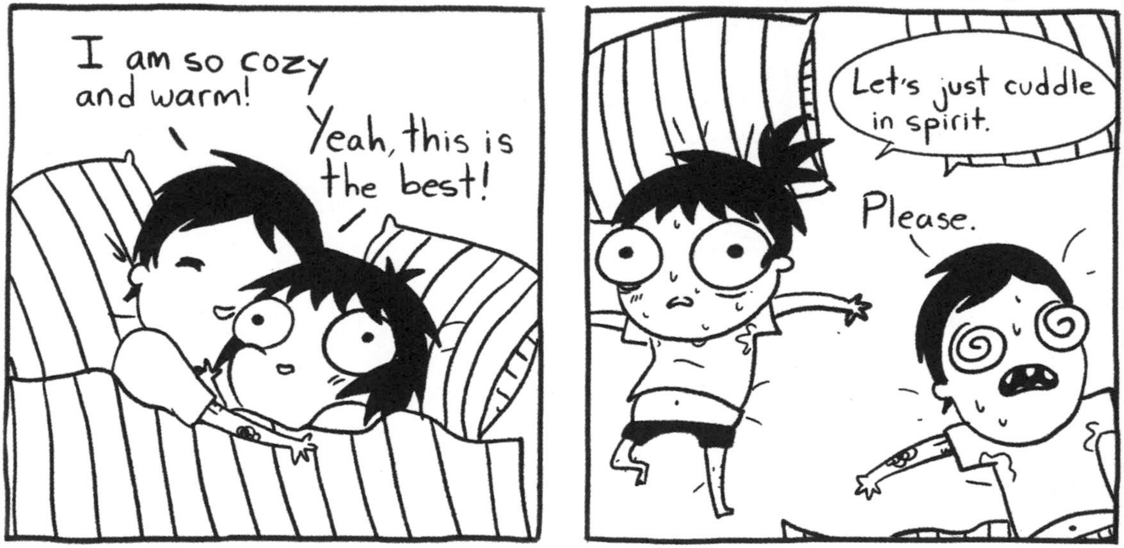
I am so cozy and warm!
Yeah, this is the best!
Let's just cuddle in spirit.
Please.

HOW SONGS GET STUCK IN MY HEAD

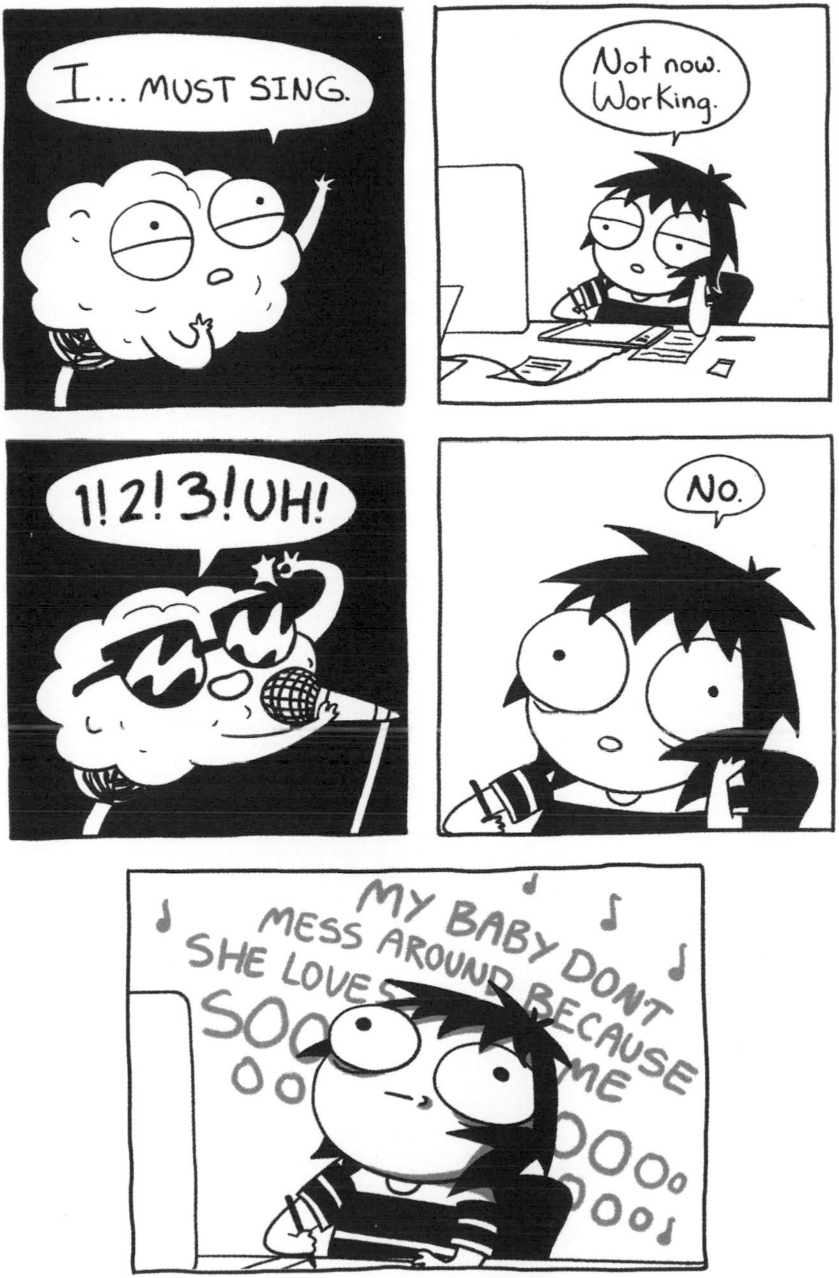
I... MUST SING.
Not now. Working.
1! 2! 3! UH!
NO.
MY BABY DONT MESS AROUND BECAUSE SHE LOVES ME SOOOOOOOOOOOOOO

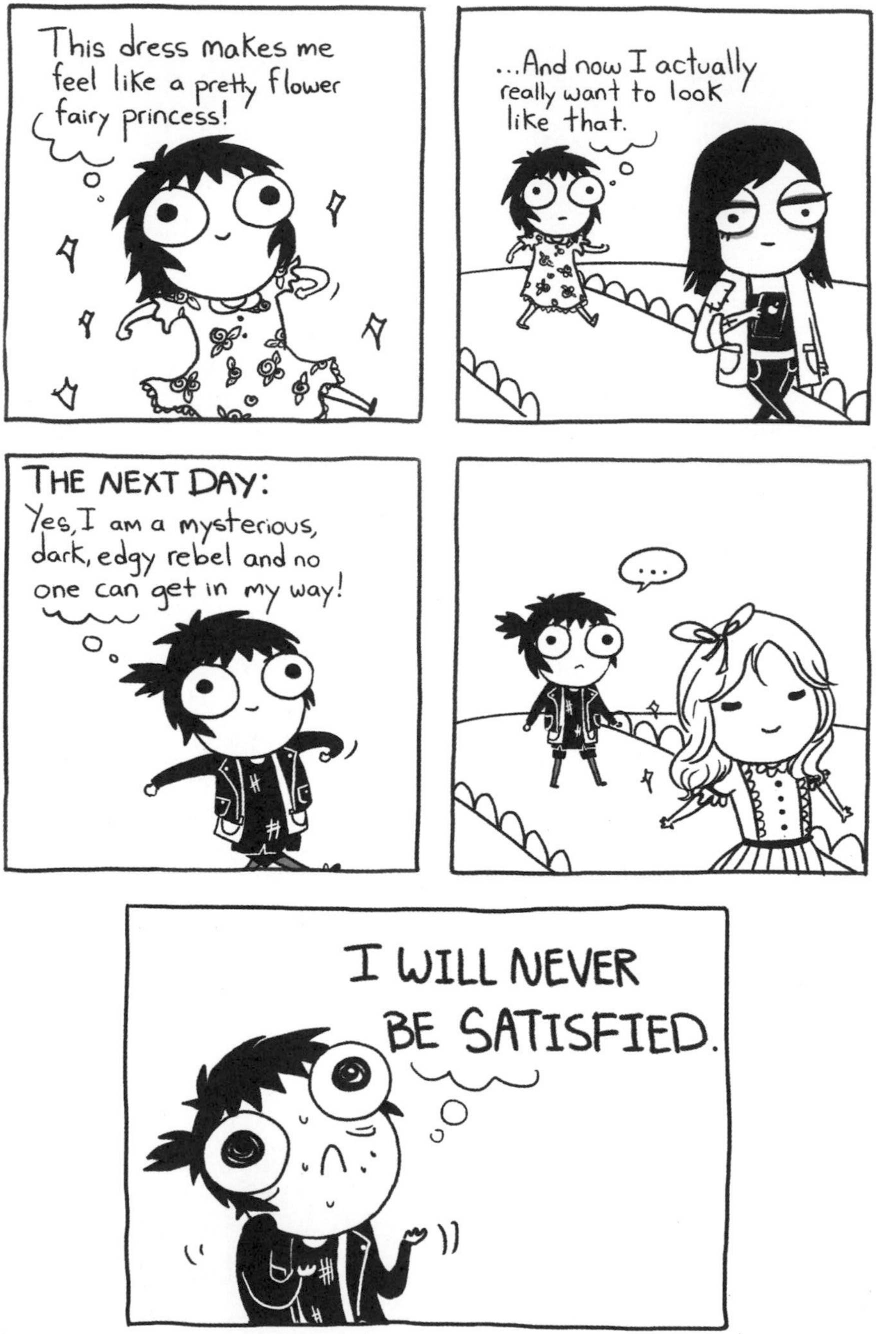
This dress makes me feel like a pretty flower fairy princess!
...And now I actually really want to look like that.
THE NEXT DAY:
Yes, I am a mysterious, dark, edgy rebel and no one can get in my way!
...
I WILL NEVER BE SATISFIED.

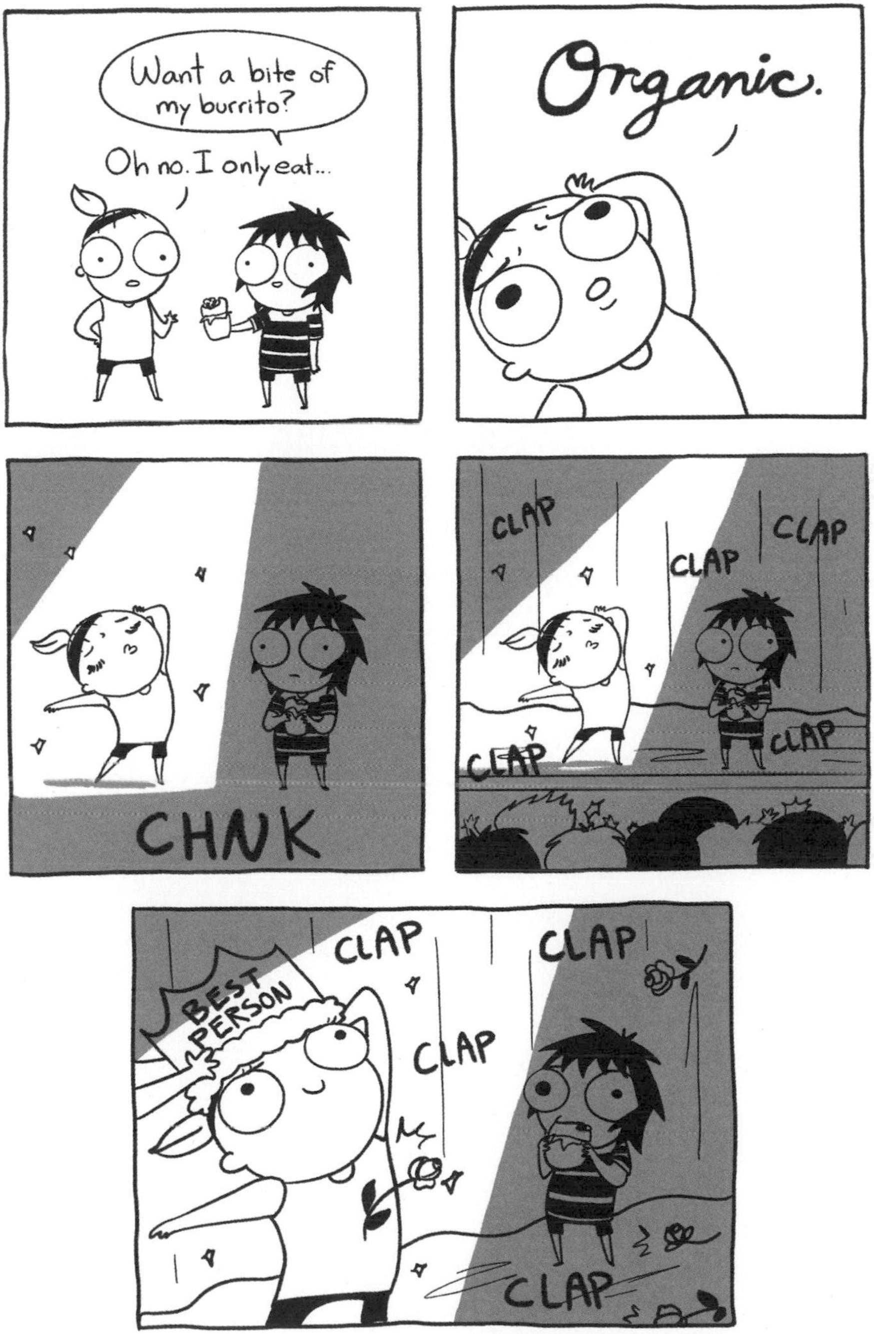
Want a bite of my burrito?
Oh no. I only eat...
Organic.
CHNK
CLAP
CLAP
CLAP
CLAP
CLAP
CLAP
CLAP
BEST PERSON
CLAP
CLAP

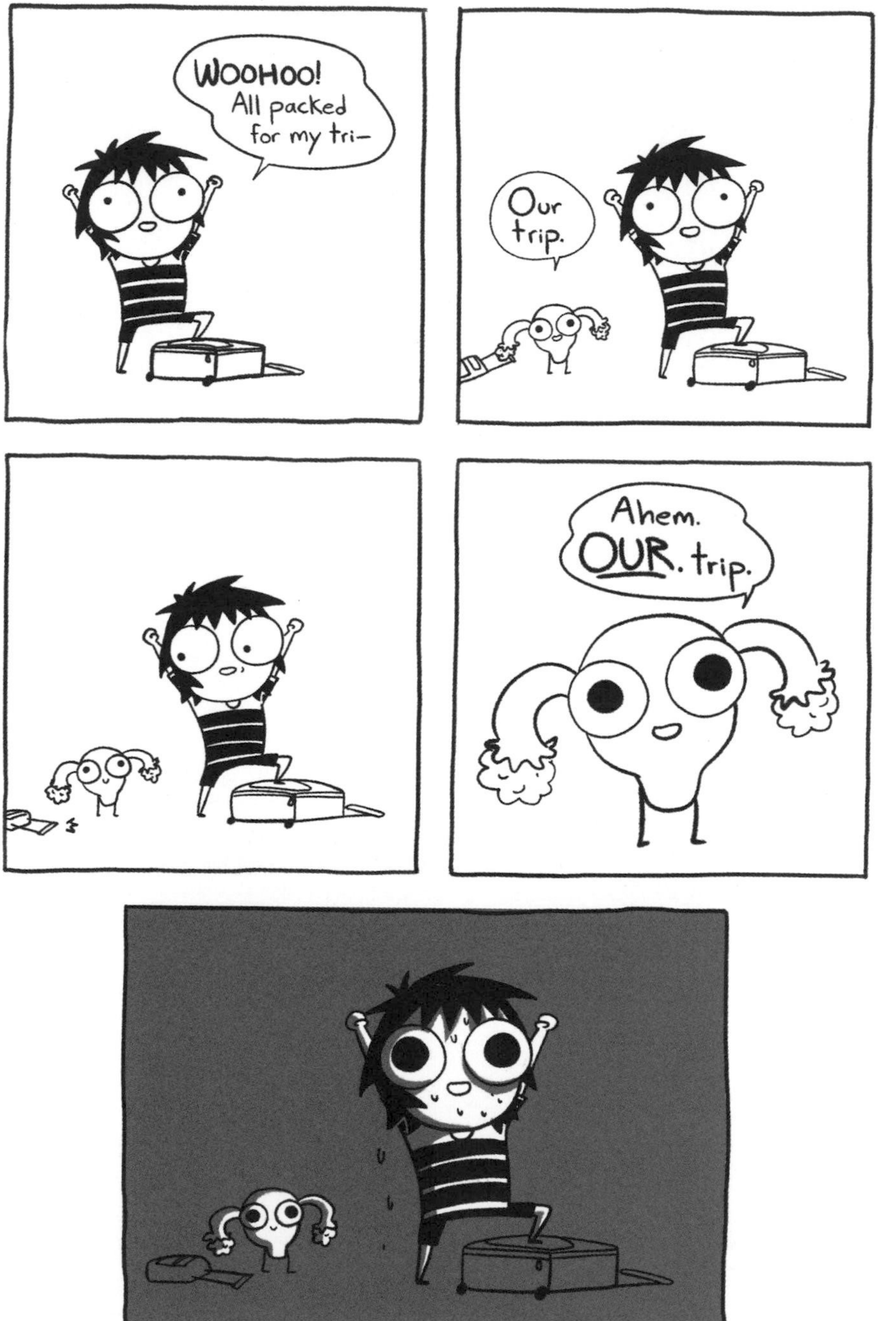
WOOHOO! All packed for my tri–
Our trip.
Ahem. OUR. trip.

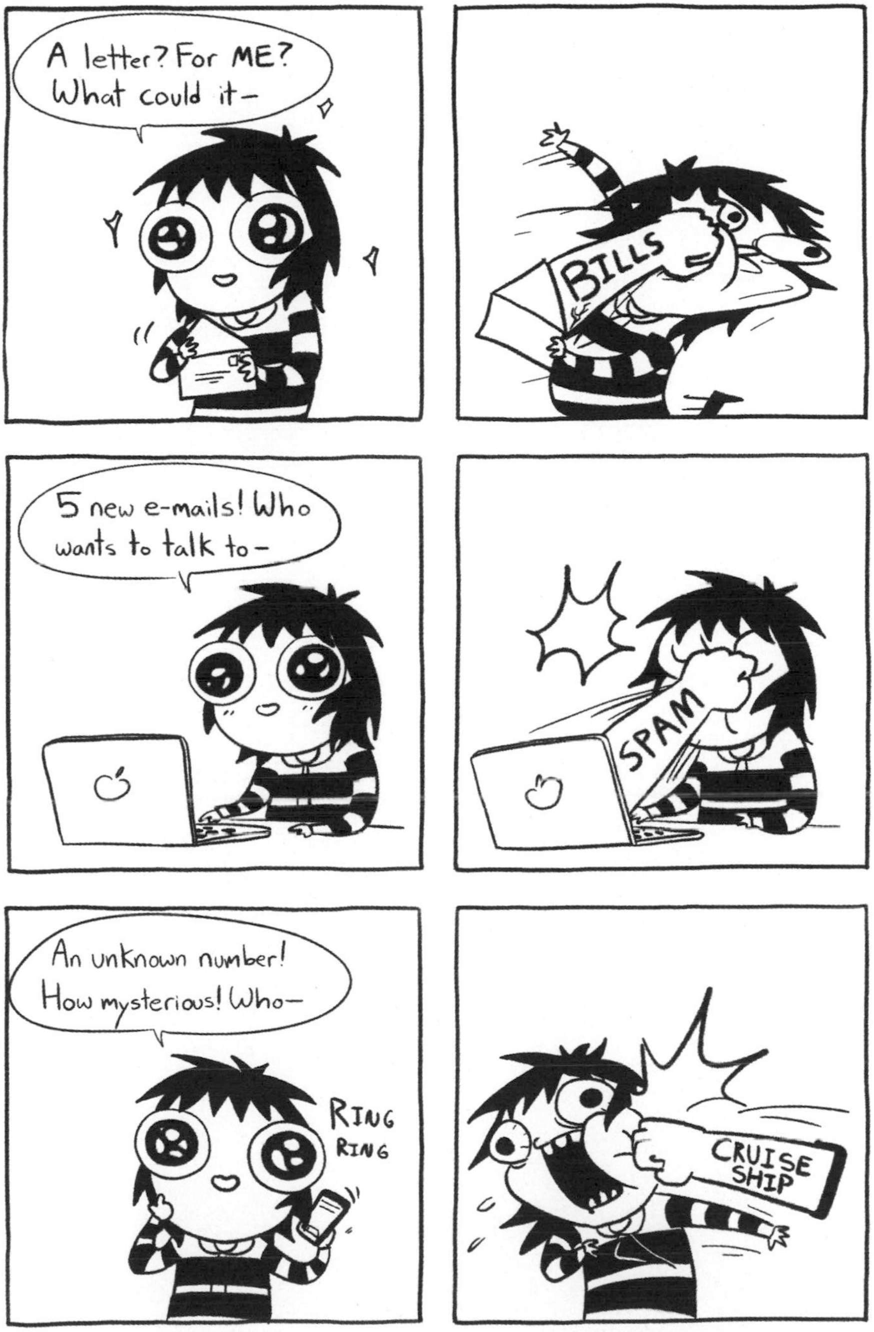
A letter? For ME? What could it-
BILLS
5 new e-mails! Who wants to talk to-
SPAM
An unknown number! How mysterious! Who-
RING RING
CRUISE SHIP

MY MEMORY

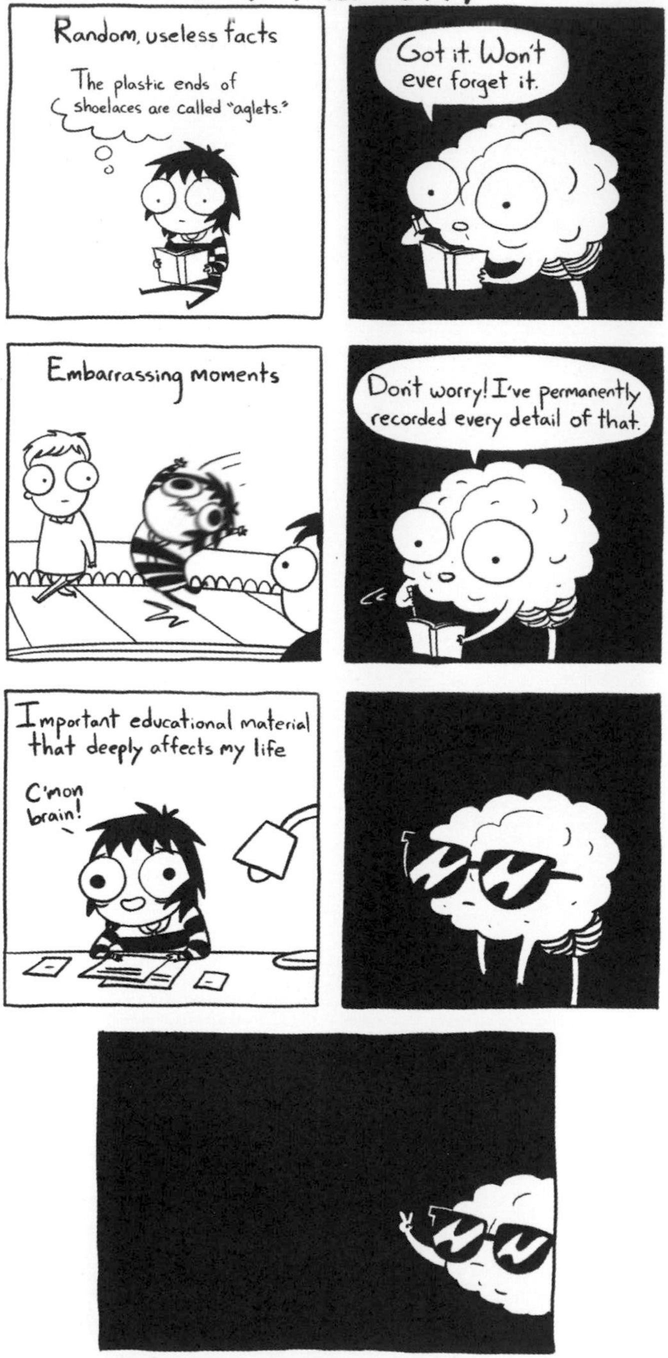
Random, useless facts
The plastic ends of shoelaces are called "aglets."
Got it. Won't ever forget it.
Embarrassing moments
Don't worry! I've permanently recorded every detail of that.
Important educational material that deeply affects my life
C'mon brain!

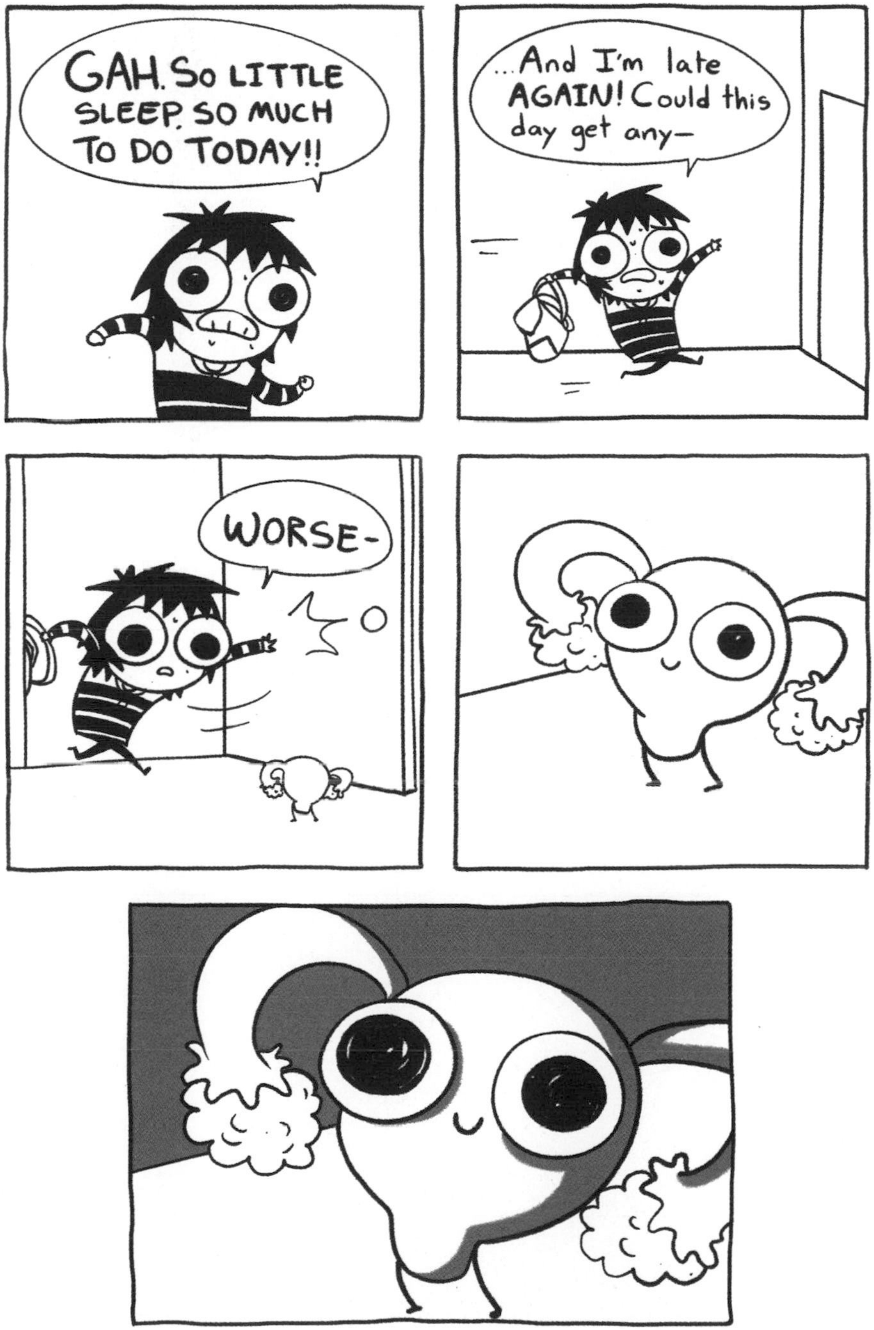
GAH. So LITTLE SLEEP. SO MUCH TO DO TODAY!!
...And I'm late AGAIN! Could this day get any—
WORSE-

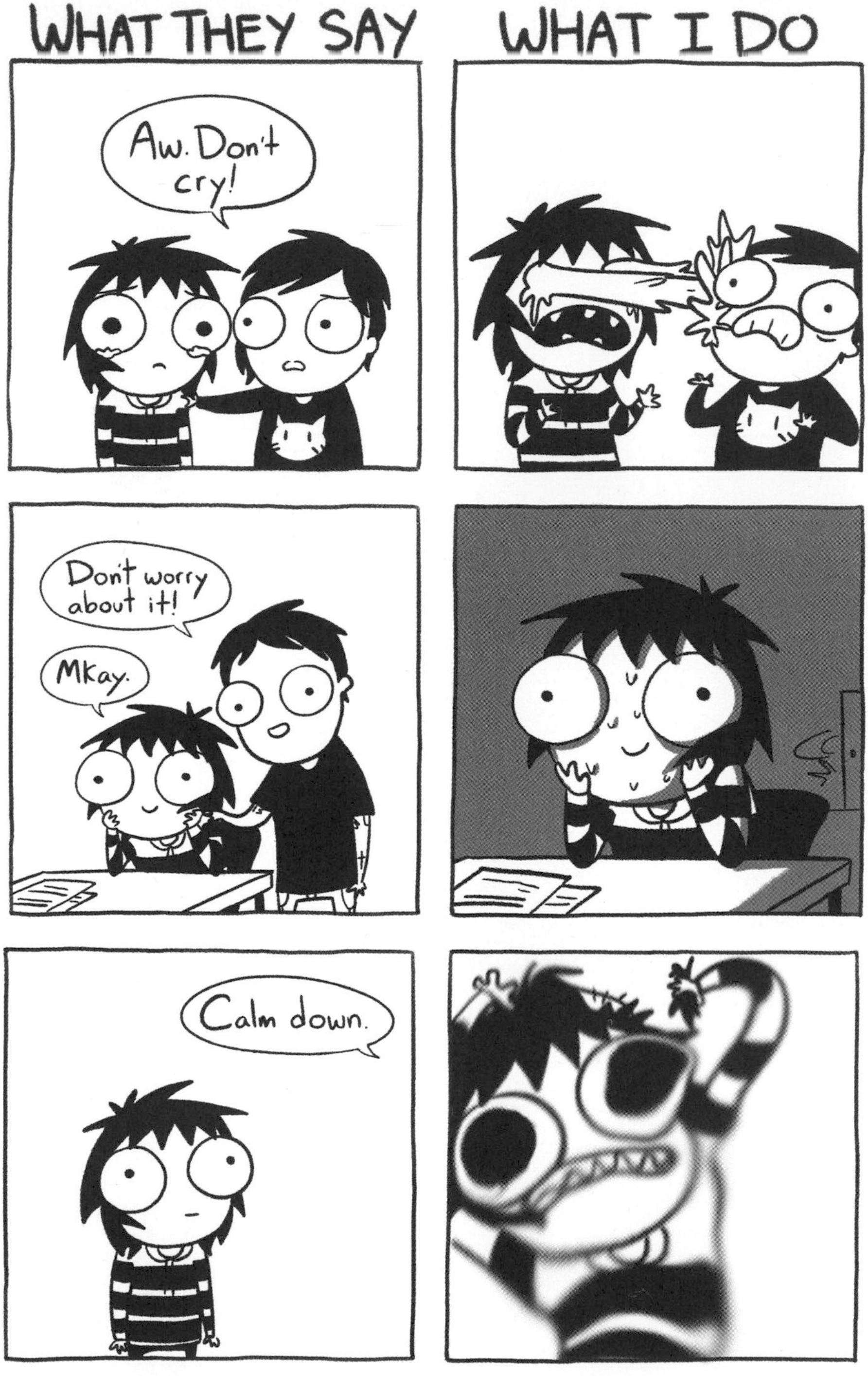
WHAT THEY SAY
WHAT I DO
Aw. Don't cry!
Don't worry about it!
Mkay.
Calm down.

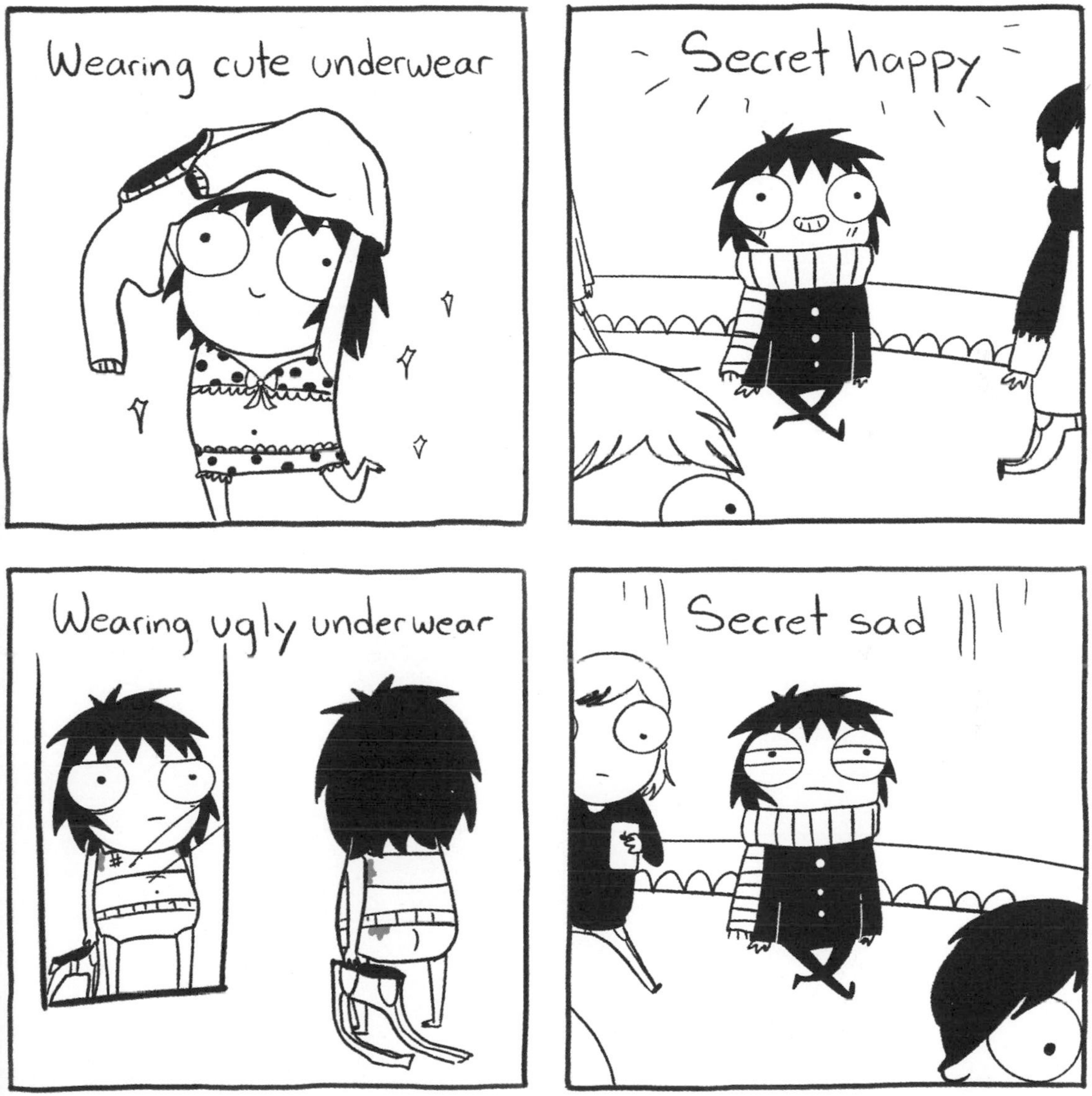
Wearing cute underwear
Secret happy
Wearing ugly underwear
Secret sad

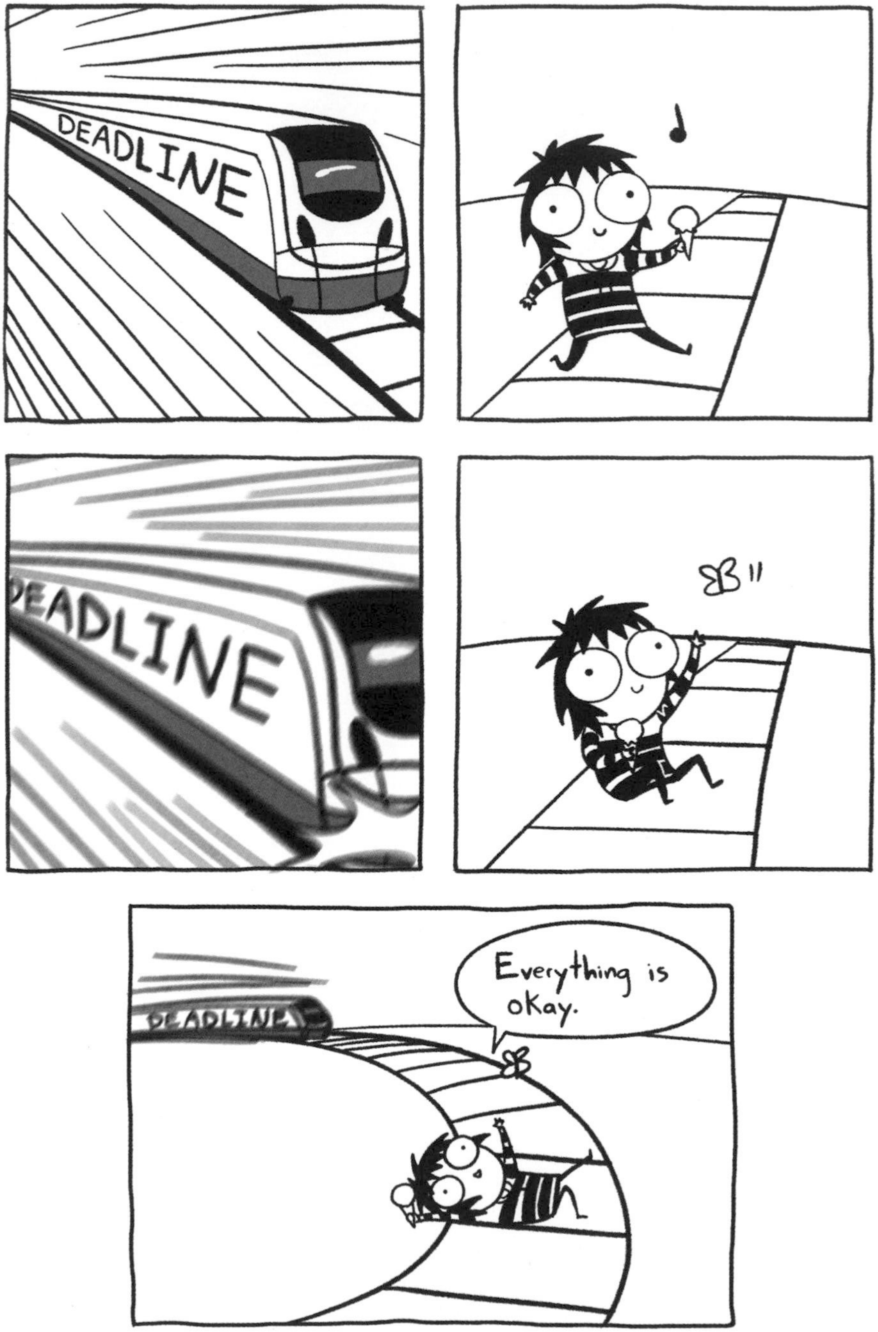
DEADLINE
Everything is okay.

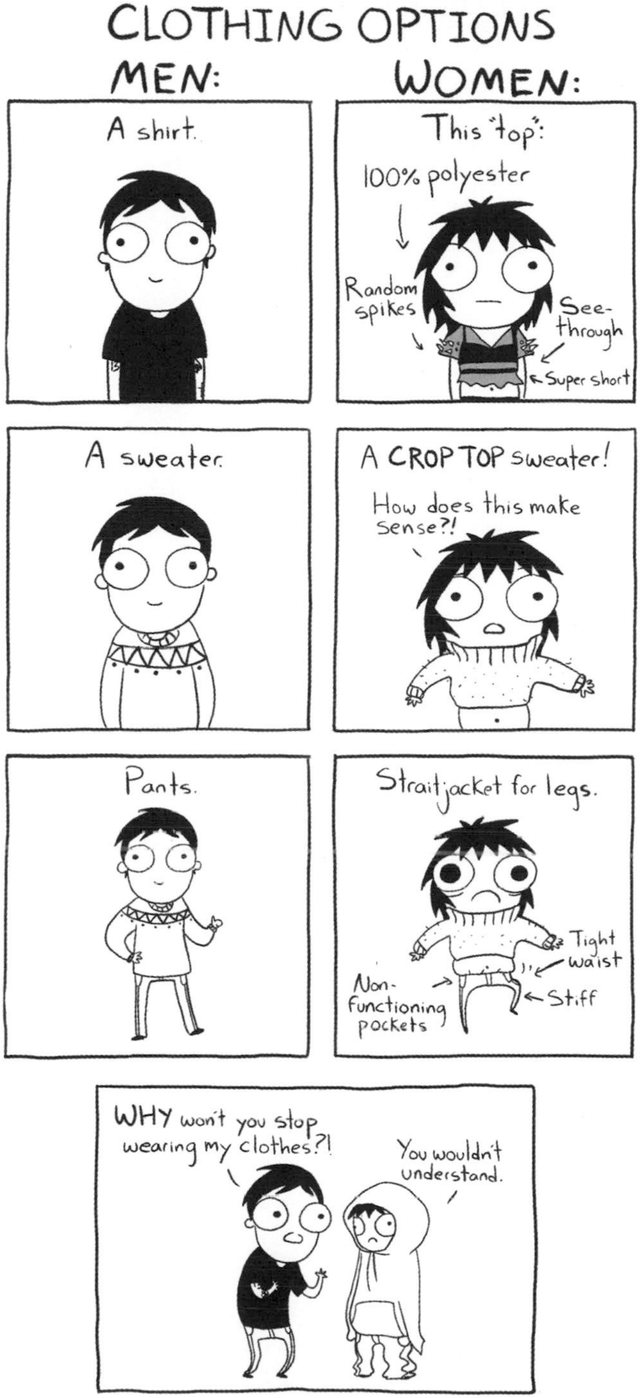
CLOTHING OPTIONS
MEN:
WOMEN:
A shirt.
This "top":
100% polyester
Random spikes
See-through
Super short
A sweater.
A CROP TOP sweater!
How does this make sense?!
Pants.
Straitjacket for legs.
Tight waist
Non-functioning pockets
Stiff
WHY won't you stop wearing my clothes?!
You wouldn't understand.

ACCOMPLISHMENTS

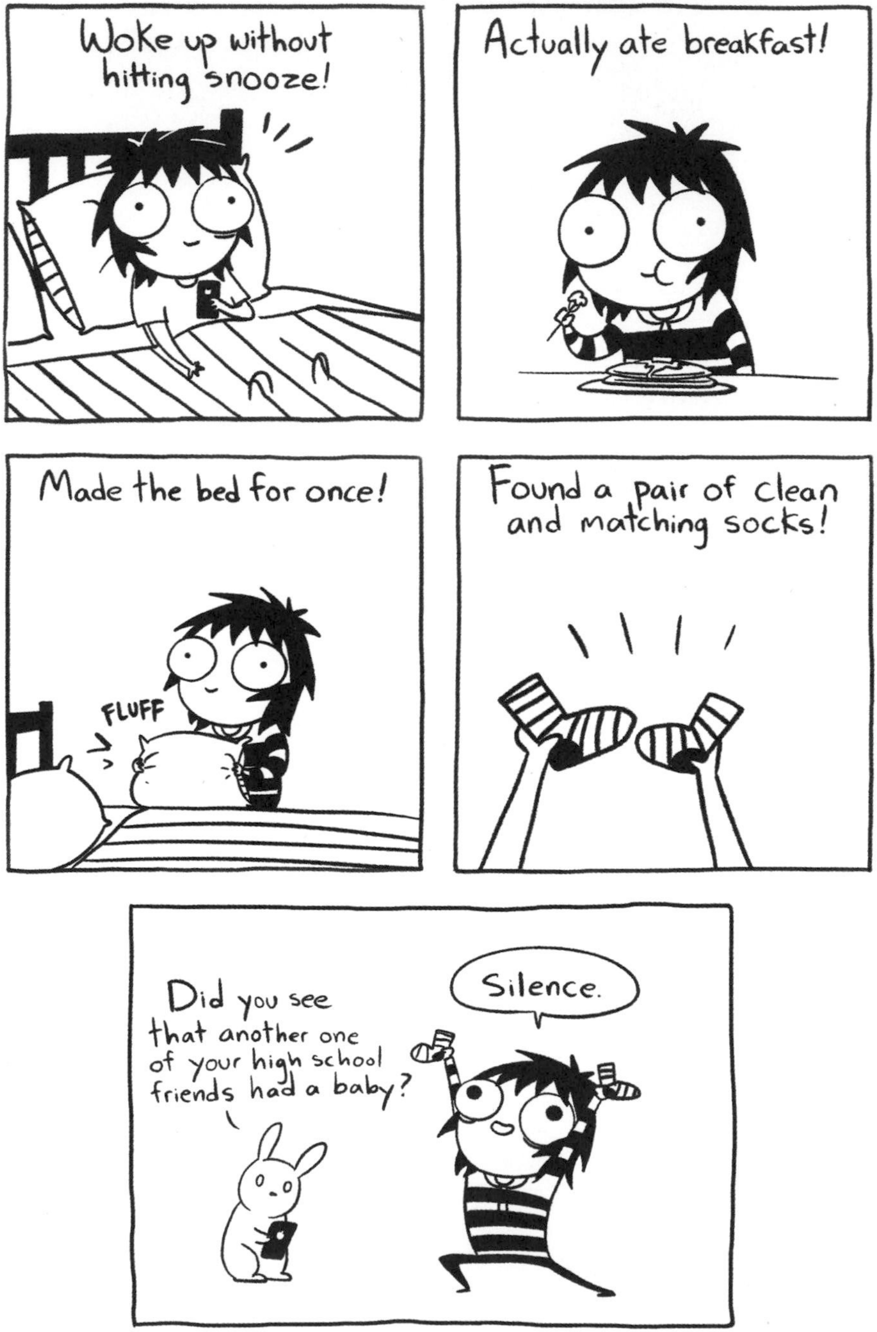
Woke up without hitting snooze!
Actually ate breakfast!
Made the bed for once!
FLUFF
Found a pair of clean and matching socks!
Did you see that another one of your high school friends had a baby?
Silence.

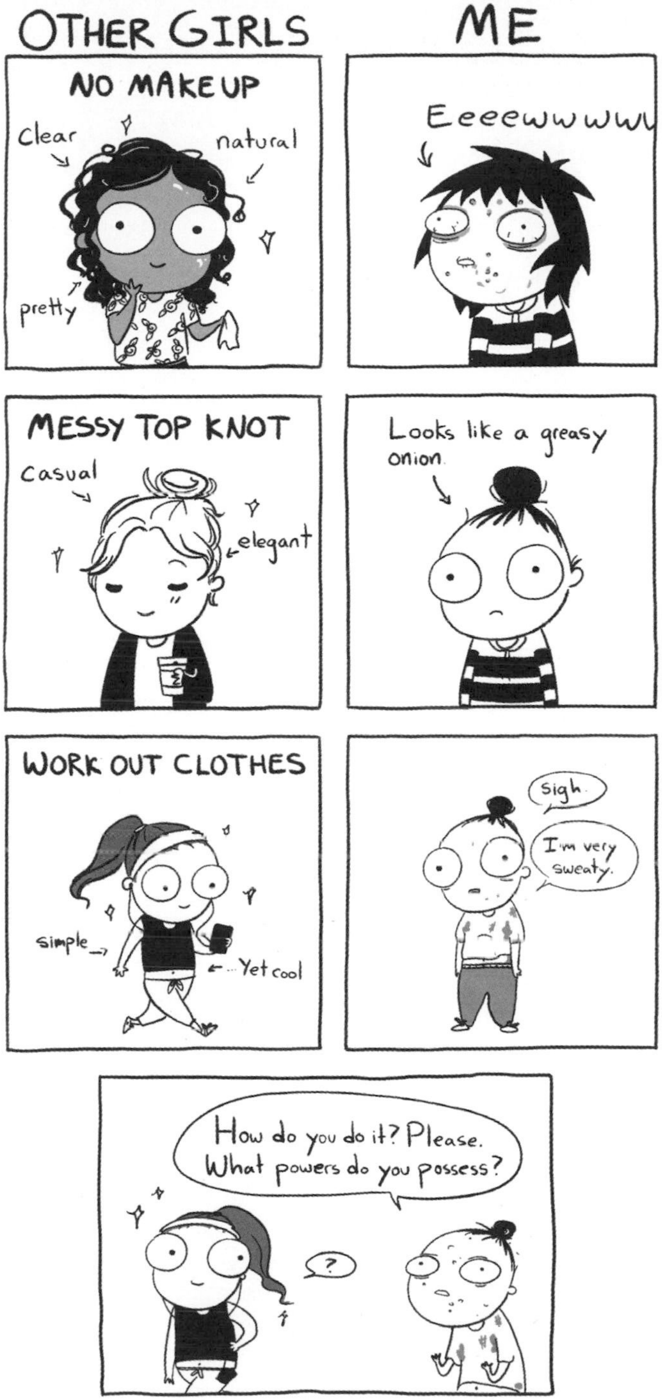
OTHER GIRLS
ME
NO MAKEUP
Clear
natural
pretty
Eeeewwwwv
MESSY TOP KNOT
casual
elegant
Looks like a greasy onion.
WORK OUT CLOTHES
simple
...Yet cool
Sigh.
I'm very sweaty.
How do you do it? Please. What powers do you possess?
?

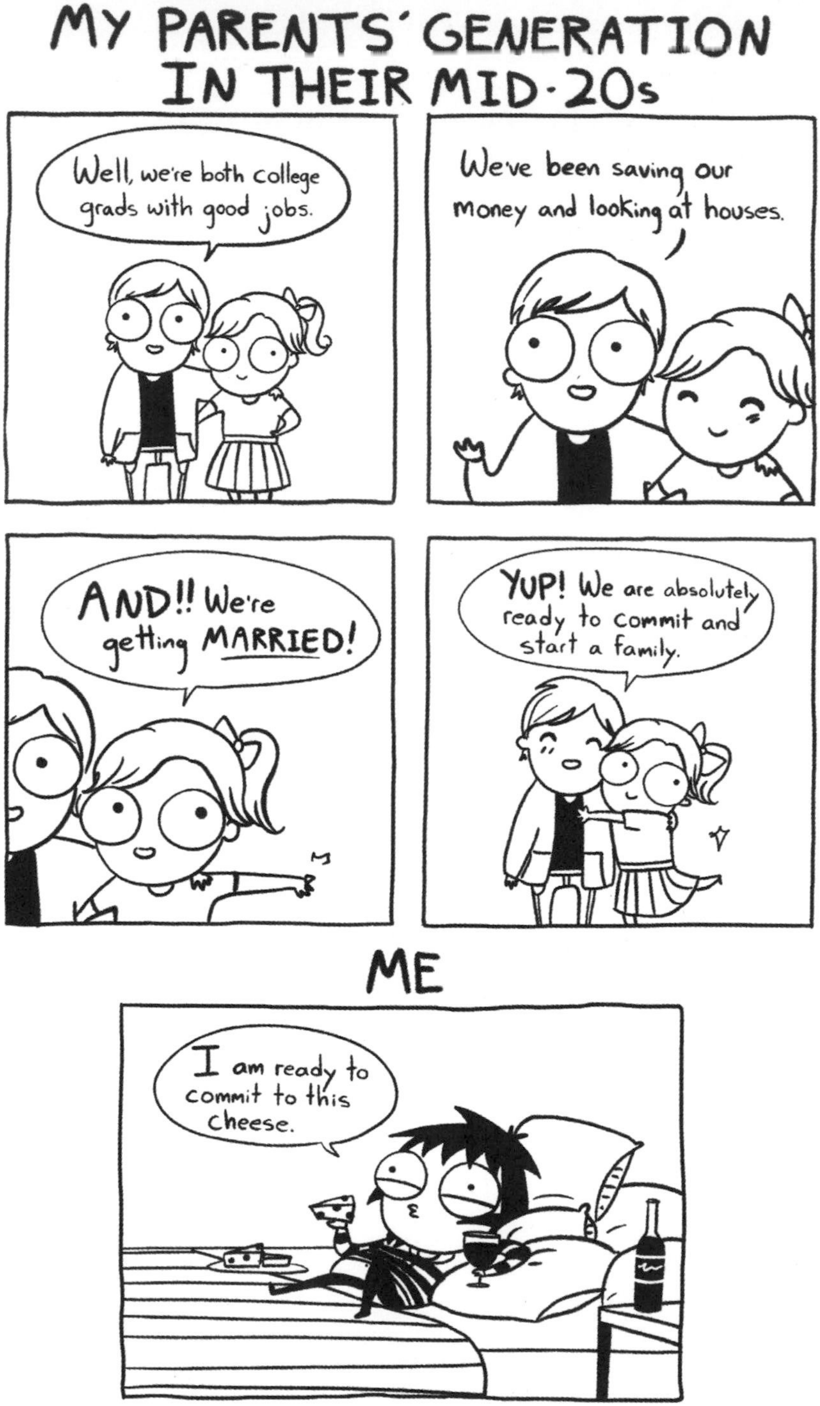
MY PARENTS' GENERATION IN THEIR MID-20s
Well, we're both college grads with good jobs.
We've been saving our money and looking at houses.
AND!! We're getting MARRIED!
YUP! We are absolutely ready to commit and start a family.
ME
I am ready to commit to this cheese.

SINGLE

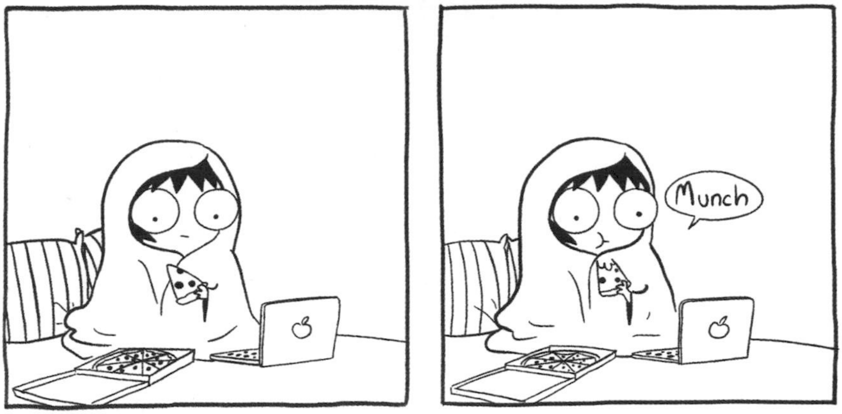
Munch

IN A RELATIONSHIP

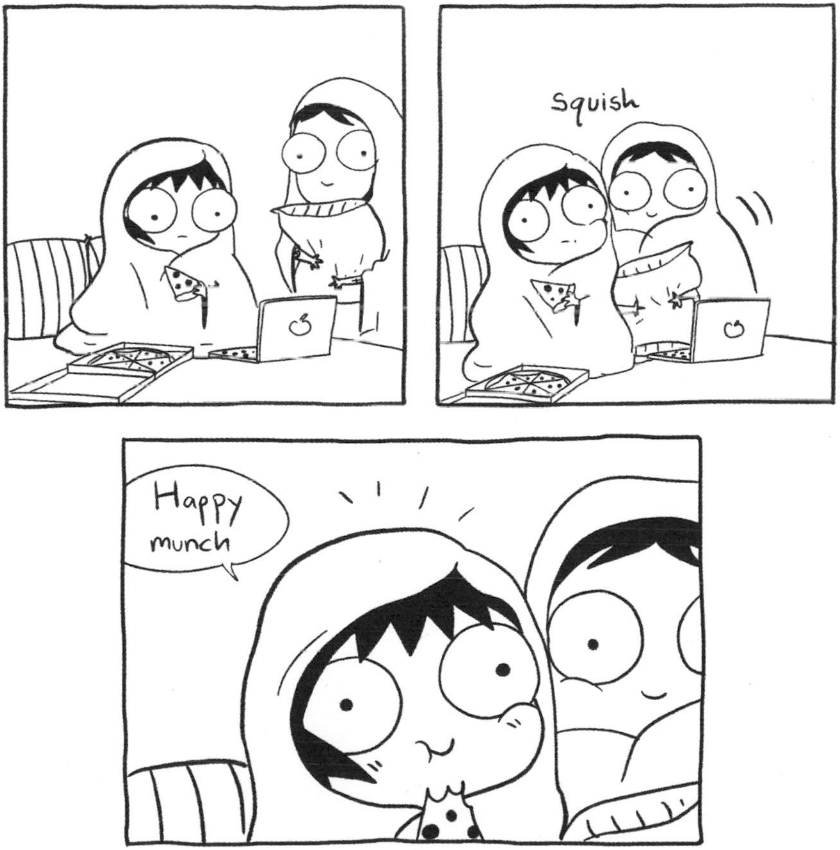
squish
Happy munch

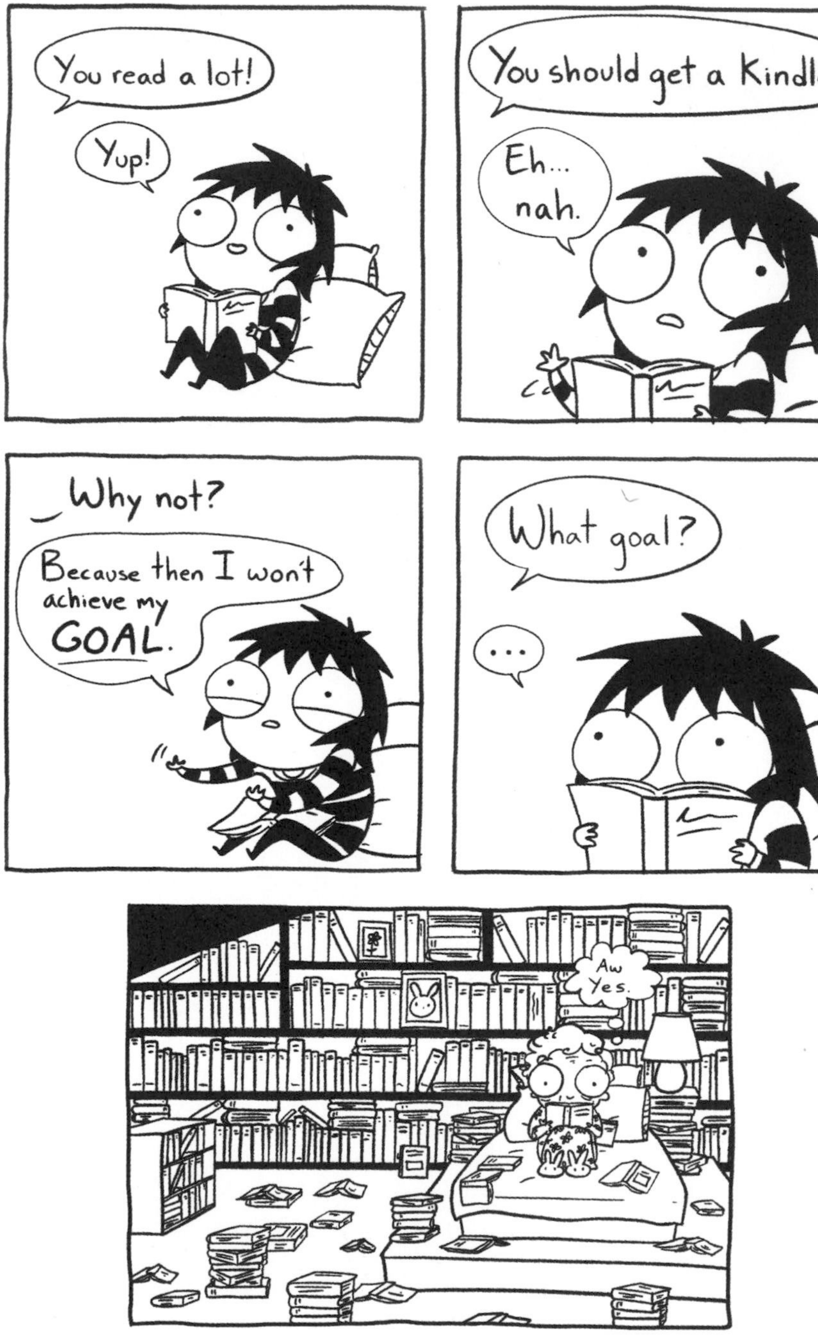
You read a lot!
Yup!
You should get a Kindle.
Eh... nah.
Why not?
Because then I won't achieve my GOAL.
What goal?
...
Aw Yes.

I DON'T KNOW HOW TO BE A PERSON

I'm not good at interacting with the world. In fact, I've *never* been good at interacting with the world.

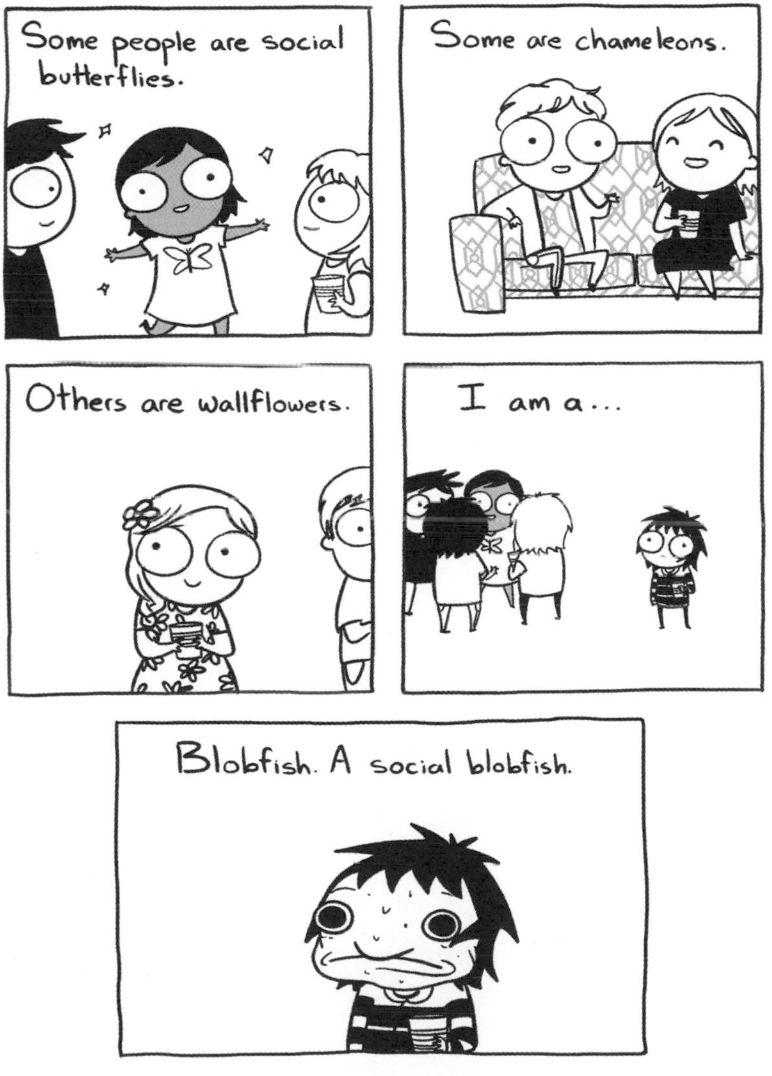

Some people are social butterflies.
Some are chameleons.
Others are wallflowers.
I am a...
Blobfish. A social blobfish.

I think I was born with a certain deadly combination of traits that would eventually wind up making me something of a misfit.

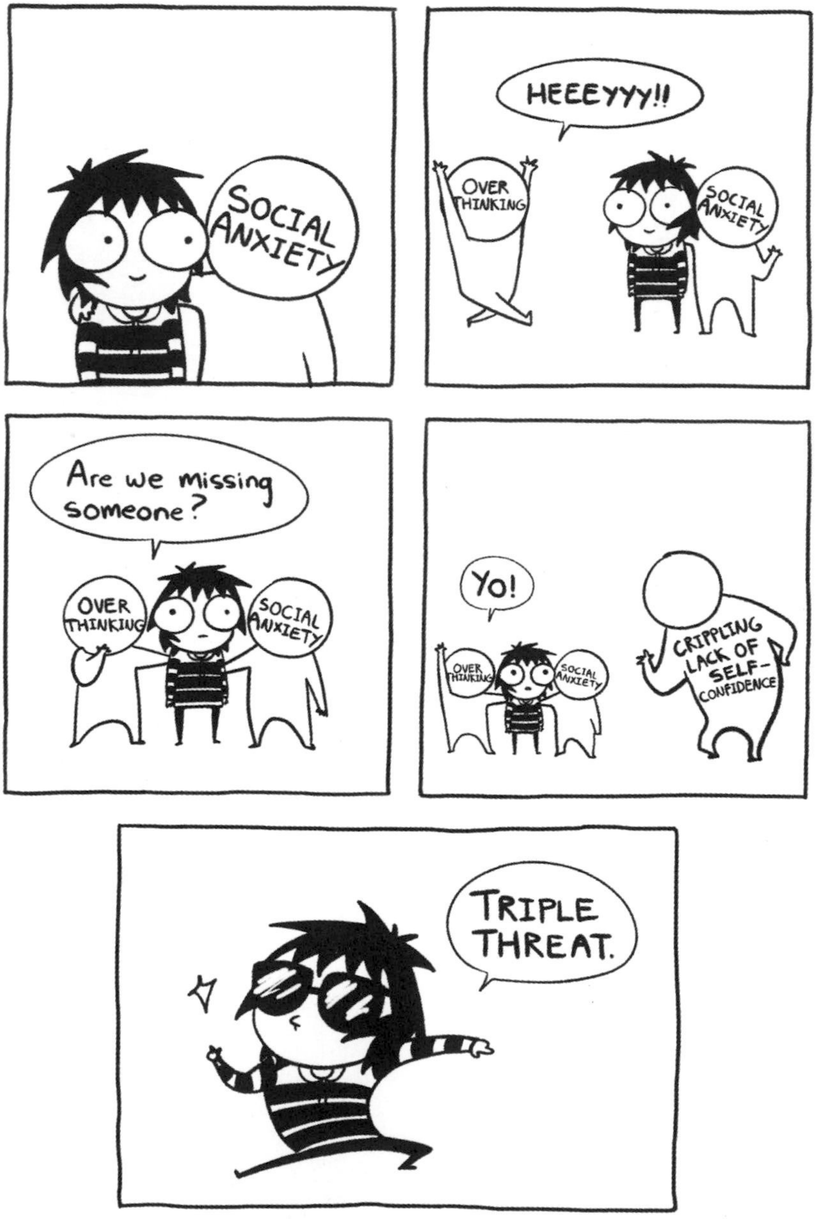
SOCIAL ANXIETY
HEEEYYY!!
OVER THINKING
SOCIAL ANXIETY
Are we missing someone?
OVER THINKING
SOCIAL ANXIETY
Yo!
OVER THINKING
SOCIAL ANXIETY
CRIPPLING LACK OF SELF-CONFIDENCE
TRIPLE THREAT.

When someone doesn't like being social, many people will assume it's because they don't like people. But that's not necessarily the case. I'm often eager to at least try to engage; it just doesn't always work out.

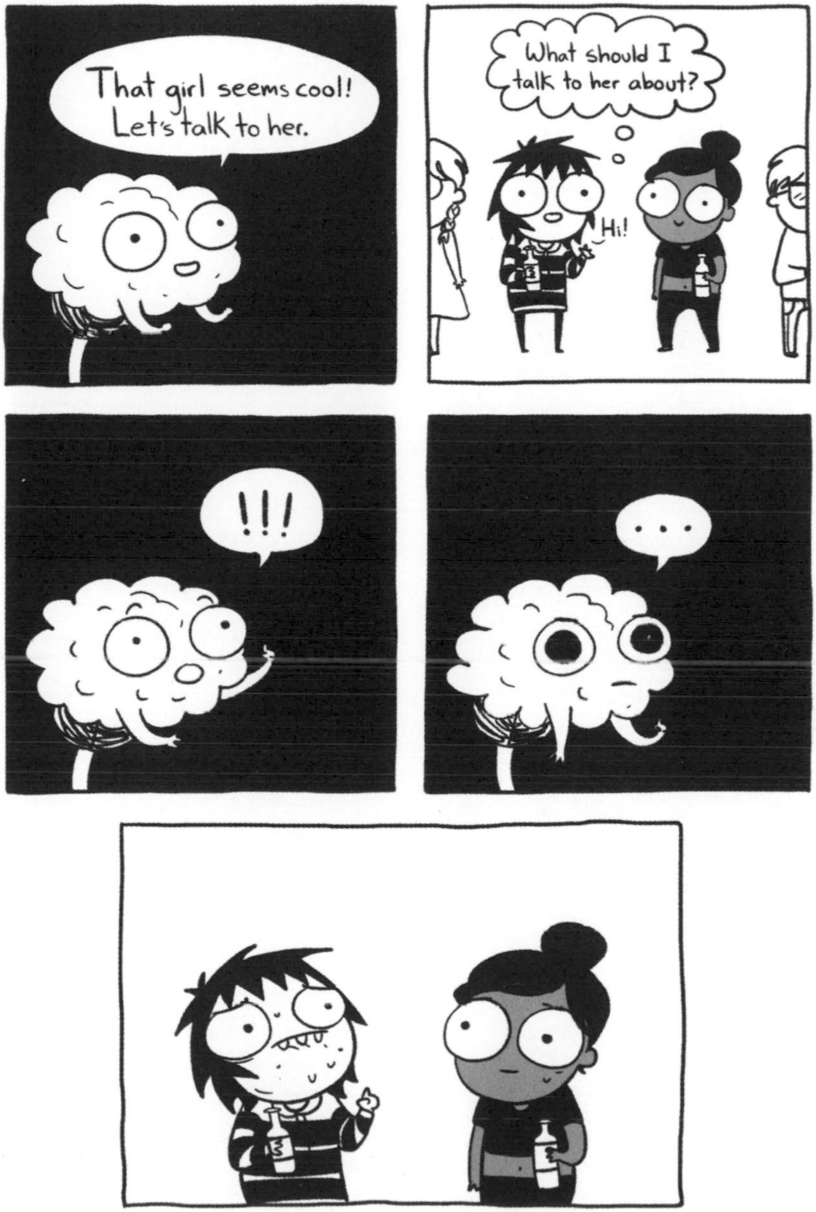

That girl seems cool! Let's talk to her.
What should I talk to her about?
Hi!
!!!
...

It's not just that I'll blank out. At times I can be like a robot suffering a severe malfunction. My brain glitches. And I know, I know! Everyone does the "you too" thing when people say, "Enjoy the movie" or "Enjoy your meal." But recently I had a brain glitch that really took the cake.

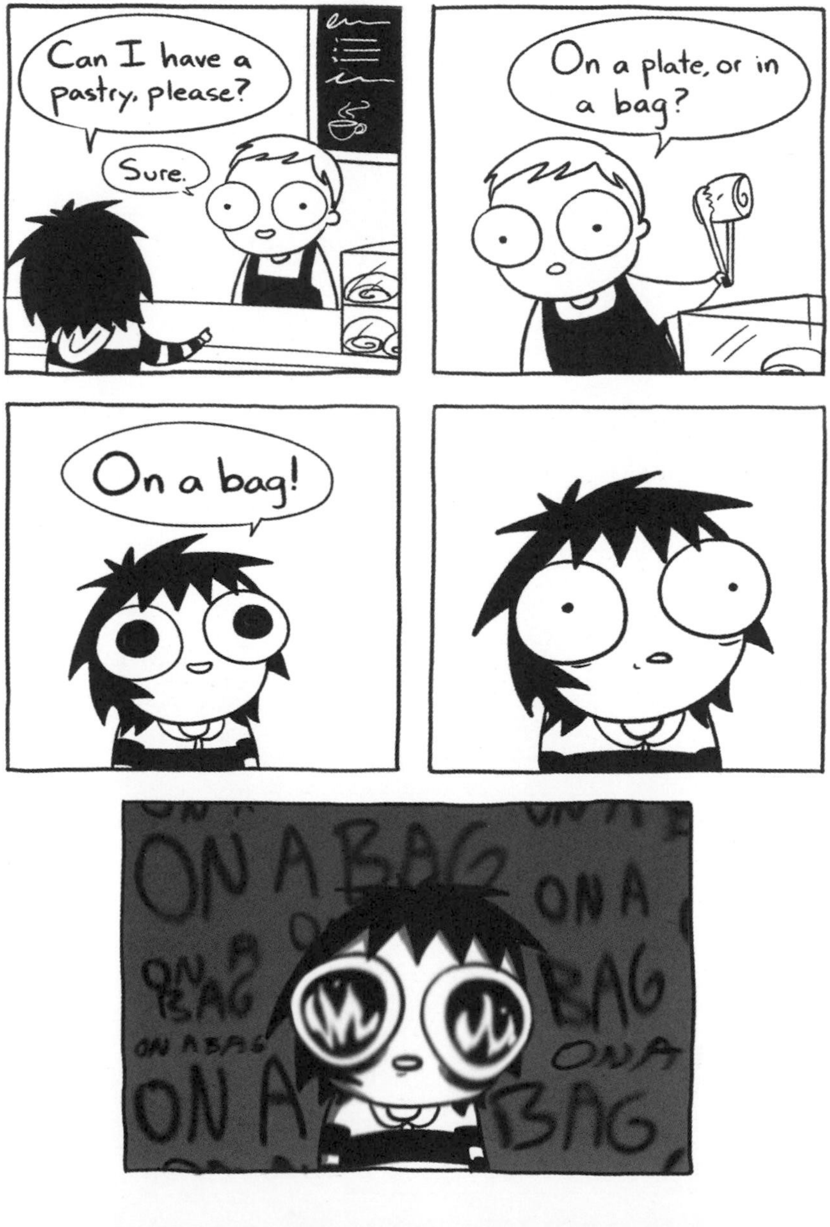
Can I have a pastry, please?
Sure.
On a plate, or in a bag?
On a bag!
ON A BAG
ON A
ON A BAG
ON A
BAG
ON A
ON A
BAG

These glitches are so, so painful. And, thanks to my good ole buddy OverThinking, the glitches continue to haunt me long after they've happened.

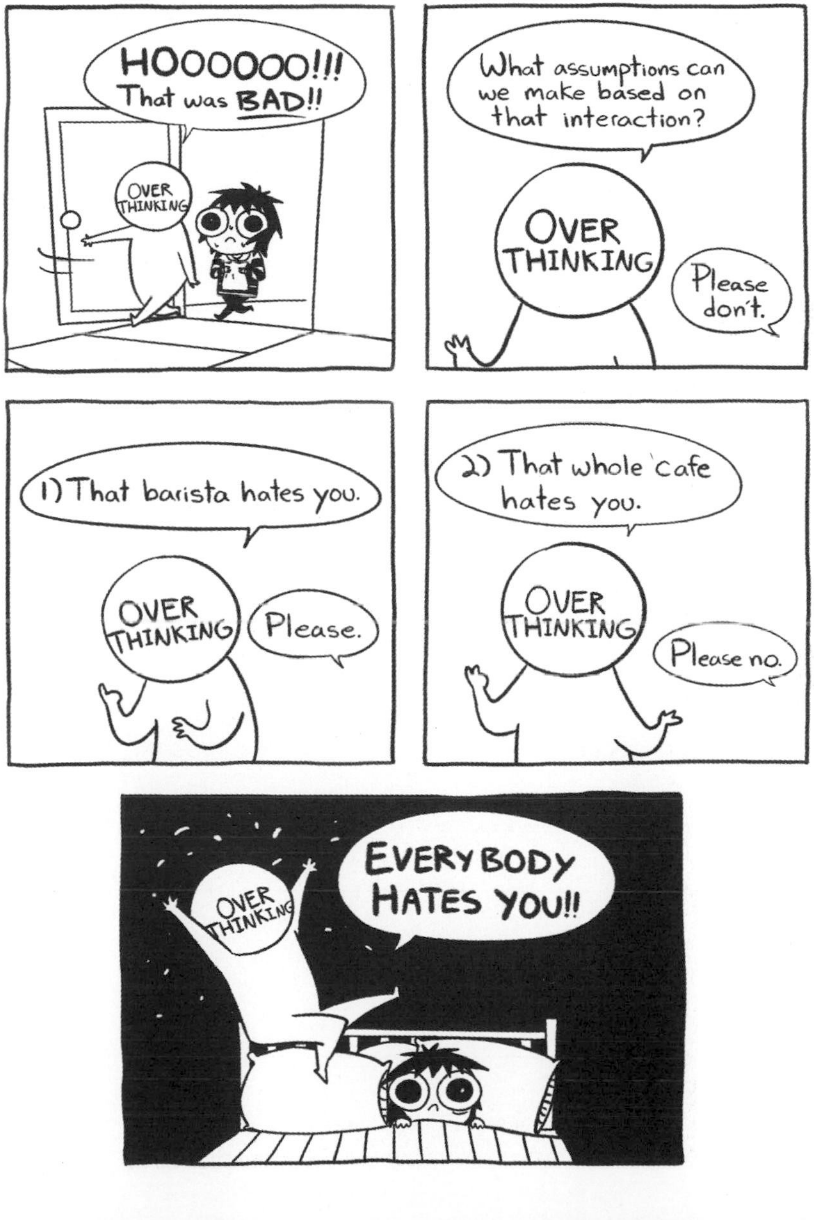
HOOOOOO!!! That was BAD!!
OVER THINKING
What assumptions can we make based on that interaction?
OVER THINKING
Please don't.
1) That barista hates you.
OVER THINKING
Please.
2) That whole cafe hates you.
OVER THINKING
Please no.
OVER THINKING
EVERYBODY HATES YOU!!

OverThinking will make sure I'll never, *ever,* forget the phrase "On a bag."

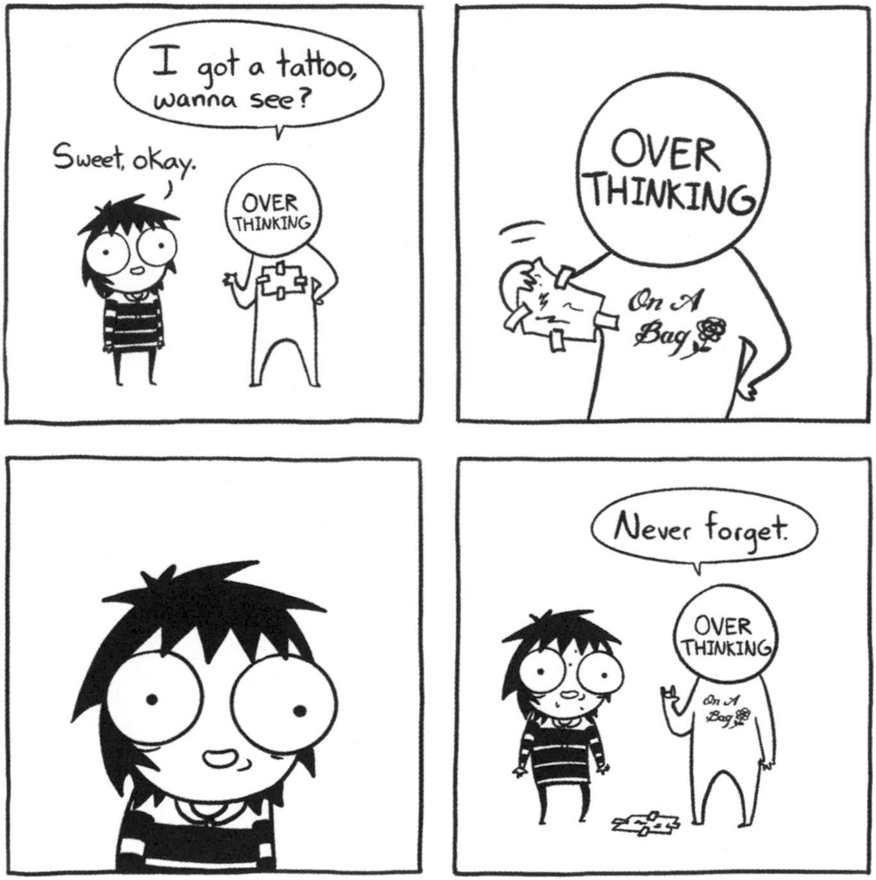
I got a tattoo, wanna see?
Sweet, okay.
OVER THINKING
OVER THINKING
On A Bag
Never forget.
OVER THINKING
On A Bag

Due to the OverThinking and whatnot, I tend to misunderstand the world's signals. I have trouble taking things at face value, and often jump dramatically to conclusions that usually aren't true.

JUMPING TO CONCLUSIONS

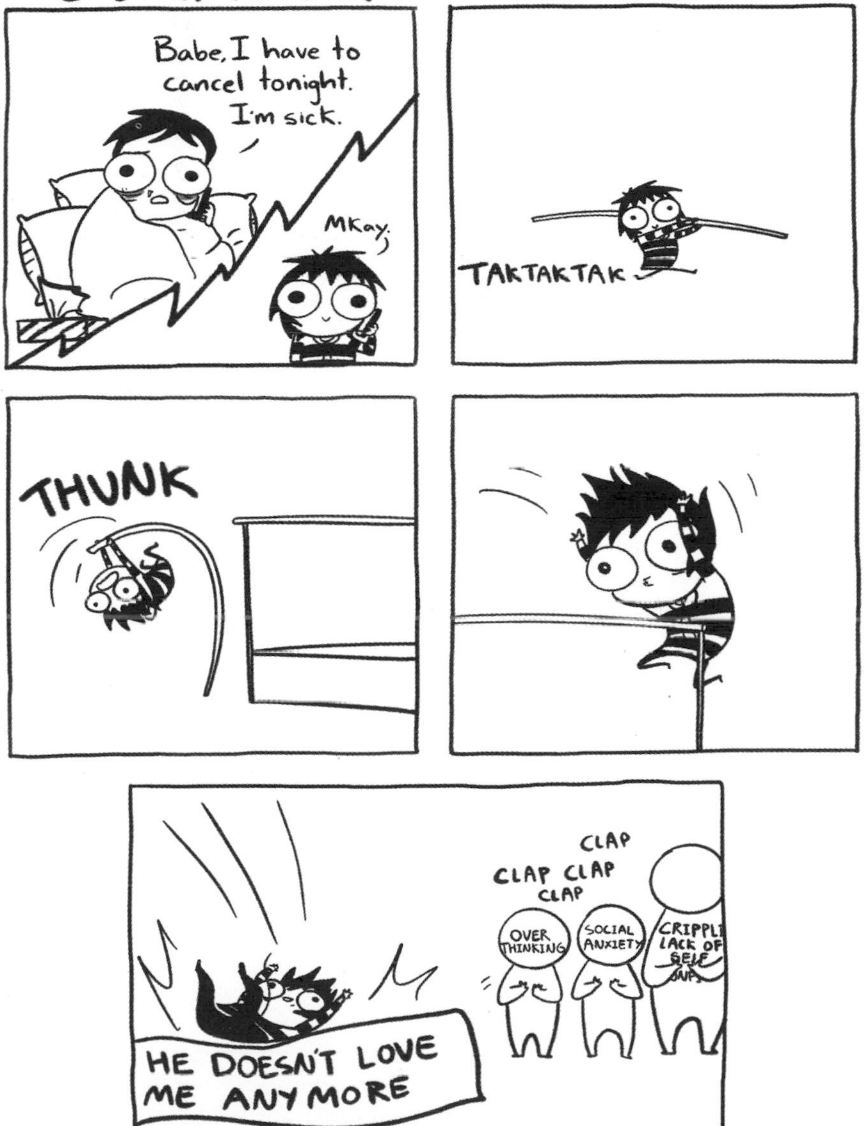
Babe, I have to cancel tonight. I'm sick.
MKay.
TAKTAKTAK
THUNK
CLAP
CLAP CLAP
CLAP
OVER THINKING
SOCIAL ANXIETY
CRIPPL LACK OF SELF
HE DOESN'T LOVE ME ANYMORE

But at the same time, I think the world misreads *me*. One of the first comments I overheard about my appearance was "she has resting bitch face." Which was a big surprise to hear. Inside I feel as harmless and bubbly as a puppy.

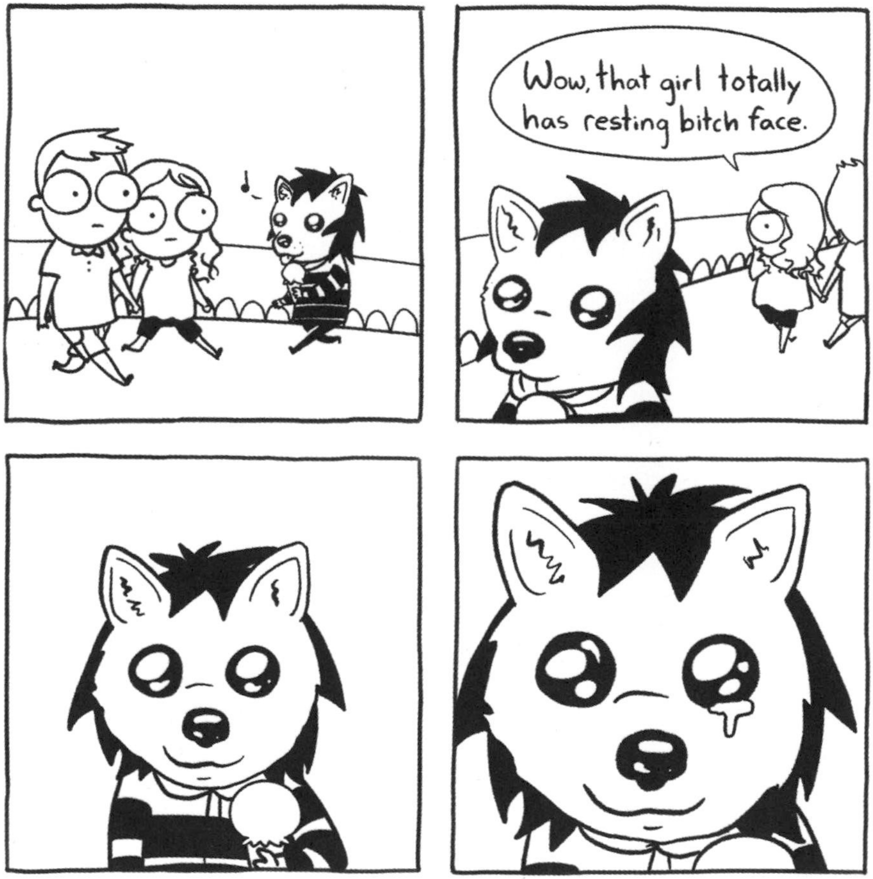
Wow, that girl totally has resting bitch face.

I also think that the world doesn't hear me sometimes. Literally! Apparently, I have a very quiet voice, even if it doesn't sound so quiet in my head.

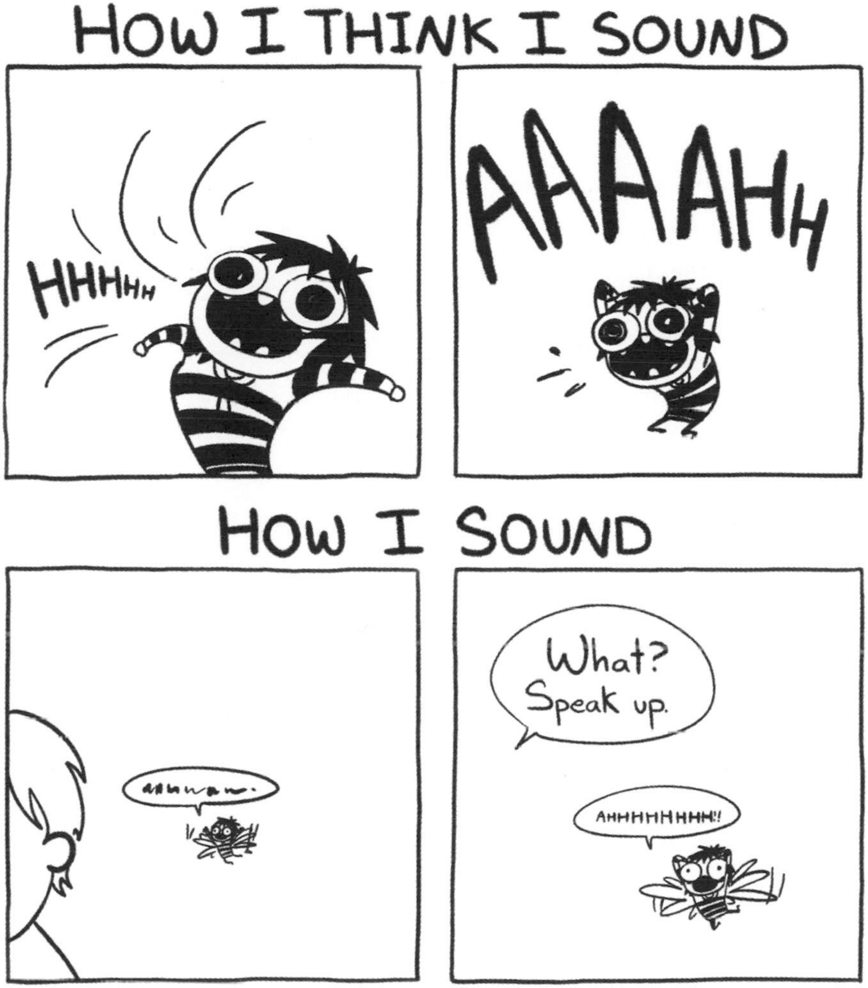
HOW I THINK I SOUND
HHHHH
AAAAAHH
HOW I SOUND
What? Speak up.
AHHHHHHHHH!!

So social interactions can be very exhausting for someone like me. I know I'm not alone. Social exhaustion is something many introverted, shy, or anxious people often suffer. But I'm also learning that if you isolate yourself *too much,* soon enough, you'll get isolation exhaustion too.

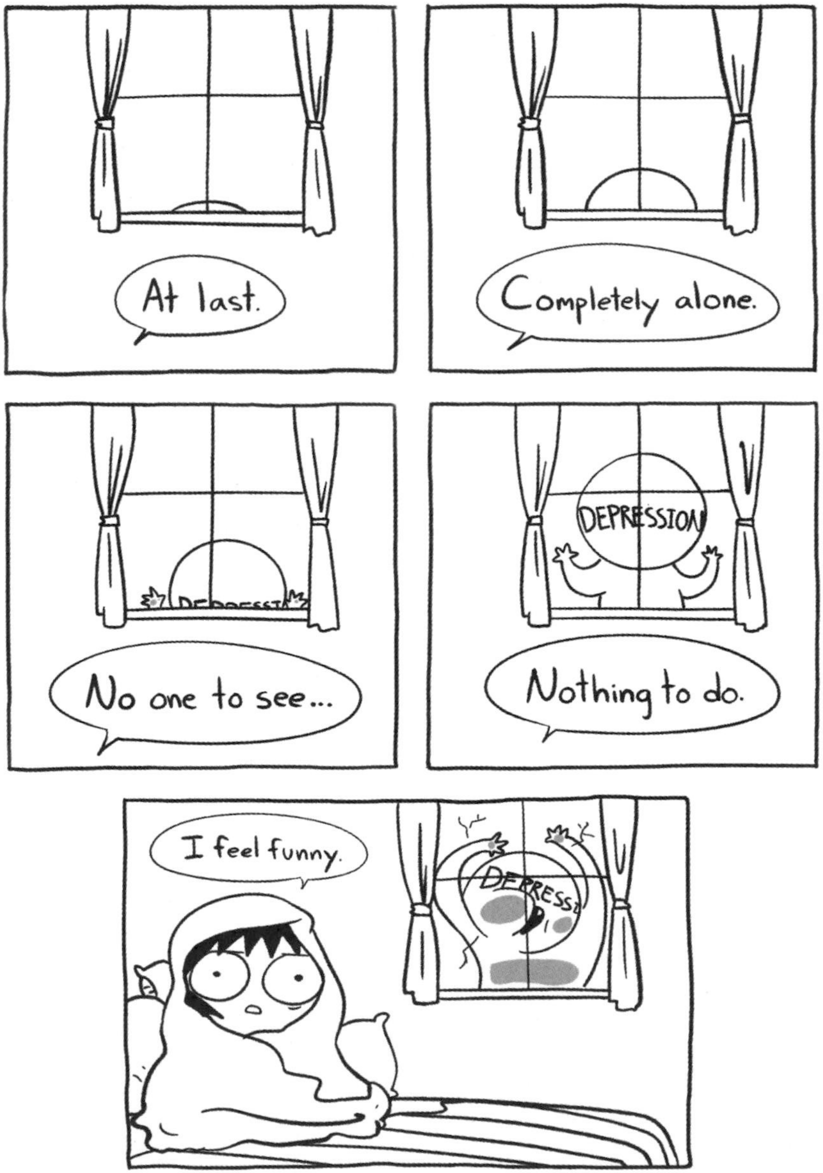
At last.
Completely alone.
No one to see...
DEPRESSION
Nothing to do.
I feel funny.

That's why I've been trying to find a balance.

NORMAL FUNCTIONING PERSON
SOCIAL OVERLOAD HELL
UTTER ISOLATION HELL
NORMAL FUNCTIONING PERSON
Just gotta...
SOCIAL OVERLOAD HELL
UTTER ISOLATION HELL
NORMAL FUNCTIONING PERSON
Squeeze in here...
SOCIAL OVERLOAD HELL
UTTER ISOLATION HELL

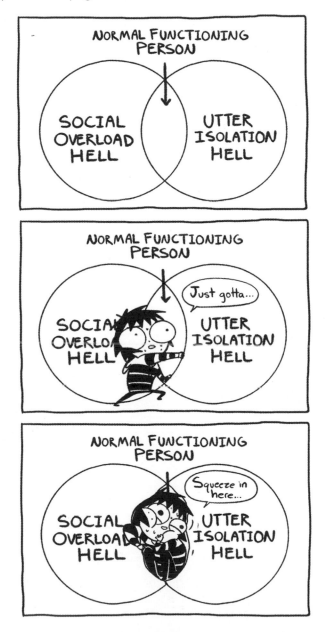

In general, I've been trying to say yes to more things. It's not easy when you've been making excuses all your life.

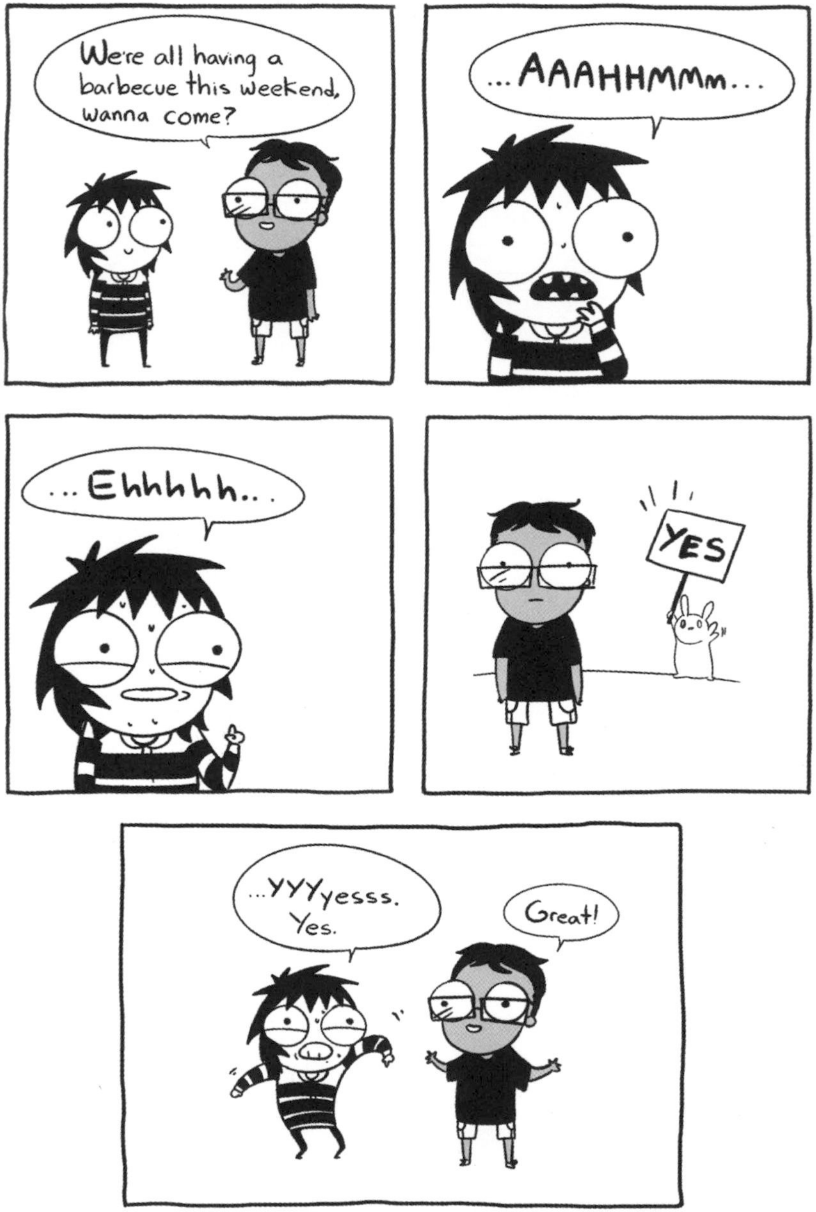

We're all having a barbecue this weekend, wanna come?
...AAAHHMMm...
...Ehhhhh...
YES
...YYYyesss. Yes.
Great!

To tone down my anxiety, I'm also trying to be more selective about what's actually worth worrying about; a sort of enforced apathy to combat the OverThinking. Imagine a superhero whose super power is the ability to say, "I don't care."

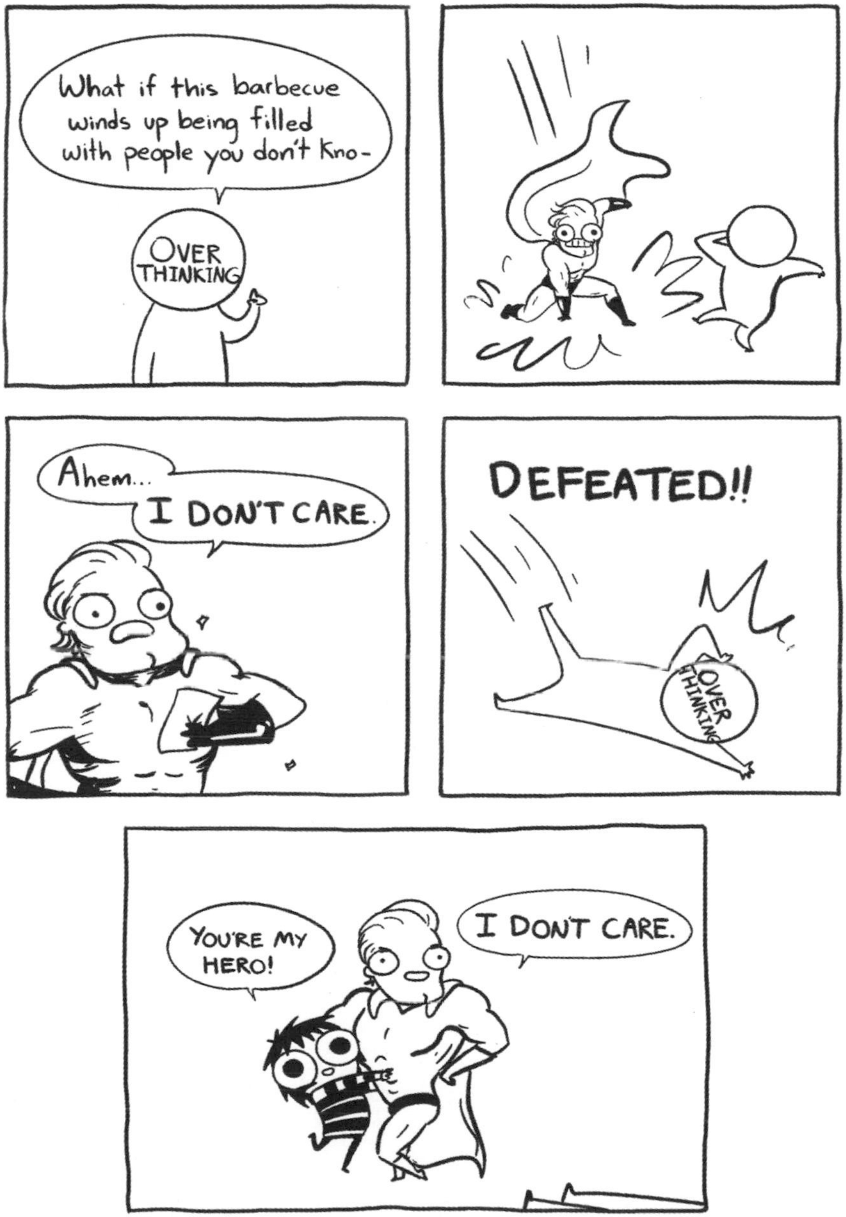
What if this barbecue winds up being filled with people you don't kno-
OVER THINKING
Ahem...
I DON'T CARE.
DEFEATED!!
OVER THINKING
YOU'RE MY HERO!
I DON'T CARE.

This is how I would apply the "I don't care" power in real life. Take, for example, awkward silences. I've been reminding myself that they really aren't a big deal, and they happen to everybody. An awkward silence here or there isn't the end of the world.

WRONG APPROACH

RIGHT APPROACH

See? Not so bad! I'm also trying to work on my conversation skills. Here's what I've learned conversation *isn't*: staying completely silent until someone brings up an obscure fact I know everything about, and then exploding into the conversation.

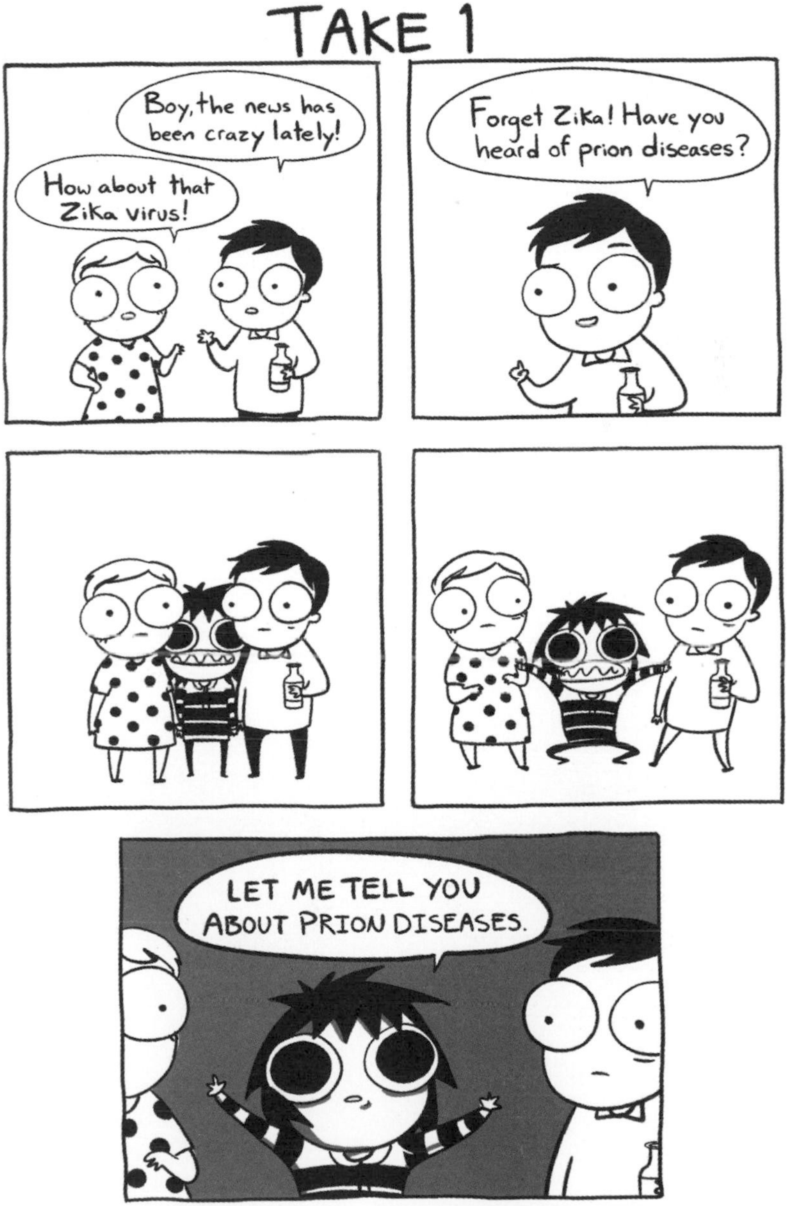
TAKE 1
Boy, the news has been crazy lately!
How about that Zika virus!
Forget Zika! Have you heard of prion diseases?
LET ME TELL YOU ABOUT PRION DISEASES.

I spend *a lot* of time on Wikipedia researching random topics. But let's try that again.

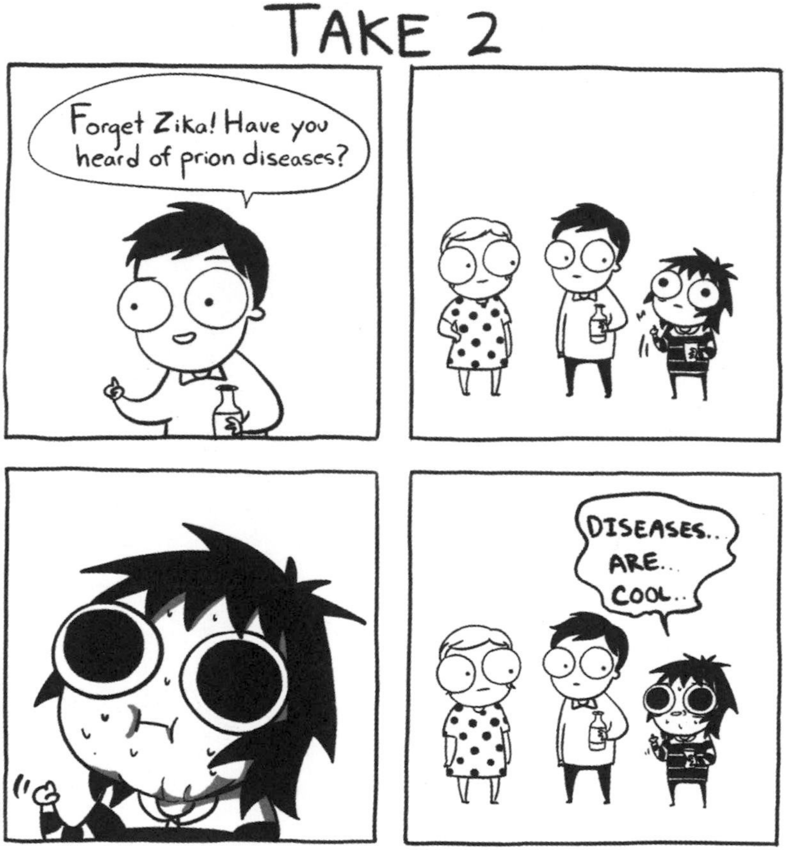
TAKE 2
Forget Zika! Have you heard of prion diseases?
DISEASES... ARE... COOL...

I think the most important thing I've learned, however, is that being social is supposed to be fun. I tend to forget this when I'm curled up in a ball, alone in my room, avoiding everything. I'm trying to remember that the point of seeing friends is to enjoy their company, not worry about their every opinion or every small misstep I take.

I'm not sure I'll ever fully get rid of the robot glitches, or the OverThinking, or dramatically jumping to conclusions. But I'm learning how to have fun anyway, despite them.

Later, losers.
SOCIAL ANXIETY
OVER THINKING

Even if they still occasionally appear uninvited.

Is that dress a little too-
OVER THINKING
I. DON'T. CARE.
OVER THINK

SADIE

(How I Learned to Get Over Myself and Love Cats)

I have a problem with liking things that are really popular. It's not a trait I'm proud of, but it's one I've always had. Deep down, I'm positive I was born a cynical, popular-thing-hating soul.

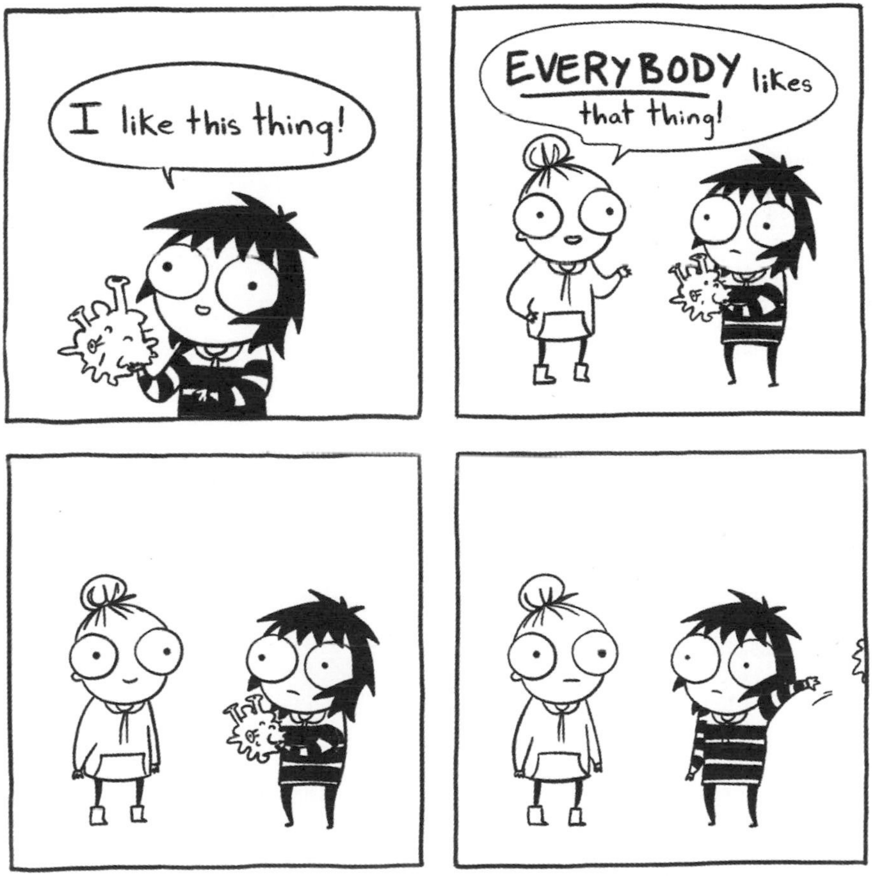
I like this thing!
EVERYBODY likes that thing!

This same logic applied to cats. Everybody seemed to love them, especially on the Internet. Logging online felt like logging into a cat-loving cult.

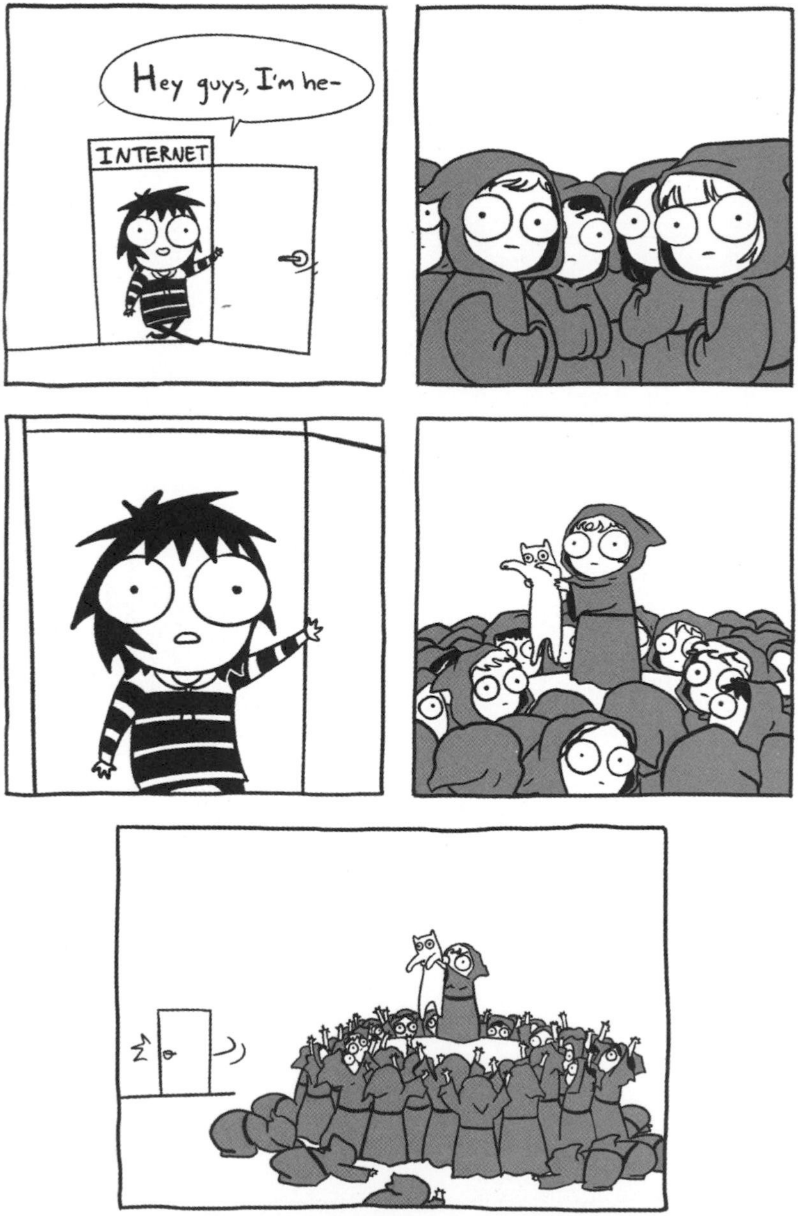
Hey guys, I'm he-
INTERNET

What's more, cats didn't particularly seem to like *me*. One of my friends had a black cat named Stormy, and we definitely didn't vibe well.

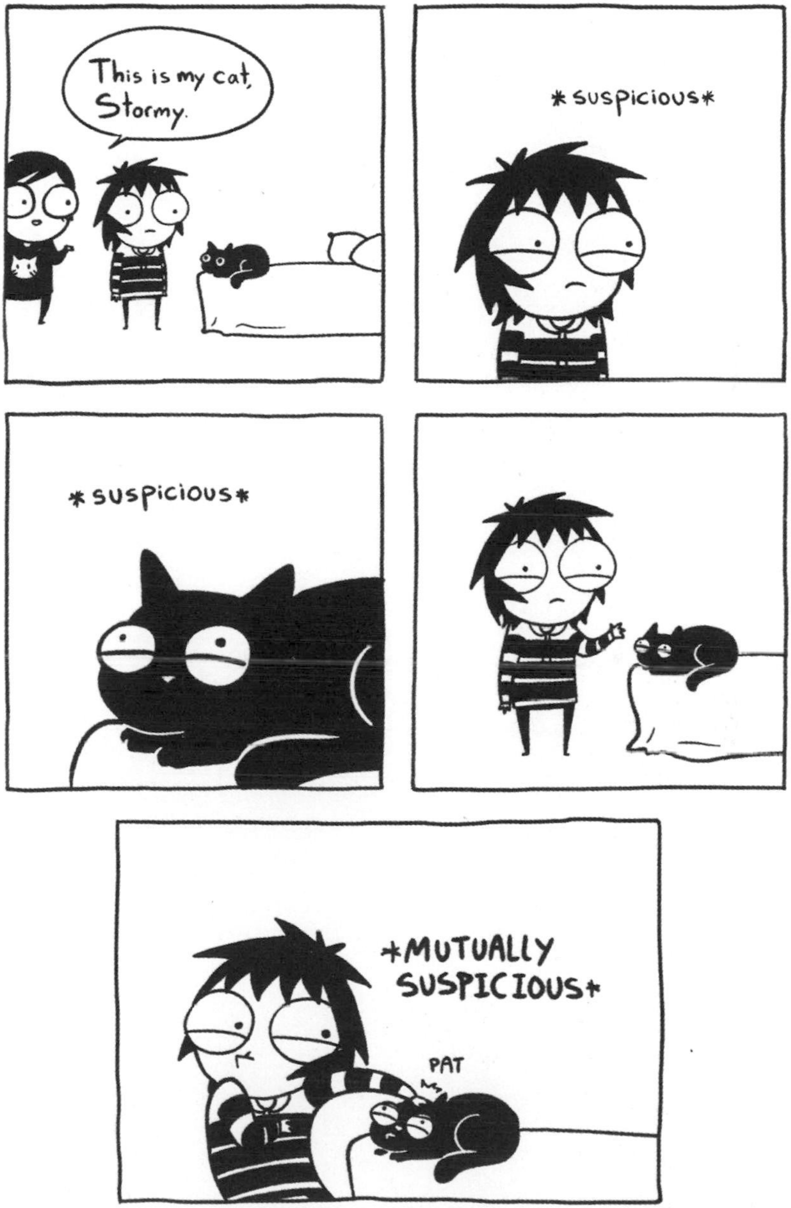

This is my cat, Stormy.
suspicious
suspicious
MUTUALLY SUSPICIOUS
PAT

I also didn't really understand what it was that cats *did* that made them so great. From what I gathered, they sat around the house and occasionally knocked things down. And people photographed their cats doing this. Oh boy, did they photograph.

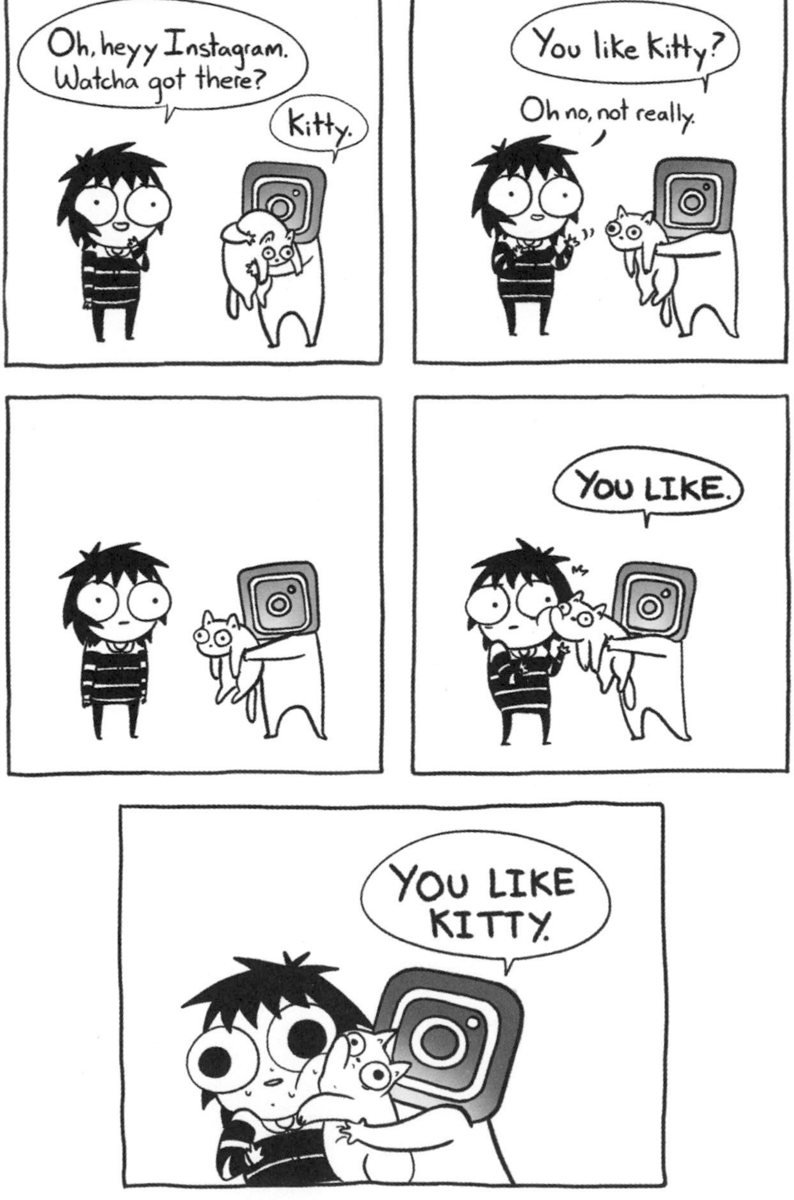
Oh, heyy Instagram. Watcha got there?
Kitty.
You like Kitty?
Oh no, not really.
YOU LIKE.
YOU LIKE KITTY.

I always imagined that cats were the Paris Hiltons of the pet world: They didn't quite deserve all the attention but they got it anyway.

Frankly, I didn't ever think I'd own a cat. But that was soon to change when, all of a sudden, my two roommates and I had a mouse problem.

It started out very small (one-small-mouse small). In hindsight, our big mistake was that we didn't just take care of it then. You see, my roommates and I are all big animal rights people. All three of us are vegetarians. And collectively, we agreed that we would avoid killing the mouse at all costs.

One mouse quickly became many mice. But we still couldn't kill them. We bought humane traps, which completely backfired, because this is what happened:

HUMANE MOUSE TRAP CYCLE

Catch mouse
WHAP
Release mouse
Mouse returns
Whazzuuuup!

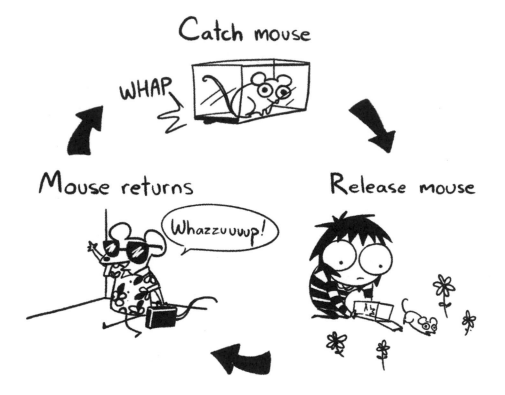

Weeks went by, and it got completely out of control. We started using insane home remedies out of our desperation not to buy lethal traps. In one instance, we sprayed down the entire apartment with peppermint.

We might as well have been doing this:

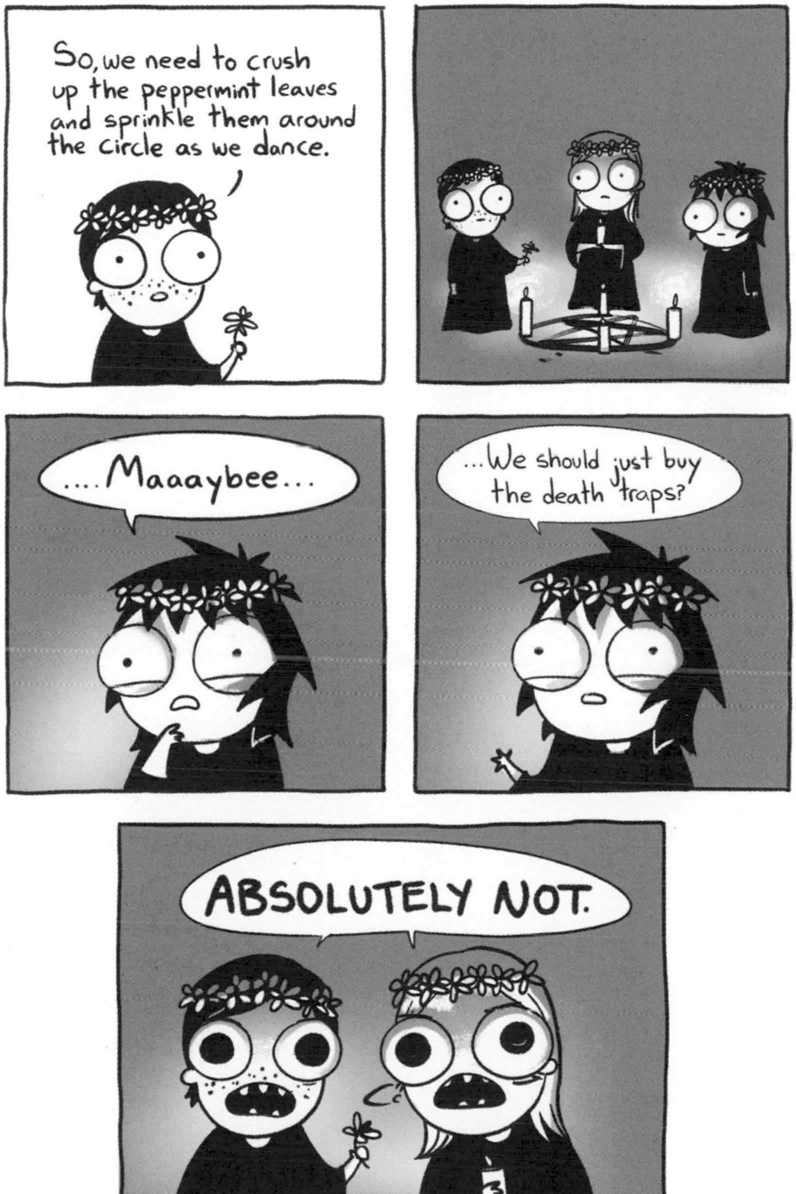
So, we need to crush up the peppermint leaves and sprinkle them around the circle as we dance.
....Maaaybee...
...We should just buy the death traps?
ABSOLUTELY NOT.

As our mouse problem was increasing, a solution appeared. My mom had just adopted a kitten because her cat Jessie was depressed and needed company.

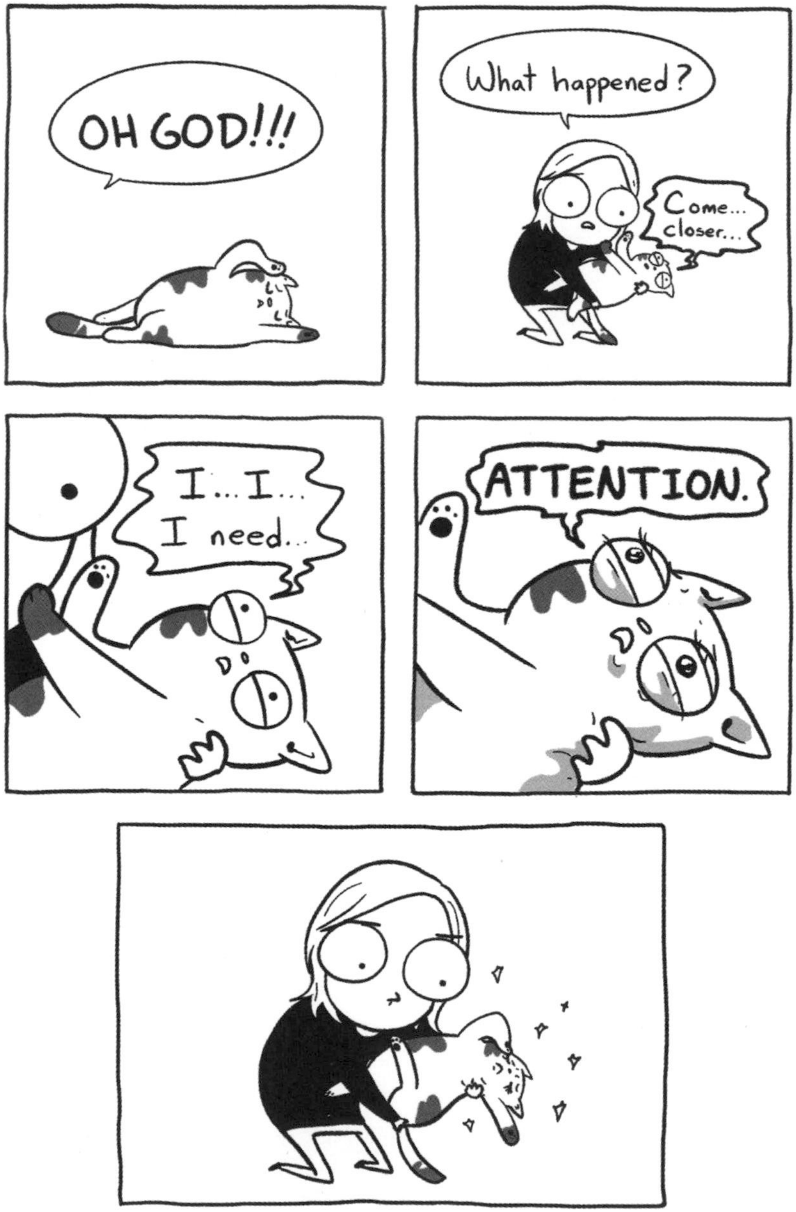
OH GOD!!!
What happened?
Come... closer...
I... I... I need...
ATTENTION.

To us, a kitten seemed like the perfect humane solution. Young kittens aren't trained, experienced hunters yet. But maybe just having a cat's scent in the apartment would scare mice away. It was a natural remedy that (hopefully) wouldn't hurt any animals. I convinced my mom to let us take the kitten for a month.

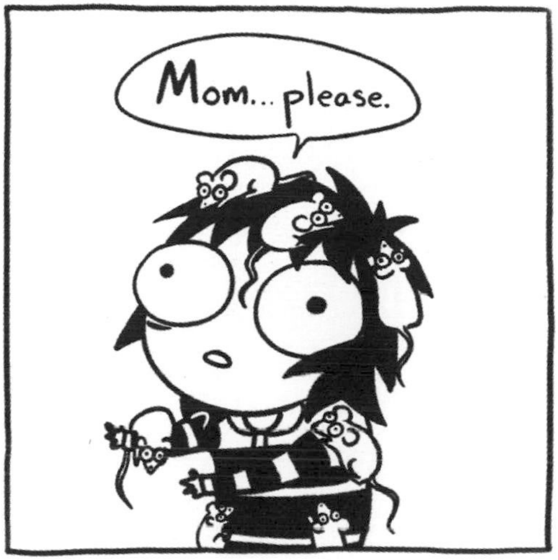
Mom... please.

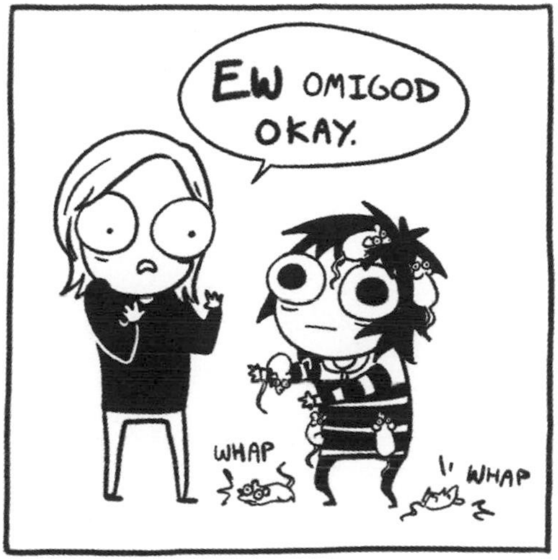
EW OMIGOD OKAY.
WHAP
WHAP

The kitten's name was Sadie. I went to pick her up, expecting the same mutually suspicious encounter I'd had with most cats before. But when I walked into the room . . . she was so . . . tiny. And her paws were so soft and . . . squishy! And her meows were so high-pitched and cute! And she was so . . . nice!

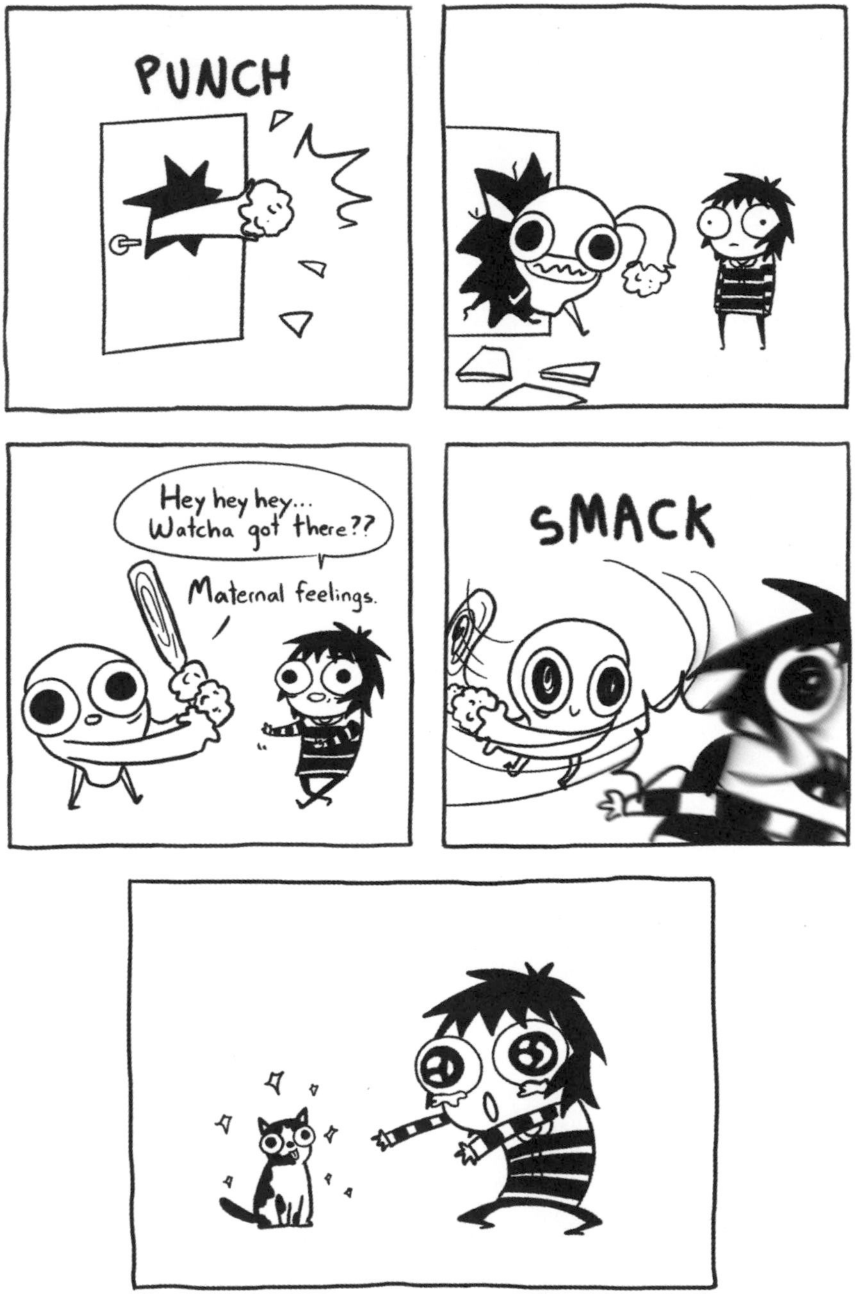
PUNCH
Hey hey hey...
Watcha got there??
Maternal feelings.
SMACK

I brought her to my apartment, and my roommates loved her too. One thing that immediately surprised me about Sadie was how social she was. We would sit around the apartment chatting and she would sit with us, looking at us intently and listening. And I was surprised at how much she liked me! A cat had never liked me before. But Sadie actually spent most of her time trying to be near me.

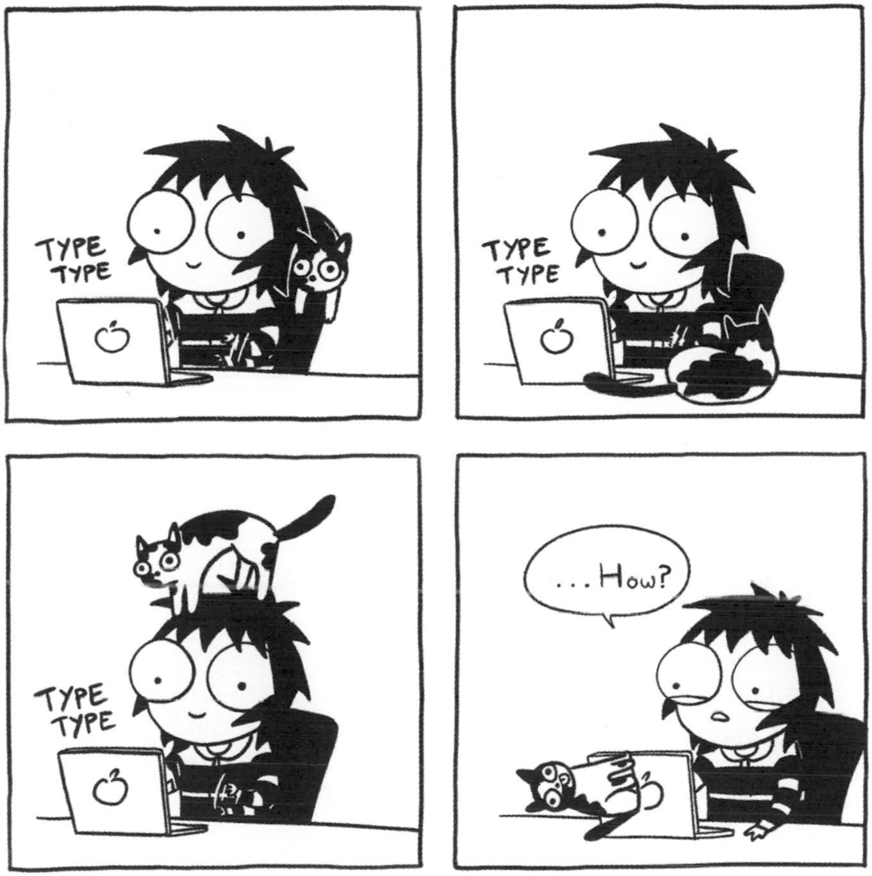
TYPE
TYPE
TYPE
TYPE
TYPE
TYPE
...How?

As the weeks went by, my affection for her grew. Seeing her just lying around in the sun was the cutest thing in the world to me. And just as she always tried to be near me, I always tried to be near her. She made me behave in strange ways.

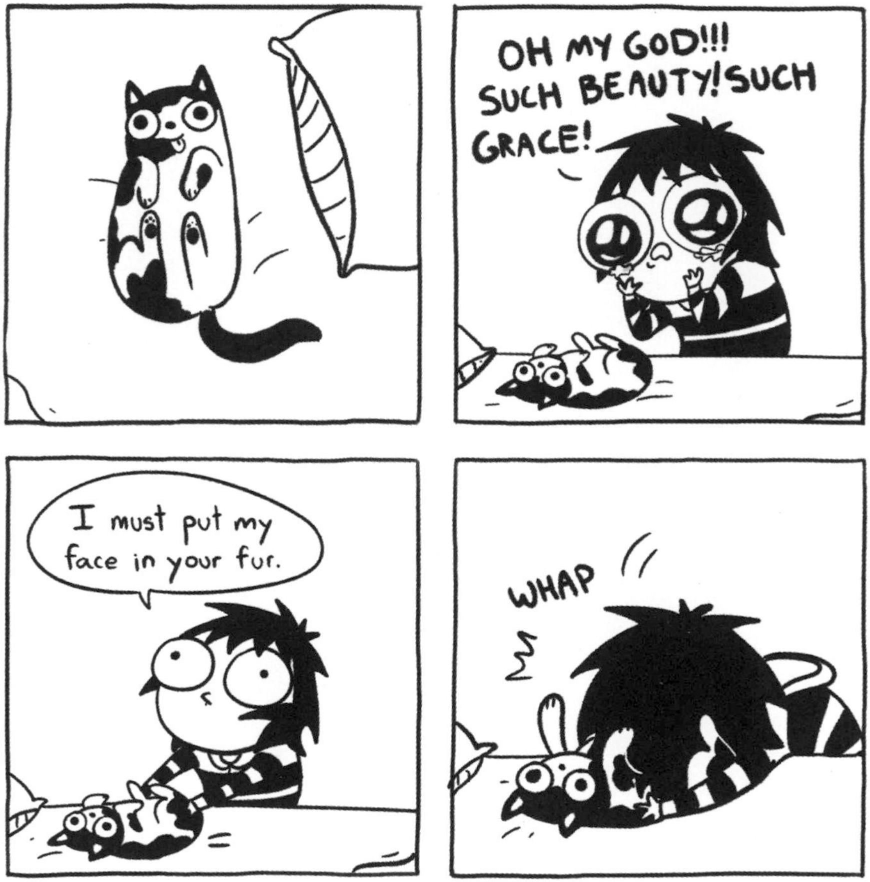
OH MY GOD!!! SUCH BEAUTY! SUCH GRACE!
I must put my face in your fur.
WHAP

I had never understood the number of photographs people took of their cats. But Sadie was so special, so extremely precious, that I needed to document her fabulousness.

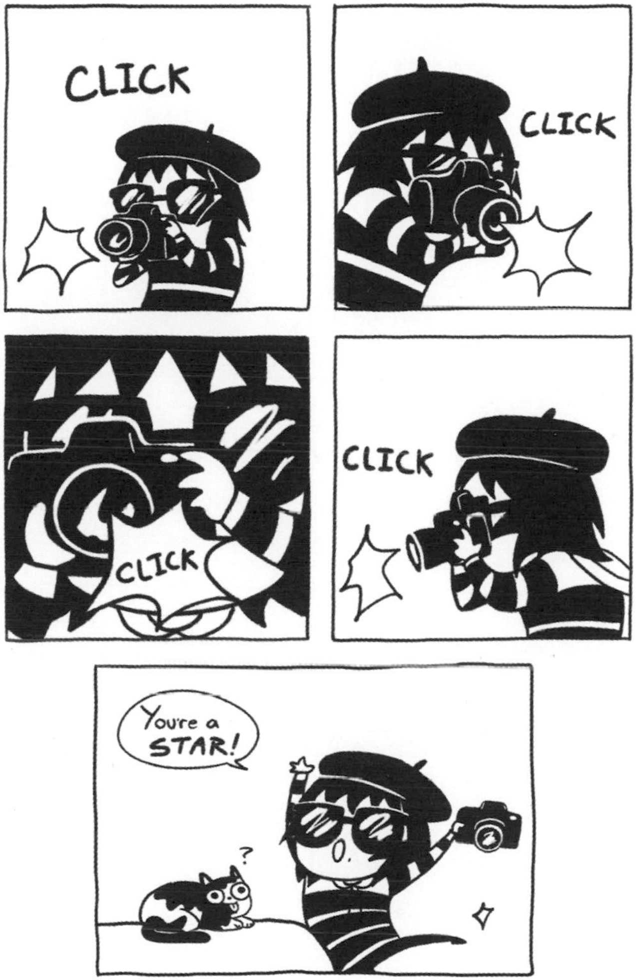
CLICK
CLICK
CLICK
CLICK
You're a STAR!
?

And she *did* get rid of the mice. One time, she actually *caught* a mouse, and we all watched in horror. But my prediction turned out to be true: Pure, naïve kitten Sadie didn't kill the mouse. It got away; my roommates and I breathed a sigh of relief. And after that, the mice never returned. We shared a blissful month in which all of our problems were replaced by a cute and cuddly ball of joy.

However, my agreement with my mom was that I could keep Sadie for a month. At the end of the month, as in a fairy tale, she demanded Sadie back. After all, the whole reason she got Sadie was for Jessie, and Jessie was lonelier by the day. I responded to my mom's perfectly legitimate request in horror.

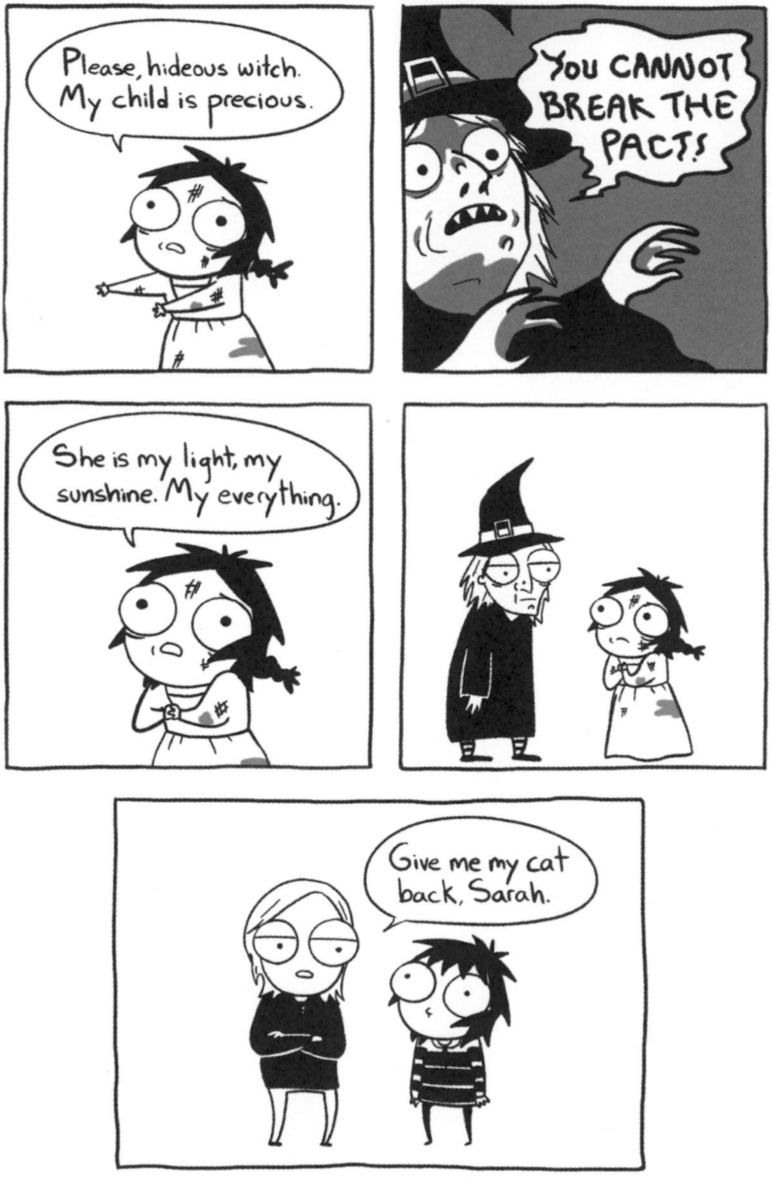
Please, hideous witch. My child is precious.
YOU CANNOT BREAK THE PACT!
She is my light, my sunshine. My everything.
Give me my cat back, Sarah.

She was right. I had to give her back. I'm no cat-napper. But I hadn't been prepared for all the feelings I had toward Sadie.

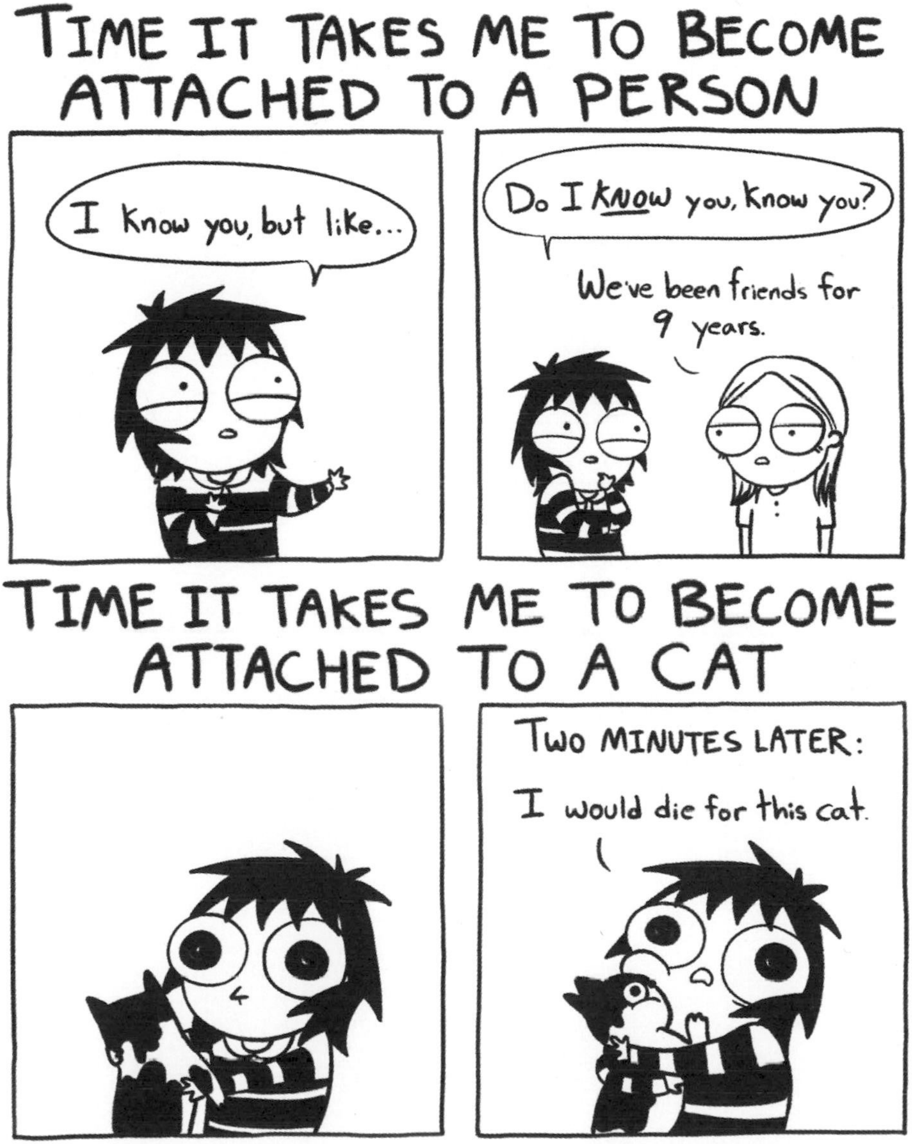
TIME IT TAKES ME TO BECOME ATTACHED TO A PERSON
I know you, but like...
Do I KNOW you, know you?
We've been friends for 9 years.
TIME IT TAKES ME TO BECOME ATTACHED TO A CAT
TWO MINUTES LATER:
I would die for this cat.

The mice were gone, and so was Sadie. Much as I wasn't prepared to feel affection toward her in the first place, I also wasn't prepared to feel as sad as I did when she left. I didn't realize how much a cat can become entwined with your daily life. I woke up with her, worked while she napped next to me, and struggled to eat meals as she attempted to steal food from me. She was a small friend I briefly shared my life with. Her tiny presence made that short time so much more joyful. When she went back to live with my mom, my room suddenly felt very empty.

But Sadie changed my life for the better. I've realized my opinions about things can radically change. For example, I'd never thought I'd be this person:

Hey! Wanna see pictures of my cat?
YES.

Liking cats has made my life much more enjoyable. And maybe this means I can learn to start liking other things that are popular too.

And the haters gonna hate hate hate hate hate
BABY I'M JUST GONNA
SHAKE SHAKE SHAKE SHAKE SHAKE SHAKE
SHAKE IT OFF

We'll see!

(For those who are curious, Sadie and Jessie are currently living together in peace. Jessie's not depressed anymore.)

THE SWEATER THIEF

I am smaller than the average human, and as a result, I am cold more frequently than most of my peers. If you're not an "always cold" person, then I'm sure you've encountered one of them before.

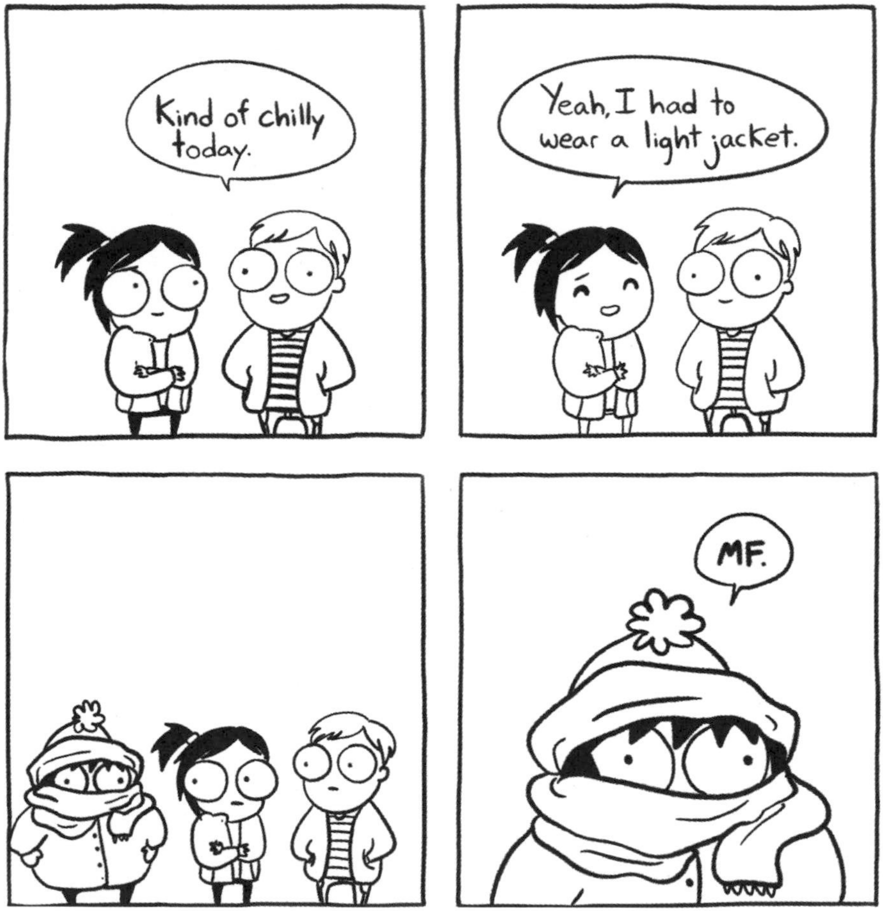
Kind of chilly today.
Yeah, I had to wear a light jacket.
MF.

This has been a problem for my entire life. It gets especially bad in the winter, when I'm frequently too cold to even leave my bed. And when it's absolutely necessary to leave out of sheer survival, I try to take my bed with me.

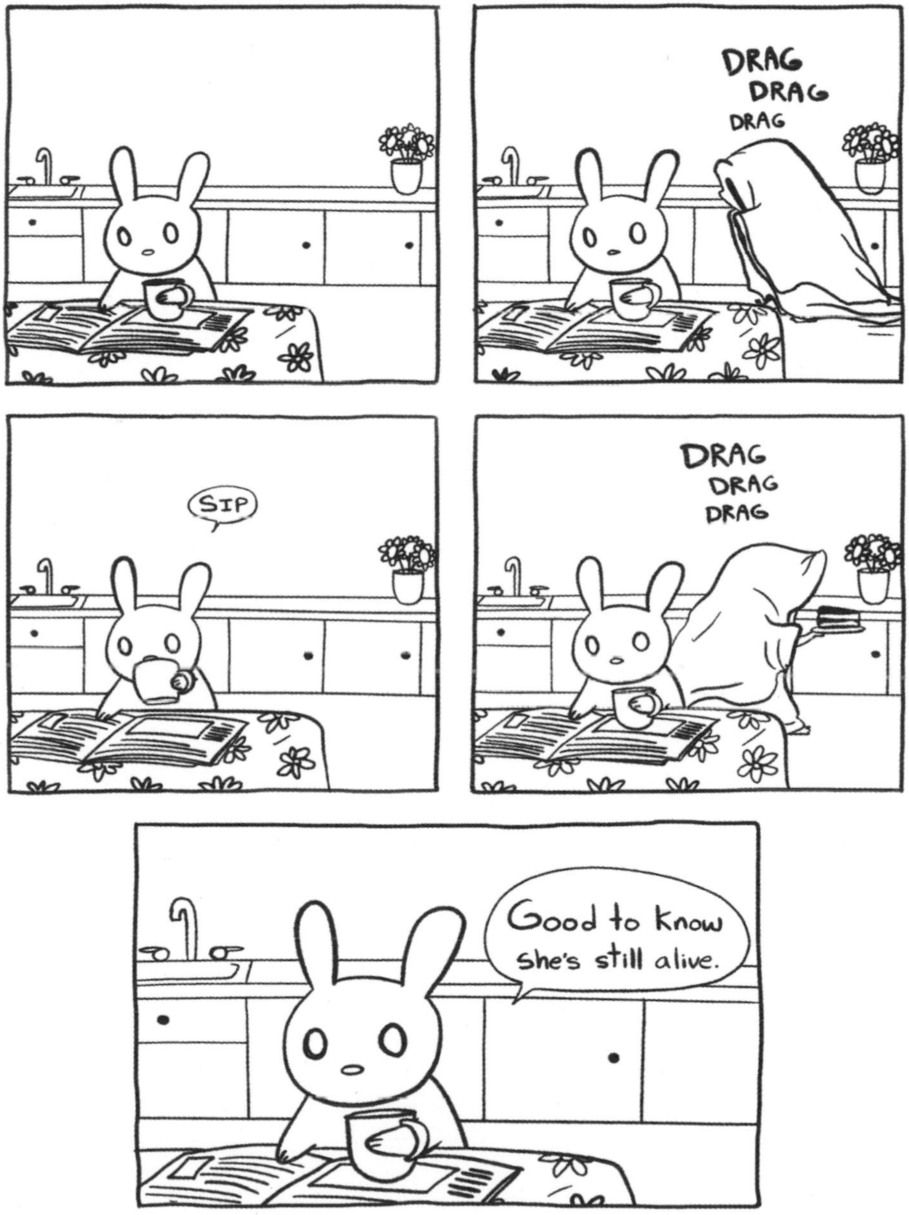
DRAG
DRAG
DRAG
SIP
DRAG
DRAG
DRAG
Good to know she's still alive.

The closest socially acceptable thing to carrying a bed around with me is a large, comfy sweater. But it goes beyond my need for warmth. I consider myself a sweater connoisseur in the same way someone would consider herself a wine expert or an art aficionado; to me each sweater is different, unique. Some are great; many are subpar.

Finding the sweet spot is harder than you might think. There are a lot of bad sweaters in this world.

EXAMPLES OF BAD SWEATERS

The itchy irritation

The Navajo nightmare

I feel like a Shaman, and as a white girl, that feels wrong.

The too-short terror

The turtleneck trap

FREE ME

As if that weren't bad enough, good sweaters for women are even harder to find.

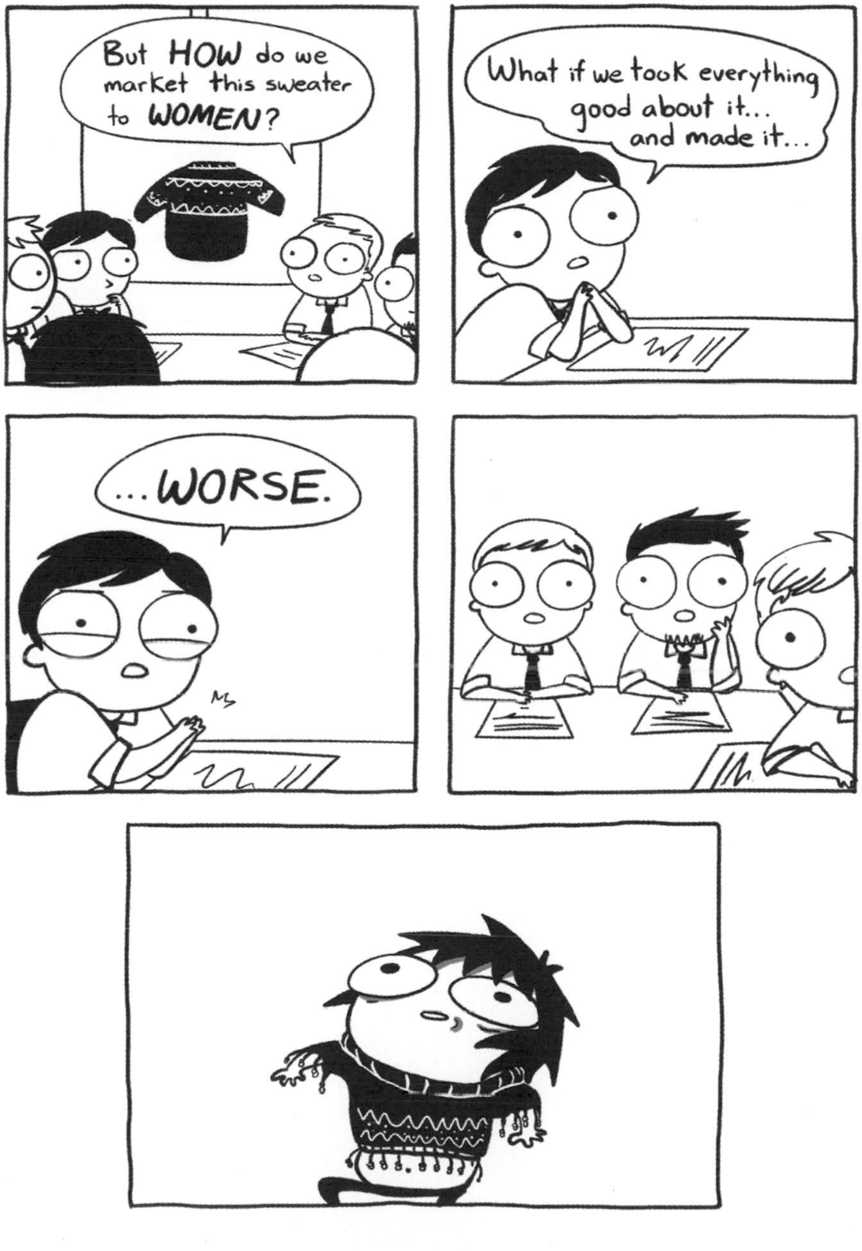
But HOW do we market this sweater to WOMEN?
What if we took everything good about it... and made it...
...WORSE.

All this is why I'm a thief of sweaters . . . men's sweaters, that is. And being a connoisseur, I can't take just *any* sweater. It needs to come from the right person.

Consider an art thief. To him, what makes a painting worth stealing isn't necessarily aesthetic beauty but the value that comes from its age, rarity, and, of course, association with a specific artist. The difference between the way an art thief sees a painting and the way I see a sweater is that no one but me recognizes a sweater's true value.

I'll go even further and say that I have pretty good taste in sweaters, even better than many of the so-called old masters did in their art. Or if not better, at least a little more . . . diverse. More well-rounded.

19th CENTURY PAINTERS

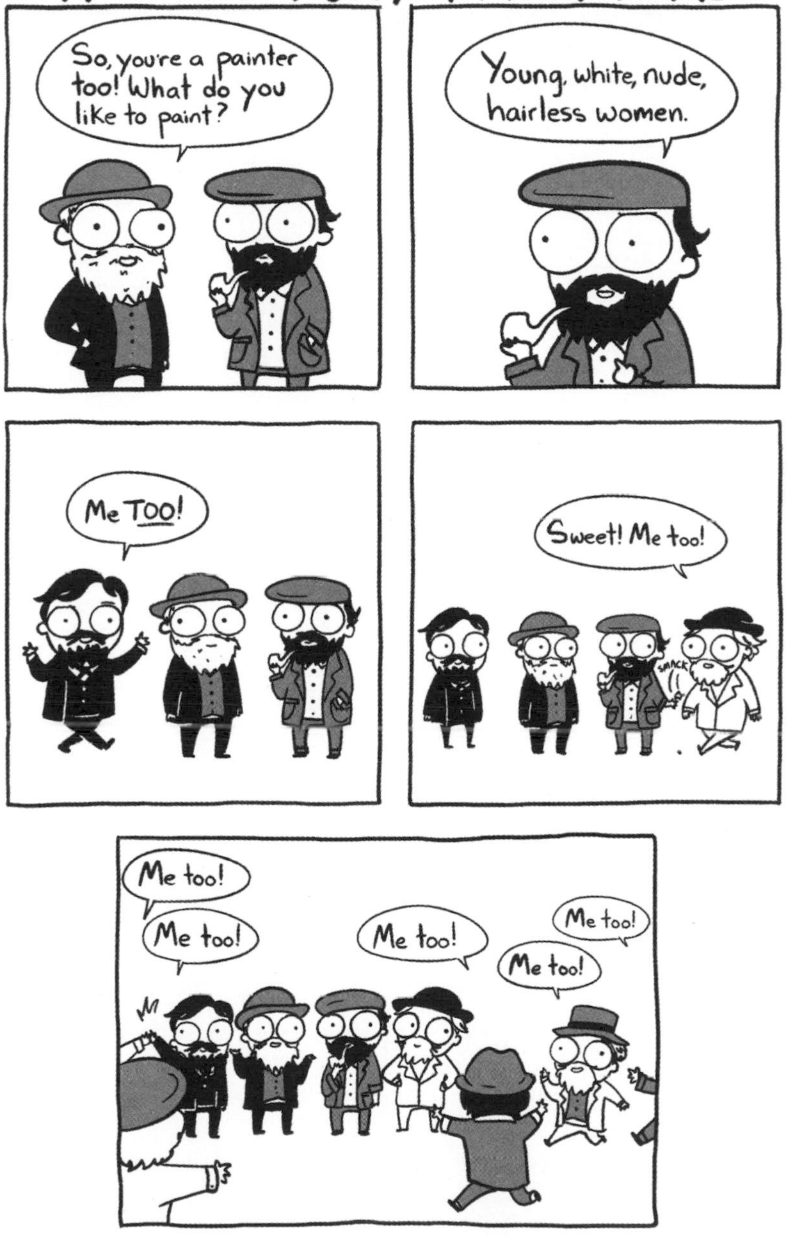
So, you're a painter too! What do you like to paint?
Young, white, nude, hairless women.
Me TOO!
Sweet! Me too!
SMACK
Me too!
Me too!
Me too!
Me too!
Me too!

Good thing we don't live in *those* times anymore!

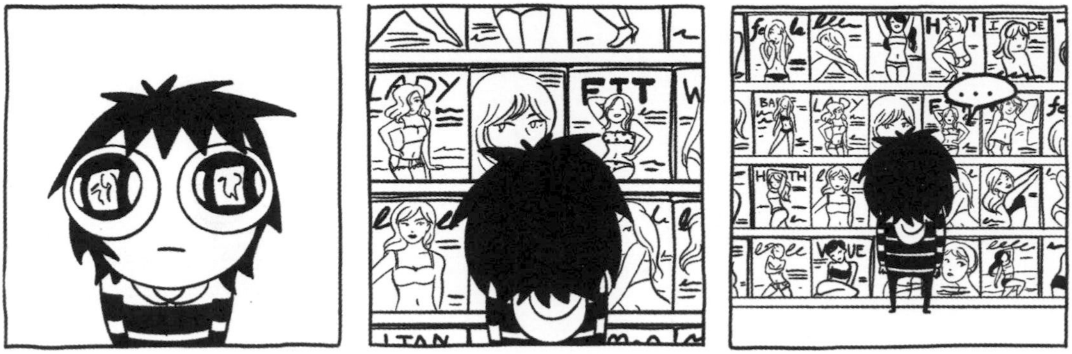
LADY
...

So anyway, back to sweaters!

A beaten-up sweater worn by the right person is as priceless to me as a Monet. Priceless because it's been worn by *the* Monet, the one and only, no other.

That's why I only steal my sweaters from the right person. The person I really, really like. In a painful way.

HOW CRUSHES FEEL

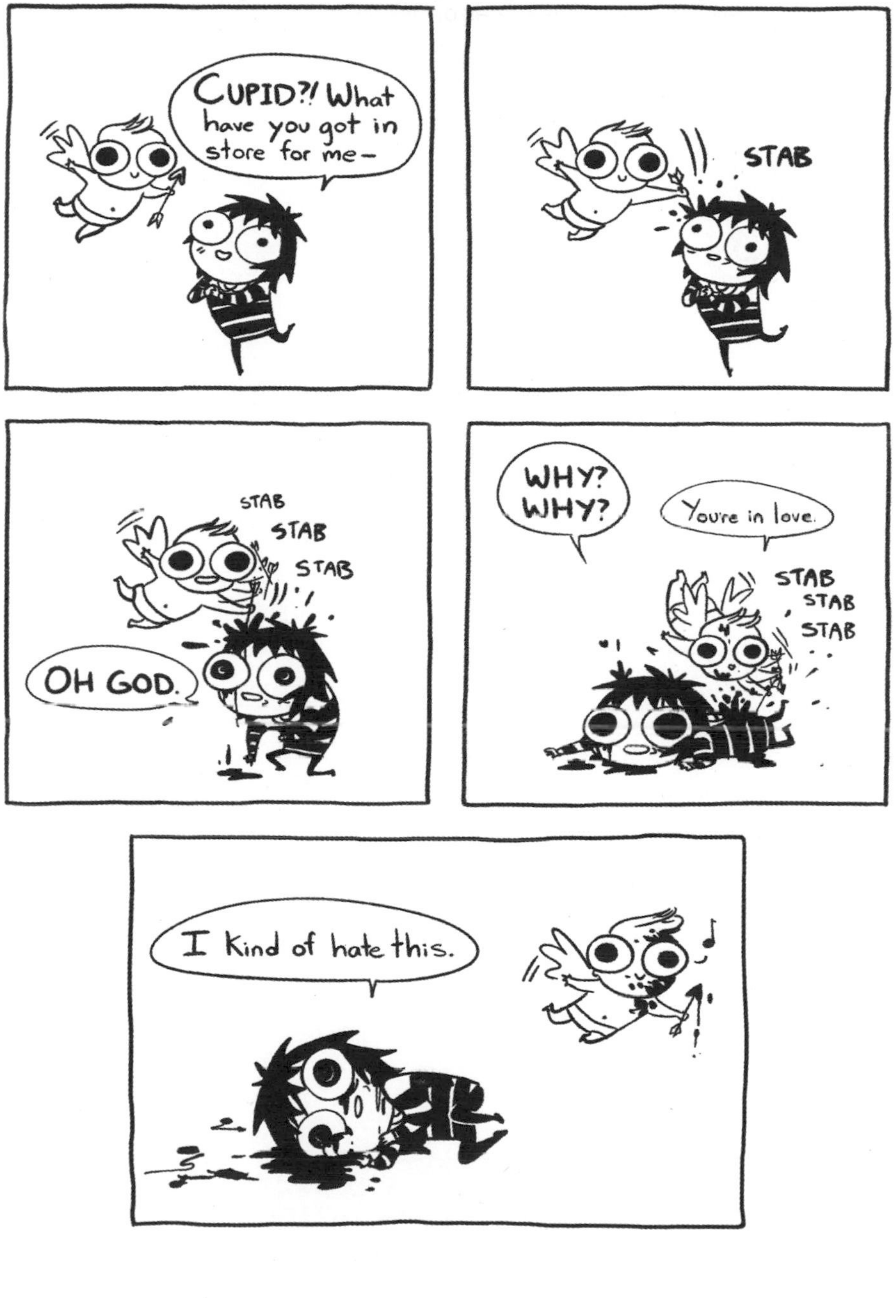
CUPID?! What have you got in store for me–
STAB
STAB
STAB
STAB
OH GOD.
WHY? WHY?
You're in love.
STAB
STAB
STAB
I kind of hate this.

It takes a very special someone to evoke that level of emotion in me.

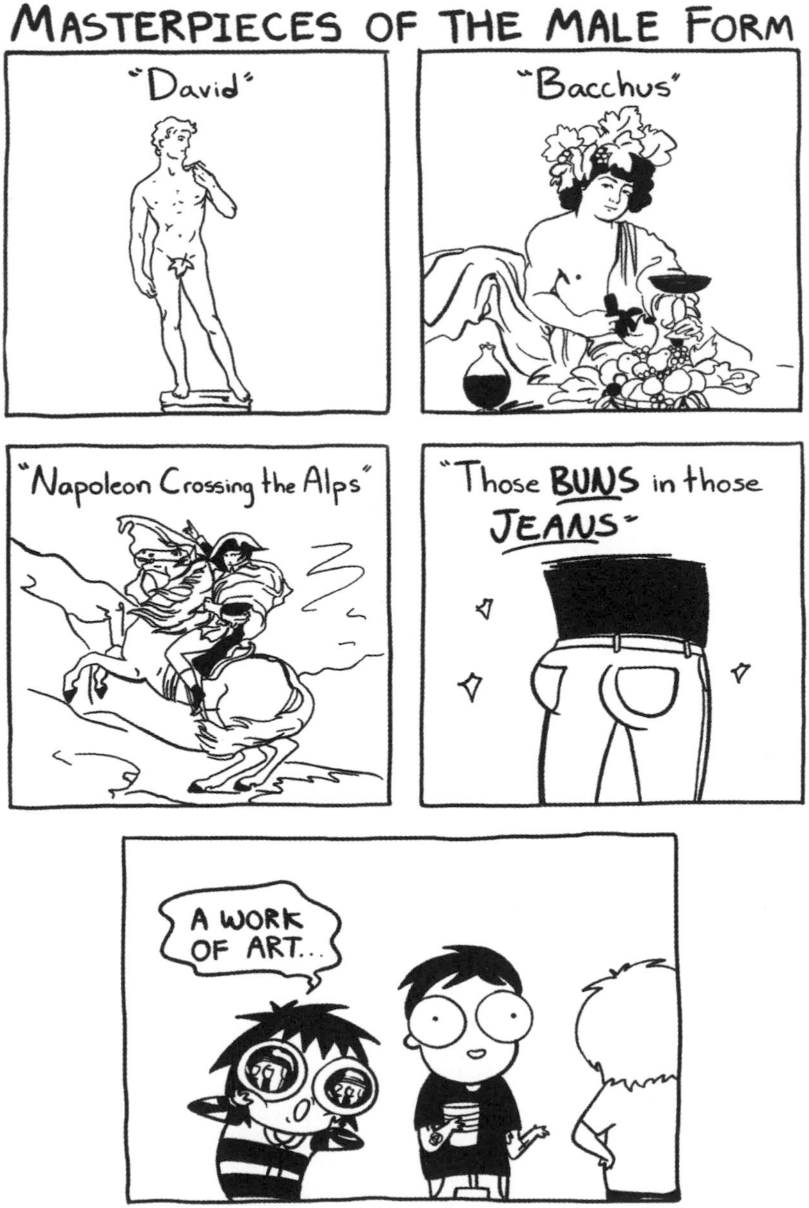
MASTERPIECES OF THE MALE FORM
"David"
"Bacchus"
"Napoleon Crossing the Alps"
"Those BUNS in those JEANS"
A WORK OF ART...

The clothes you take from someone almost always smell like them. Smell is so important. Pheromones are powerful and addictive. When someone smells good, my lizard brain instincts kick in.

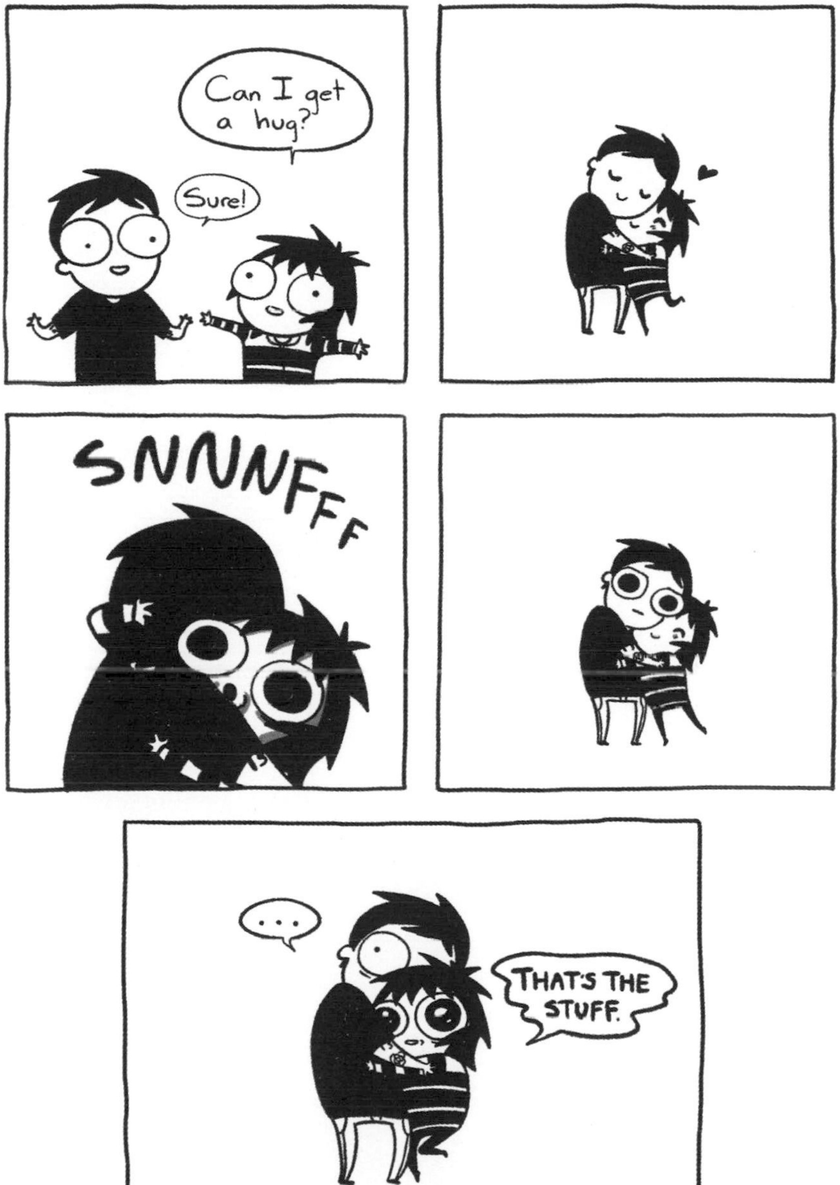
Can I get a hug?
Sure!
SNNNFFFF
...
THAT'S THE STUFF.

It's not just the delicious smell. Putting on a sweater from the right person instantly transports me to all the feelings I have when I'm with that person.

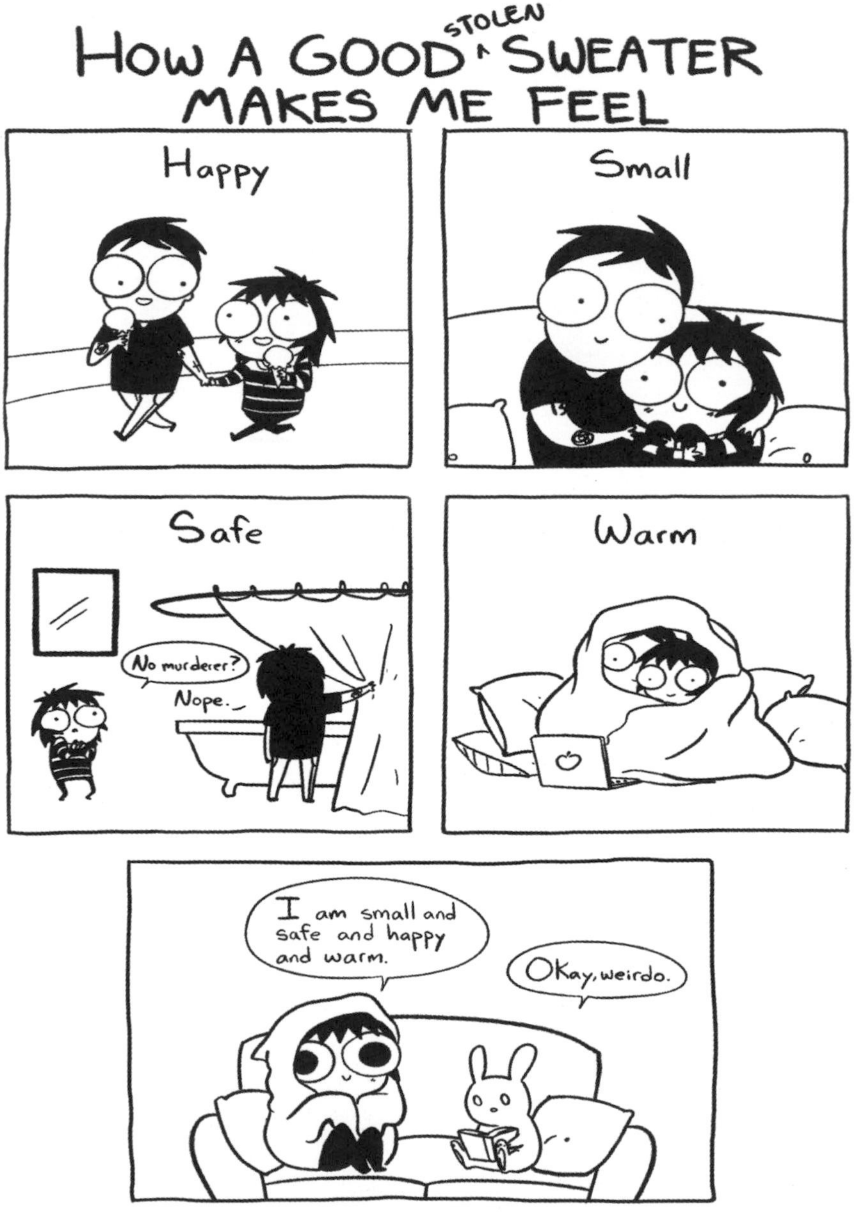
HOW A GOOD STOLEN SWEATER MAKES ME FEEL
Happy
Small
Safe
No murderer?
Nope.
Warm
I am small and safe and happy and warm.
Okay, weirdo.

But *acquiring* the sweater is a different story. Let me clarify. I am not a sweater borrower. I am a sweater *thief*. I belong to a long line of art fraudsters and forgers. Though admittedly, art fraud has gotten a little easier over the years.

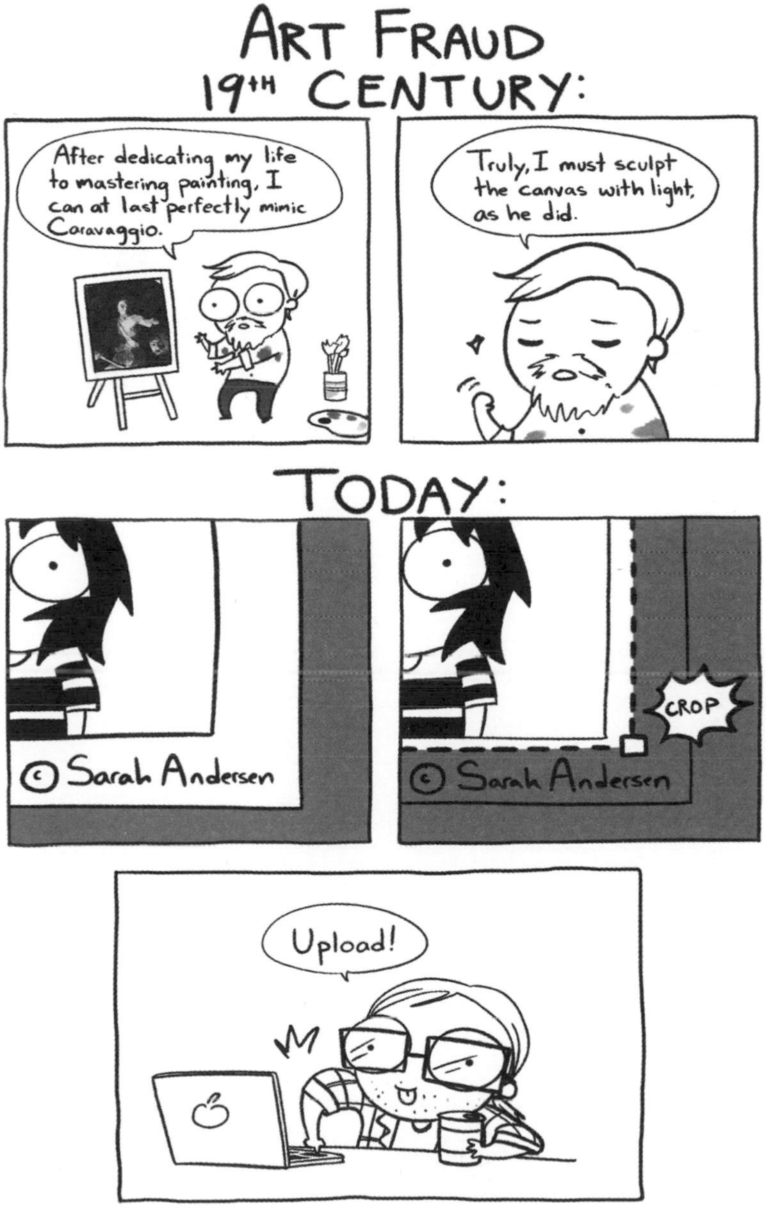

ART FRAUD
19TH CENTURY:
After dedicating my life to mastering painting, I can at last perfectly mimic Caravaggio.
Truly, I must sculpt the canvas with light, as he did.
TODAY:
© Sarah Andersen
© Sarah Andersen
CROP
Upload!

My own theft technique is a careful game of misinterpration and willful ignorance. When someone tells me I can use a sweater for the day, little do they know they are transferring ownership of that sweater over to me. Forever.

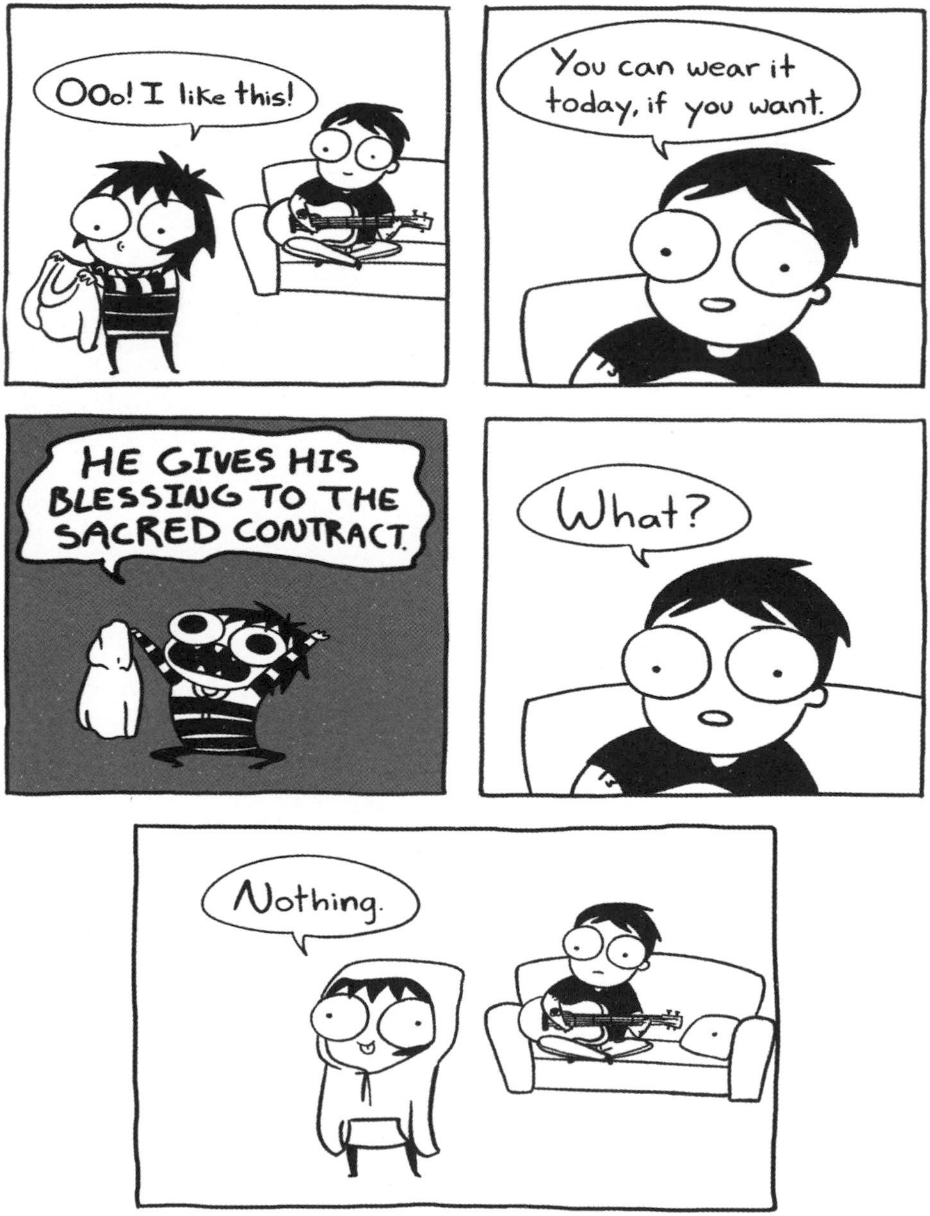
OOo! I like this!
You can wear it today, if you want.
HE GIVES HIS BLESSING TO THE SACRED CONTRACT.
What?
Nothing.

Usually they start to catch on to what I'm actually doing.

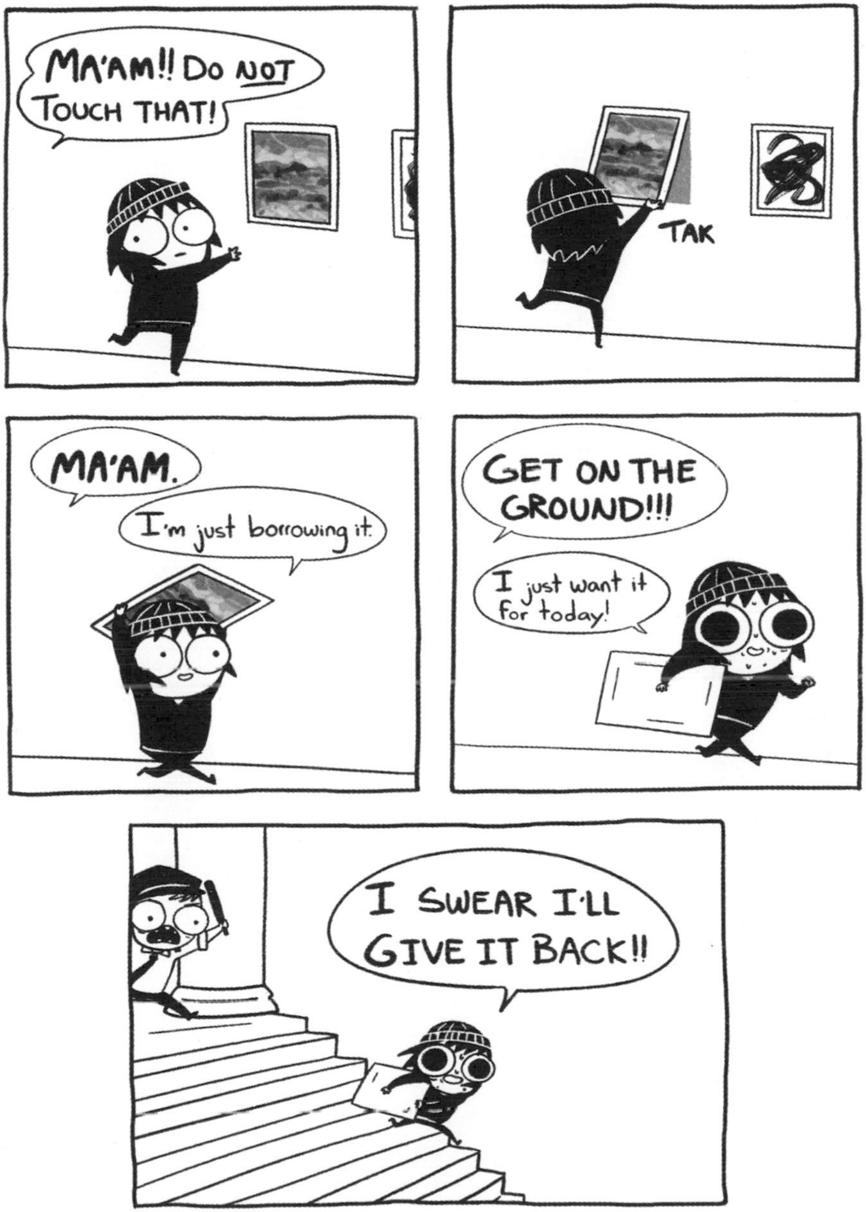
MA'AM!! DO NOT TOUCH THAT!
TAK
MA'AM.
I'm just borrowing it.
GET ON THE GROUND!!!
I just want it for today!
I SWEAR I'LL GIVE IT BACK!!

But by then it's too late.

By the time they realize what I've been doing, they've been living in a sea of lies for far too long.

I'm not getting it back am I-
NOPE.

Because if anything is guaranteed in a relationship with me, it's that I won't ever stop being a sweater thief.

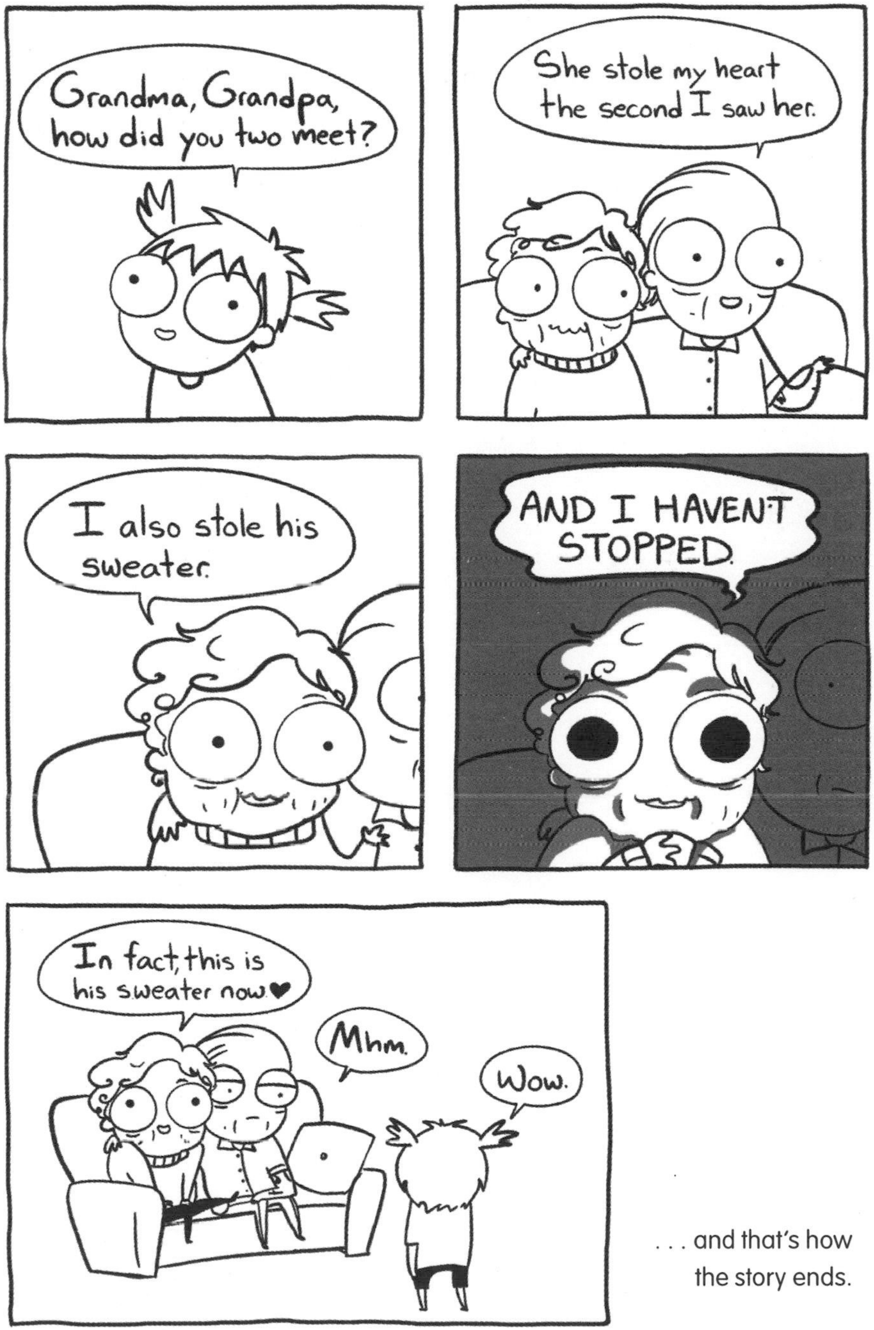
Grandma, Grandpa, how did you two meet?
She stole my heart the second I saw her.
I also stole his sweater.
AND I HAVEN'T STOPPED.
In fact, this is his sweater now.♥
Mhm.
Wow.

. . . and that's how the story ends.

INTROVERT FRIENDS

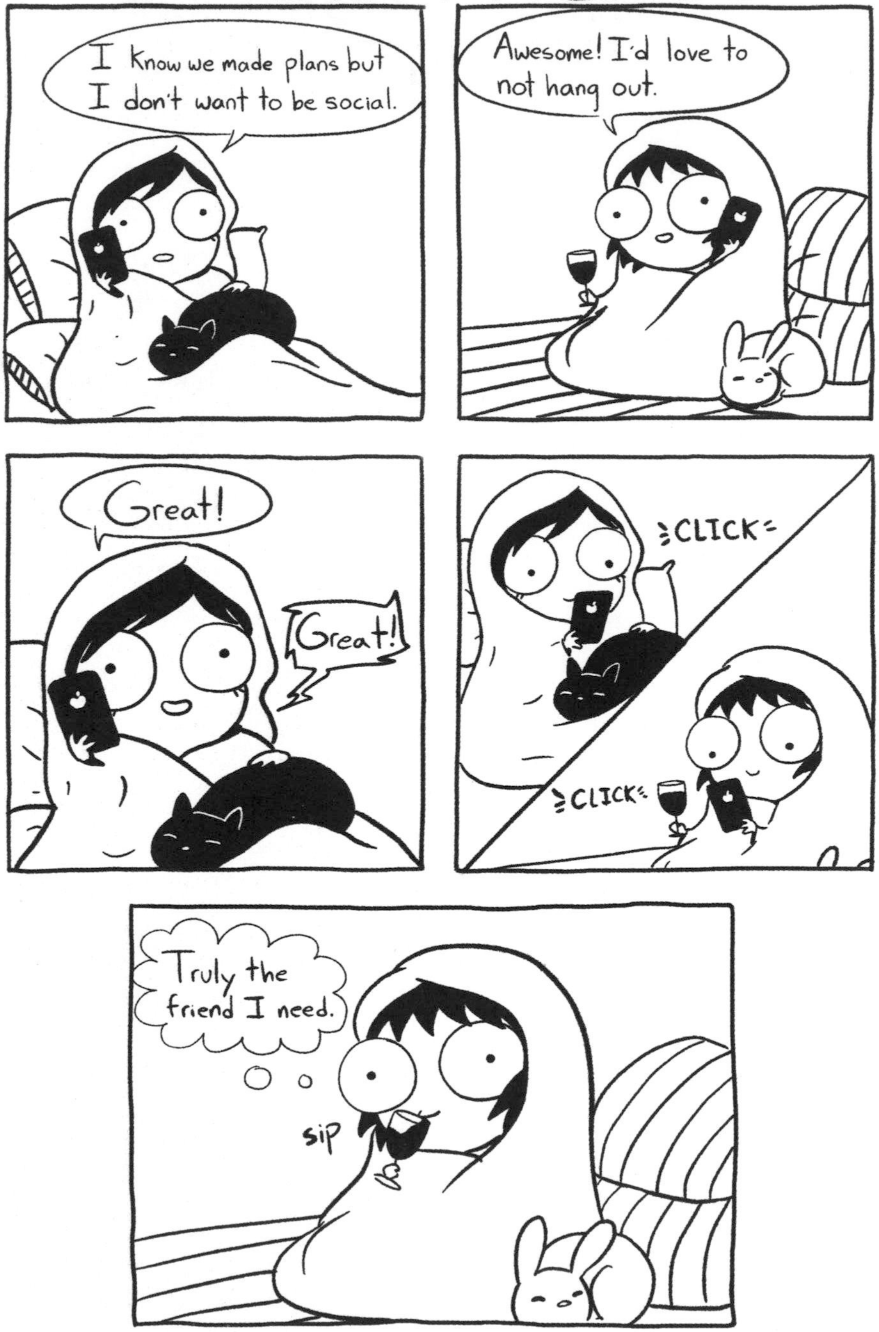
I know we made plans but I don't want to be social.
Awesome! I'd love to not hang out.
Great!
Great!
CLICK
CLICK
Truly the friend I need.
sip

SPRING/SUMMER

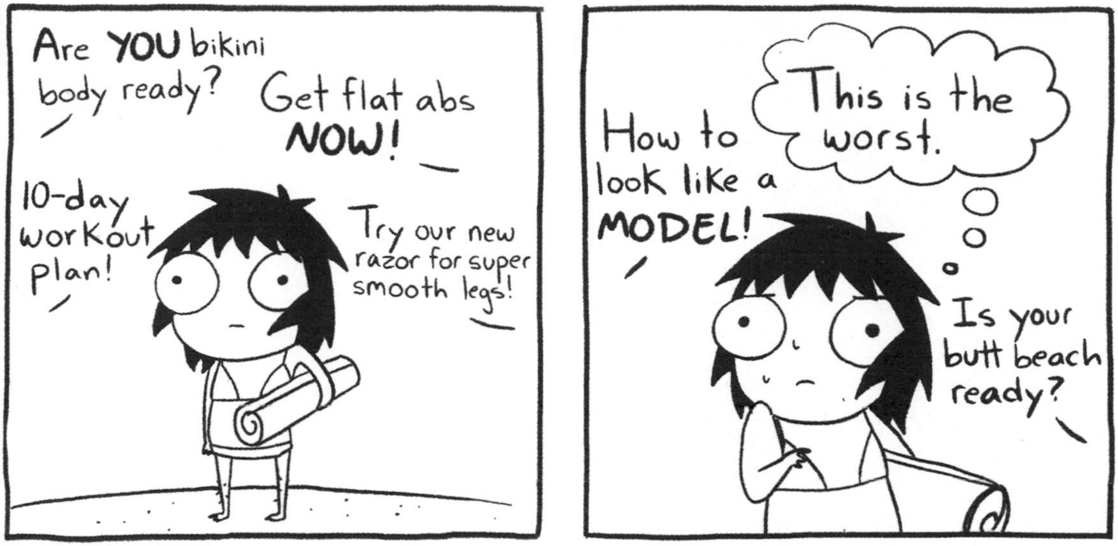
Are YOU bikini body ready?
Get flat abs NOW!
10-day workout plan!
Try our new razor for super smooth legs!
How to look like a MODEL!
This is the worst.
Is your butt beach ready?

FALL/WINTER

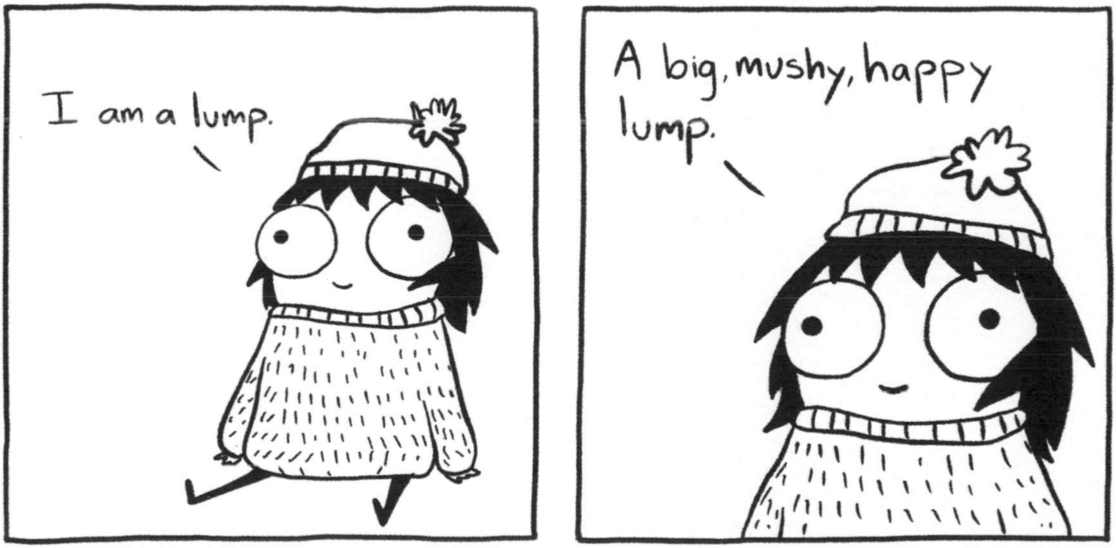
I am a lump.
A big, mushy, happy lump.

BIG MUSHY HAPPY LUMP

Andrews McMeel Publishing
a division of Andrews McMeel Universal
1130 Walnut Street, Kansas City, Missouri 64106

www.andrewsmcmeel.com

17 18 19 20 21 TEN 10 9 8 7 6 5 4 3 2

ISBN: 978-1-4494-7961-9

Library of Congress Control Number: 2016951399

Editor: Grace Suh
Art director and designer: Diane Marsh
Production editor: Erika Kuster
Production manager: Tamara Haus

ATTENTION: SCHOOLS AND BUSINESSES
Andrews McMeel books are available at quantity discounts with
bulk purchase for educational, business, or sales promotional use.
For information, please e-mail the Andrews McMeel Publishing
Special Sales Department: specialsales@amuniversal.com.